Google® SketchUp® and SketchUp® Pro 7 Bible

Google® SketchUp® and SketchUp® Pro 7 Bible

Kelly L. Murdock

Wiley Publishing, Inc.

Google SketchUp® and SketchUp® Pro 7 Bible

Published by
Wiley Publishing, Inc.
10475 Crosspoint Boulevard
Indianapolis, IN 46256
www.wiley.com

Copyright © 2009 by Wiley Publishing, Inc., Indianapolis, Indiana

Published simultaneously in Canada

ISBN: 978-0-470-29229-7

Manufactured in the United States of America

10 9 8 7 6 5 4 3 2 1

For general information on our other products and services or to obtain technical support, please contact our Customer Care Department within the U.S. at (800) 762-2974, outside the U.S. at (317) 572-3993 or fax (317) 572-4002.

Library of Congress Control Number: 2009920911

There's sketching for pleasure

And sketching for pain,

And psychologists sketch inkblots

To find the insane.

There's sketching by architects

And inventors to boot,

And sometimes you sketch

Cause you don't give a hoot.

Some sketches amuse

Some sketches explain

Concepts and ideas

That in words aren't so plain.

My sketches show boxes

Lines and circles galore

And the sides of my notebooks

Are never a bore.

With folders full of sketches

That are easy to find,

It's obvious that sketchy

Describes well my mind.

To Jeff and Michelle. 2008

About the Author

Kelly Murdock has been authoring computer books for many years now and still gets immense enjoyment from the completed work. His book credits include various 3D, graphics, multimedia, and Web titles, including nine previous editions of *3ds Max Bible*. Other major accomplishments include *Edgeloop Character Modeling for 3D Professionals Only, Maya 6 and 7 Revealed, LightWave 3D 8 Revealed, Poser 6 and 7 Revealed, 3D Game Animation For Dummies, gmax Bible, Adobe Atmosphere Bible, Master VISUALLY HTML and XHTML, JavaScript Visual Blueprint,* and co-authoring duties on two editions of the *Illustrator Bible* (for versions 9 and 10) and three editions of the *Adobe Creative Suite Bible*.

With a background in engineering and computer graphics, Kelly has been all over the 3D industry and still finds it fascinating. He's used high-level CAD workstations for product design and analysis, completed several large-scale visualization projects, created 3D models for feature films and games, worked as a freelance 3D artist, and even done some 3D programming. Kelly's been using 3D Studio since version 3 for DOS. Kelly has also branched into training others in 3D technologies. He teaches at the local university and is a frequent speaker at various conferences.

In his spare time, Kelly enjoys the outdoors while rock climbing, mountain biking, or skiing.

Credits

Acquisitions Editor
Courtney Allen

Project Editor
Sarah Cisco

Technical Editor
Lee Musick

Copy Editor
Kim Heusel

Editorial Manager
Robyn Siesky

Business Manager
Amy Knies

Sr. Marketing Manager
Sandy Smith

Vice President and Executive Group Publisher
Richard Swadley

Vice President and Executive Publisher
Barry Pruett

Project Coordinator
Kristie Rees

Graphics and Production Specialists
Stacie Brooks
Andrea Hornberger
Jennifer Mayberry
Christin Swinford
Ronald Terry

Quality Control Technician
Melanie Hoffman

Media Project Manager 1
Laura Moss-Hollister

Media Associate Producer
Josh Frank

Media Quality Control
Kit Malone

Proofreading and Indexing
Christine Spina Karpeles
Christine Sabooni

Contents at a Glance

Contents

Contents

Contents

Contents

Part VII: Extending SketchUp   463

Part VIII: Appendixes   487

Contents

Preface

SketchUp is an example of a great idea that has succeeded because it accomplishes exactly what it is setting out to do. It allows an alternative medium for all those visual thinkers that frequently sketch out ideas and concepts on napkins or whatever scraps of paper happen to be around.

I am one of those people, and I find that I am very reluctant to throw away any little scrap that has a sketch on it. These scraps become a source of inspiration and the building blocks upon which great ideas are formed. But, this habit has the unfortunate result of filling my office filing cabinet with folders full of little scraps.

These folders and scraps aren't the easiest system to search through, so finding the exact scrap that I need to inspire me isn't always easy. Another drawback to this system is that often in my hurry to capture a great idea, the concept is lost in the poor representation that I scribble down in my hurry. Let's see was that a circle or a square knot?

SketchUp provides a solution for both of these dilemmas and often makes it possible for me to springboard my rough sketch into more than the scribbled scrap of paper can show. I've found that SketchUp hasn't replaced my constant need to scribble, but by redrawing the quickly drawn sketches into SketchUp, new concepts are revealed and SketchUp lets me look at the drawing in a whole new way.

SketchUp provides a way to flesh out the crude drawing and refine it so that I can more easily share the idea it represents with others. I've even been able to throw away some scraps once I know that a better and more complete copy has been created in SketchUp.

Acknowledgments

No man is an island and no book project was ever completed without help from a host of key people. First on the list is Courtney Allen, whose kind reminders and frequent contacts have made this book a reality. Close behind is Sarah Cisco who managed the production cycle and main editing. Sarah was tasked with asking the tough questions and finding solutions to those questions.

Thanks also to Lee Musick, who was in charge of technically editing the book and for making sure that what I said was at least close to the truth. Thanks also for the other editors, indexers, cover copy, CD production team, and the staff at Wiley for their efforts.

Thanks to the Google SketchUp development team for creating such a great product and for Tricia Stahr, who helped me get started with the new version.

Thanks, as always, to my wife, Angela and my two sons, Eric and Thomas, who I'm asking once again to please go to bed.

Introduction

SketchUp isn't a new piece of software. It has actually been around since 2000. It was developed by @Last Software, based in Boulder, Colorado. It has won numerous awards for its innovative design and flexible implementation. Part of SketchUp's flexibility allowed it to use plug-ins to extend its set of features. One such plug-in allowed SketchUp files to be integrated with Google Earth.

The team at Google must have been impressed with the software and the plug-in because they acquired the company and its development team in 2006. Development has continued on the software and in 2008, version 7 was released. The Google team has also given SketchUp a home and an ongoing development life. We can only hope that the program will continue to improve and keep the attention of a strong corporate entity that gives it the attention it deserves.

SketchUp is quite unique from other graphics packages. It uses a paradigm that is the most accessible to all users — sketching your ideas on a simple piece of paper. I myself have sketched on my share of paper scraps, but I must say that it is easier to keep them organized in SketchUp than littering my study. My wife has learned not to throw out any papers that have odd scribbles on them no matter how strange, but I still end up losing the most important scraps unless I get them into my computer.

SketchUp removes many of the time-consuming frustrations of learning how to use the software before you can get something close to your idea into a project. From the very first couple of lines, you should feel right at home with the software. SketchUp is designed to be easy to use. To create a line, you simply drag with the mouse; the software automatically makes it straight and attaches it to other lines in the project. Lines can be made into surfaces that can be pushed and pulled to create 3D objects. The simplicity of the software makes it extremely quick to take a sketch and recreate into any 3D object.

SketchUp has the experience of years of designers packed into its design, and with these smarts, it can often guess pretty closely what you're trying to do. It also automates much of the manual processes for you, leaving you free to play with the design.

SketchUp was initially embraced by the architecture and construction industries, but over time it has become an indispensable tool for product designers, interior designers, landscape and gardening designers, urban planners, film and theater directors, inventors, game designers, and many other professions where visualizing objects is key.

Part I

Getting Started with Google SketchUp

Quick Start

Building a Windmill

I f you can't decide for sure where to start, I suggest that you start right here with this Quick Start. It is designed to give you a quick whirlwind tour of the major SketchUp features using tutorials.

Each stage of this Quick Start is also saved on the book's CD and available as a reference if you get off track. And if you are inspired to take the model in a different direction, feel free to do so.

The example project for this Quick Start is a windmill. SketchUp is really good at creating architectural designs such as buildings and homes. It also is good at visualizing machines, and a windmill is both.

Finding a Reference Image

One of the best places to start is to look for a reference image that is similar to what you want to build. A quick search on the Internet enabled me to find a windmill that is fairly close to what I want to build. This image is used as a reference that gives me the correct relative dimensions and shapes.

Because the reference image is flat, you can load it into the drawing area and use the image as you line up different dimensions. You can load the reference image as a background image, but the scaling may be off, so you'll load it onto a flat planar surface that you can position wherever you want.

Tutorial: Loading a reference image

Loading and positioning a reference image will take a little bit of work, but it is worth it as you begin to build.

To load a reference image, follow these steps:

1. **Open SketchUp and create a new file.** Choose File ⇨ New menu.

2. **Rotate the view so you're looking down the green axis. You can rotate the view by dragging in the drawing area with the scroll wheel button pressed down.**

3. **Select the Rectangle tool from the toolbar (or by choosing Draw ⇨ Rectangle) and drag at the back of the drawing area to create a large plane object.** Make the plane taller than it is wide.

4. **Choose Window ⇨ Materials to open the Material Browser.**

5. **Select the In Model category from the drop-down list.** Click the Create Material button in the upper-right corner of the browser to open the Create Material dialog box.

6. **In the Create Material dialog box, select the Use Texture Image option.** Browse to the Quick Start folder on the CD-ROM and load the Windmill reference.jpg image. Click OK to close the Create Materials dialog box.

7. **With the new windmill image texture selected in the Material Browser, select the Paint Bucket tool from the toolbar (or by choosing Tools ⇨ Paint Bucket) and click on the rectangular plane in the drawing area.** The texture is applied as a bunch of small tiles.

8. **With the Select tool (which is the first tool on the toolbar; you can also access it by choosing Tools ⇨ Select), click on the rectangular plane face to select it, then choose Edit ⇨ Face ⇨ Texture ⇨ Position.** Four colored icons appear in the center of the plane. Drag the red move pin to the lower-left corner, then drag the green scale and rotate pin to the right to scale the image to fill the plane, as shown in Figure QS.1.

FIGURE QS.1

The reference plane provides some guidance as you build.

Building the Windmill

When the reference image is in place, you can begin building the actual geometry. This is where SketchUp shines, and with relatively few steps you should have a geometry in good shape.

Tutorial: Building the base structure

The next task is to create the base of the windmill. If you look closely at the reference image, you can see that the base is composed of a cylinder structure with a cone object on top of it and a pointed hexagon tower on top of the cone. These objects are fairly easy to create using the default shapes and the Push/Pull tool.

To make sure that the dimensions are set correctly, you start with the lines to use as guides. These are temporary lines that can be deleted later.

To build the base structure, follow these steps:

1. **Drag with the scroll wheel to move the view up above the scene.**

2. **Select the Line tool (Draw ⇨ Line) and click on the reference image where the base of the windmill touches the ground on the left side and drag a line perpendicular to the reference plane.** Release the mouse when the line is green, indicating that the line is parallel to the Y-axis. Then repeat to create a guide line that extends from the right side of the reference windmill. These two lines give you the radius of the windmill base.

3. **Select the Circle tool (Draw ⇨ Circle) and drag from the center between the two guide lines to create a circle that touches both guide lines.** Select the circle's face with the Select tool.

4. **Drag with the scroll wheel to change to a side view and then drag the circle face with the Push/Pull tool (Tools ⇨ Push/Pull) upward to match the height of the cylinder in the reference image.**

5. **Drag back to a top view, and drag from the circle's center to a little beyond the circle's edge with the Circle tool to create the base of the cone shape.**

6. **Select the larger circle, switch back to the side view, and drag upward with the Push/Pull tool again to create the height for the cone shape.**

7. **With both edges of the larger circle selected, choose Tools ⇨ Scale.** Then drag on each of the opposite corners to scale down the top circle's edges to make a cone shape.

8. **From a top view, choose Draw ⇨ Polygon.** Then type the number 6 and press Enter to change the number of sides in the Measurements Toolbar to 6 and drag from the center of the circle to the inner edge of the circle.

9. **From the side view, drag with the Push/Pull tool to extrude the polygon face upward to match the reference image.**

10. **Select the Polygon tool again and draw another hexagon at the top of the base that is aligned with the lower hexagon.** Then extrude the new face with the Push/Pull tool and select and scale the top hexagon edge to near a point, as shown in Figure QS.2.

Tutorial: Adding the fins

This tutorial adds the fins to the windmill. The fins are all copies: when one is built, you simply clone and rotate the others into position. To build one fin, it is easier to change to a top view and use the base plane to lay out the fin's pieces.

To build the windmill fins, follow these steps:

1. **Drag with the scroll wheel to move the view up above the scene.**

2. With the Rectangle tool, click-and-drag a long rectangular edge that is aligned with the red axis, then use the Push/Pull tool to give the strut some height.

3. With the Rectangle tool click-and-drag a box that is perpendicular to the first strut, and give it some height.

4. **Select the second box with its edges and select the Move/Copy tool.** Press and hold down the Ctrl key and click-and-drag the box to the right to create another strut. Continue until struts are all along the first box.

5. Repeat Steps 2 through 4 to create and duplicate the crossing struts.

6. Use the Push/Pull tool to extend one end of the first strut where it connects to the center.

7. **With a single fin completed, select all the objects in the first fin and choose Edit ⇨ Make Group.** This adds all the objects to a single group that moves as one object. Figure QS.3 shows the completed grouped fin.

CROSS-REF You can learn more about grouping objects in Chapter 8.

FIGURE QS.2

The base structure for the windmill is complete.

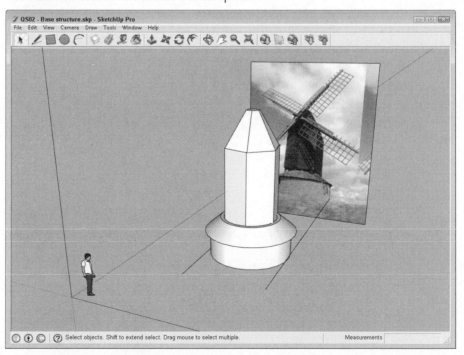

FIGURE QS.3

One fin is completed and grouped.

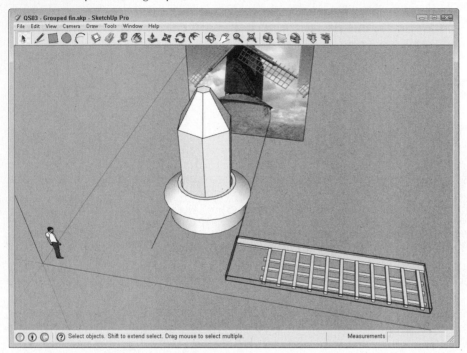

Tutorial: Aligning the fins

In this step, you align the completed fin and then copy and align the duplicates. The scale of the fin also needs to be addressed. When rotating the duplicates into place, you want to center the rotation pivot at the center of the drive shaft.

To align the windmill fins, follow these steps:

1. **Select the Rotate tool (Tools ⇨ Rotate) and click on the end of the fin to set the rotation dial.** Then click and rotate the fin 90 degrees to face the windmill base.

2. **Choose Tools ⇨ Scale and drag on the corner of the fin to scale it to match the reference image.** Make sure that the vertical fins don't reach so far that they touch the ground.

3. **Select the Move/Copy tool and move the fin into place in front of the windmill base.**

4. **Select the first fin and choose Edit ⇨ Copy and then Edit ⇨ Paste in Place.** With the Rotate tool, click the point closest to the windmill axle and rotate the duplicated fin 90 degrees.

5. Repeat the Steps 1 through 4 to create and duplicate all four fins.

6. Create a new block with the Rectangle and Push/Pull tools and align it to be the fin's axle.

7. Select the axle and all fins, and rotate them 45 degrees to be at an angle to the windmill like the reference image, as shown in Figure QS.4.

FIGURE QS.4

The fins are now aligned and connected to the windmill.

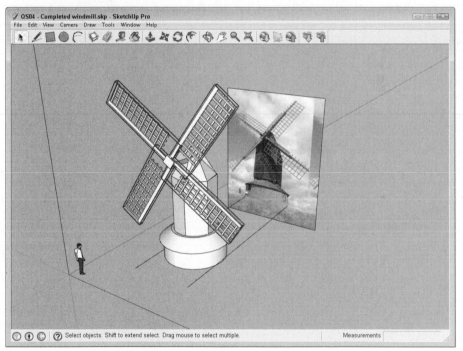

Adding Materials and Styles

With the geometry building completed, the next task is to add materials to the objects. Materials can include simple colors and/or textures and transparency. All of these material properties add a lot to the final look of the drawing.

Materials are added using the Material Browser. The Material Browser includes multiple preset materials that you can use. The Paint Bucket tool is used to apply the selected material to objects in the scene.

Materials take care of the object's colors, but you can also change the scene's environment by applying a different style. Styles can display the model using a sketchy style as if the model were hand-drawn.

Tutorial: Applying materials to the windmill

Using the preset materials in the Material Browser lets you quickly add materials to the windmill.

To add materials to the windmill objects, follow these steps:

1. **Choose Window ⇨ Materials to open the Material Browser.**

2. **From the Stone category, select the Stone_Sandstone_Ashlar_Light material.** Then with the Paint Bucket tool click on the lowest cylinder in the base structure.

3. **From the Roofing category, select the Roofing Shingles Multi material and apply it to the base cone object.**

4. **From the Wood category, select and apply the Wood_Floor_Dark material to the hexagonal base object.** This material needs to be applied to each face.

5. **Also from the Wood category, select the Wood_Lumber_ButtJoined material and apply it to the axle and fin objects.** Figure QS.5 shows the windmill with applied materials.

FIGURE QS.5

The windmill looks much better after materials are applied.

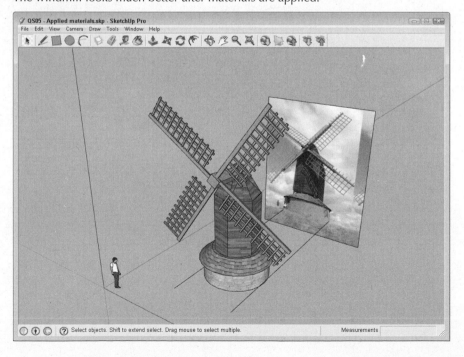

Tutorial: Adding a style

The Styles Browser, like the Material Browser, also includes a large number of presets that you can choose.

To add a style to the drawing, follow these steps:

1. **Choose Window ⇨ Styles to open the Styles Browser.**
2. **From the Assorted Styles category, select the Google Earth style.** This style has a nice sky and ground look.
3. **Select and delete the guide lines and the reference plane.**
4. **Select the entire windmill and move it down so it contacts the ground plane.** Figure QS.6 shows the windmill with its environment.

If you want to clean up the scene at this point, you can delete or hide the reference photo and guide lines.

FIGURE QS.6

Adding a style gives the scene an environment.

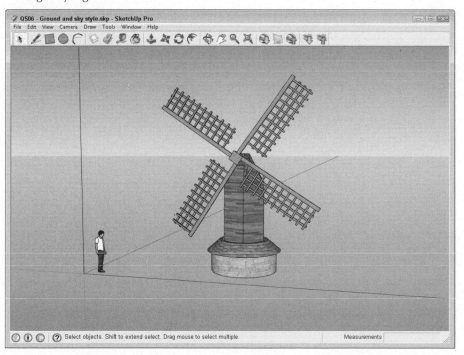

Enabling Shadows

One of the last touches to add to a drawing is to include shadows. By enabling shadows, the model gets a much needed sense of depth. Shadows can be configured based on the time of day and the month of a year.

Tutorial: Adding shadows

Shadows are enabled and configured using the Shadow Settings dialog box.

To enable shadows, follow these steps:

1. **Choose Window ⇨ Shadows to open the Shadow Settings dialog box.**
2. **Select the Display Shadows option.** Then set the Time slider to about 4 in the afternoon. Figure QS.7 shows the model with shadows.

FIGURE QS.7

Adding shadows gives the model a sense of depth.

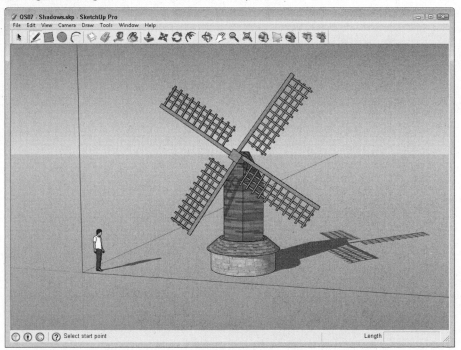

Summary

The goal of this Quick Start was to run through a complete example from start to finish showing off the major SketchUp features. These tutorials showed how to build a model using a number of tools, and how to apply materials, styles, and shadows.

This Quick Start covered the following topics:

- Loading a background reference image
- Building a windmill with the various tools
- Adding materials and styles to the scene
- Enabling shadows for a sense of depth

Chapter 1 dives into SketchUp by first looking at where SketchUp came from and its intended purpose.

Chapter 1

Introducing Google SketchUp

IN THIS CHAPTER

Designing with SketchUp

Understanding the different versions of SketchUp

Getting help

It would be interesting to determine the number of great ideas that started out as rough sketches on a restaurant napkin. If you've ever had a brilliant idea, you know that they don't always come at the most convenient times. When ideas come, you really need to quickly jot them down and sketch them out or you'll likely forget them before they can be captured.

Once an idea is captured on a napkin, a scrap of paper, or scratched into the nightstand, the next step is to flesh out the idea into something more substantial. That is where SketchUp comes in. SketchUp is a program that enables anyone, regardless of his or her drawing ability, to quickly and easily create a realistic 3-D drawing. Finally, you can throw away that folder full of napkins and paper scraps that is cluttering your desk.

Designing with SketchUp

SketchUp is quite unique compared to other graphics packages. It works similarly to sketching your ideas on a simple piece of paper, which makes it accessible to all users. I have sketched on my share of paper scraps, but it is easier to keep them organized in SketchUp than littering my study. My wife has learned not to throw out any papers that have odd scribbles on them no matter how strange, but I still end up losing the most important scraps unless I get them into my computer.

Because SketchUp is easy to use, you won't be spending all of your time learning how to use the software; instead you'll be able to start getting your idea into a project. From the very first couple of lines, you should feel right at home with the software. SketchUp is designed to be easy to use. To create a line, you simply click and drag with the mouse; the software automatically makes it straight and attaches it to other lines in the project. Lines can be made into surfaces that can be pushed and pulled to create 3-D objects. The simplicity of the software makes it extremely quick to recreate any of your 2-D sketches into 3-D objects.

SketchUp has the experience of years of designers packed into its design, and with these smarts it can often guess pretty closely what you're trying to do. It also automates many of the manual processes for you, leaving you free to play with the design.

SketchUp was initially embraced by the architecture and construction industries, but over time it has become an indispensable tool for product designers, interior designers, landscape and gardening designers, urban planners, film and theater directors, inventors, game designers, and many other professions where visualizing objects is key.

Understanding the Different Versions of SketchUp

What could be better than a unique graphics package like SketchUp? How about two versions of SketchUp; and better than that, one of those versions is free. Google SketchUp is available as a free download from the Google Web site.

For users who need a little more functionality, a professional version is also available. SketchUp Pro has all the features found in the standard version and includes many additional advanced features. There is a trial version of SketchUp Pro available that you can download and try out. You can find the trial version at www.sketchup.com.

Google SketchUp

Google SketchUp is the standard version of the software. It can be downloaded for free from the SketchUp Web site at www.sketchup.com. The current version is 7. This version includes the features for building, viewing, and modifying 3-D content. It also allows you to apply materials to objects and even upload your creation to Google Earth. Figure 1.1 shows a product description page, which can be accessed by going to http://sketchup.google.com/product_suf.html

ON the CD-ROM   **The standard version of Google SketchUp 7 is also available on the book's CD.**

FIGURE 1.1

Google SketchUp standard can be downloaded from the Web.

Google SketchUp Pro 7

The Pro version of SketchUp can be bought online. Making an online purchase gives you a license to use the software and gives you access to product support. The Pro package adds the ability to import and export SketchUp models to a number of different formats.

The Pro version also ships with LayOut, a separate software package that lets you combine 3-D models with 2-D images to create interactive presentations. These finished presentations can be exported as PDF files for distribution on the Web.

 More information on LayOut is covered in Chapters 24 and 25.

Google SketchUp Pro 7 trial versions

If you want to try the Pro version, a trial version is available on this book's CD, or you can download it from the SketchUp Web site at http://sketchup.google.com/product_sup.html, as shown in Figure 1.2. The trial version works for eight hours after being installed.

FIGURE 1.2

An eight-hour trial version of Google SketchUp Pro is available on the Web.

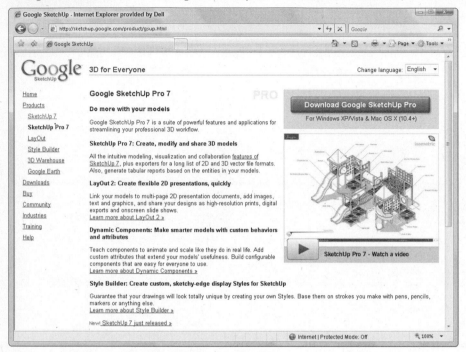

Getting Help

There are several help resources available for learning SketchUp. This book is intended to be not only a complete reference, but a resource that offers multiple examples and step-by-step tutorials to help you get up to speed with the software.

Many additional help features are available including the Learn panel in the Welcome dialog box, the Help Center, the online Help pages, and several online videos.

Learn panel

The Learn panel in the Welcome to SketchUp dialog box, shown in Figure 1.3, is a panel that shows simple videos of specific SketchUp tasks. Once a video is done, you can replay the video or connect online to view more videos.

There is also an Always show on startup check box at the bottom of the dialog box that you can disable to hide this dialog box when starting up.

> **TIP** Because there aren't a ton of video clips to watch, I suggest you scroll through them once and then disable the Always show on startup option so this dialog box doesn't get in your way.

The Learn panel in the Welcome dialog box is a good place to start when learning to use SketchUp.

You can close the Welcome dialog box by clicking the Start Using SketchUp button in the lower-right corner of the dialog box. If you ever want to revisit this dialog box, you can open it again by choosing Help ⇨ Welcome to SketchUp.

Quick Reference Card

The Quick Reference Card, shown in Figure 1.4, can be accessed from the Additional Resources tab in the Learning Center dialog box, from Help ⇨ Quick Reference Card, or by double-clicking the QuickReferenceCard.pdf file located in the Resource folder where SketchUp is installed. Selecting any of these links or menus opens the Quick Reference Card within Adobe Reader where you can print it.

The Quick Reference Card shows the names of all the various tool icons and explains how the Ctrl, Alt, and Shift keys can be used with each tool. It also shows how the three-button mouse can be used to navigate the current scene. The real benefit of the Quick Reference Card is when it is printed and posted next to your computer for quick reference.

> **TIP** There is also a Quick Reference Card for LayOut 2, which is located in the LayOut folder where SketchUp 7 is installed.

FIGURE 1.4

The Quick Reference Card gives each tool icon a name and shows you how to navigate with the mouse.

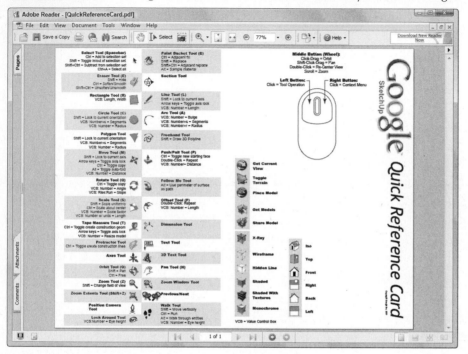

Help Center

Choosing Help ⇨ Help Center opens the SketchUp Help pages within a web browser. The Help pages are organized by categories that are listed in a panel to the left. The Help pages also make extensive use of blue links to jump to corresponding Help pages. Using the browser's navigation arrows, you can move forward and backward through the visited pages. You can also bookmark specific pages.

One of the drawbacks of the Help pages is that there isn't a way to search all categories for information. You can use the browser's search feature to search within the current page, but that is the extent of the search capability. You can do a search through multiple categories using the Help Center.

The Help Center also offers answers and help using a question-and-answer format. There is also a search feature for finding help to specific questions. The Help Center also includes an online version of the SketchUp Help pages complete with Table of Contents, Index, and Search features, as shown in Figure 1.5. There is also access to SketchUp Support, which requires a valid license number to access, and links to the SketchUp Forum.

FIGURE 1.5

The Online Help Pages include the ability to search for specific features.

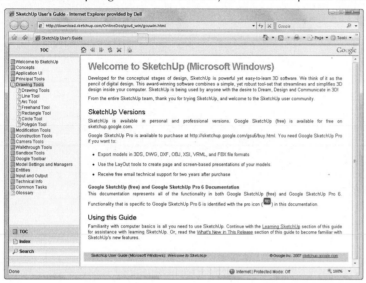

You can provide feedback to the SketchUp team using the Help ↪ Contact Us menu. This menu opens a Web browser and takes you to an online Web page, shown in Figure 1.6, where you can take a product survey, provide feedback, or report a bug.

FIGURE 1.6

You can contact the SketchUp team online to report problems or provide feedback.

The SketchUp forum

If you have a specific question, the online forum can be searched. This forum lets you post questions for experienced users that can help you if you get stuck. There are separate Help Groups for SketchUp and SketchUp Pro, as shown in Figure 1.7.

FIGURE 1.7

The SketchUp help groups provide a community forum for getting answers from experienced users.

Self-Paced Tutorials

If you learn best by doing, then you're probably a visual learner and you'll love the tutorial examples sprinkled throughout this book. The SketchUp Help Center also has some basic tutorials.

The Introduction tutorial, shown in Figure 1.8, uses 16 pages to explain how to navigate the scene, how to draw, and how to push/pull rectangles. You can navigate the tutorial pages by clicking the tabs located at the top of the interface.

FIGURE 1.8

The Self-Paced Tutorials provide a step-by-step guide to specific aspects of the software.

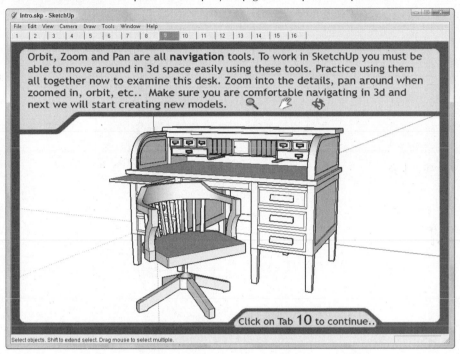

Help Center also has links where you can download and install several additional tutorials from the SketchUp Web site at `http://sketchup.google.com`. Each of these tutorials is saved as an SKP file.

Accessing other tutorials

If you search for tutorials in the 3D Warehouse, you'll find a huge number of links to step-by-step tutorials produced by existing SketchUp users. These tutorials walk you through a diverse number of tasks and show you how to model everything from airplanes and teddy bears to submarines and chess sets.

CROSS-REF To learn how to search for items within the 3D Warehouse, see Chapter 15.

Viewing the video tutorials

Help Center also includes many video tutorials. These tutorials open a Web browser with a page of videos on the SketchUp Web site, as shown in Figure 1.9. The page contains three categories of video tutorials; the first covers features new to SketchUp 7, the second covers modeling for Google Earth, and the third covers videos for the previous edition of SketchUp. Each category has multiple videos and each video can be streamed or downloaded.

 **If you download the latest videos for viewing locally on your system, you need to also download and install the EnSharpen codec in order to view the videos.**

FIGURE 1.9

The online video tutorials explain and show you different aspects of the software.

Instructor window

When learning the various SketchUp tools, the Instructor window can be helpful. It is accessed using the Window⇨Instructor menu. This window, shown in Figure 1.10, explains all the details about the current tool. If a different tool is selected, then the Instructor window is updated to show the features of the new tool.

For each tool, the Instructor window shows how to use the tool, explains any modifier keys, such as Shift, Ctrl, and Alt, and includes links for getting more information on advanced operations.

FIGURE 1.10

The Instructor window includes detailed information about the selected tool.

Summary

This chapter serves as a brief introduction to the SketchUp software, but if you have this book, then you are probably already sold on the software and have a desire to learn how to use it.

This chapter covered the following topics:

- How SketchUp is unique
- Available versions
- Help resources

The next chapter looks at the SketchUp interface, how the software works, and how to use the various buttons.

Chapter 2

Exploring the SketchUp Interface

One of the key goals of Google SketchUp is to make the software easy to use, and the interface reflects this goal. The interface is so simple that when you first start, it looks almost sparse, but under the covers are all the various tools and features that you need. These tools and features are cleverly hidden in palettes and toolbars that you can access when you need them and hide them away again to maximize your work area.

Even though the interface is simple, it has a lot of power under the hood that you can only take advantage of if you know it's there. This chapter not only shows you the elegance of the simple interface, but it also unveils the hidden power features.

Learning the Interface Elements

When SketchUp opens, several interface elements are immediately visible that allow you to get right to work. Figure 2.1 shows the various interface elements that are available when you first start. These elements include the following:

- **Title Bar:** The title bar appears at the very top edge of the interface. It displays the current filename and which version of SketchUp you are using. It can also be used to drag and reposition the interface window on the desktop. The title bar also includes icons to minimize, maximize, and close the interface window.

- **Menus:** The menus are the default source for most commands, but also one of the most time-consuming interface methods. The menus are found along the top edge of the SketchUp window.

- **Toolbars:** SketchUp includes several toolbars of icon buttons that provide single-click access to features. These toolbars can float independently or can be docked to an interface edge. The Getting Started Toolbar is the only toolbar that is initially visible.

- **Drawing area:** The drawing area makes up the bulk of the interface. This is the area where you do your work. There are axis guidelines displayed in the center of the drawing area.

- **Status Bar:** Along the lower edge of the interface is the Status Bar. This element displays helpful information about how to use the current tool. It also explains what SketchUp expects you to do next.

- **Measurements Toolbar:** To the right side of the status bar is the Measurements Toolbar. Within this box, the current value is displayed based on the tool that is currently selected. You can also type values directly into this field.

- **Resize Handle:** In the lower-right corner of the interface is the resize handle that you can use to resize the size of the interface window.

In addition to these default elements are several additional interface elements that aren't initially visible when SketchUp is first loaded. These additional interface elements include the following:

- **Additional toolbars:** Several specialized toolbars are available. You access them by choosing View ➪ Toolbars. Almost every command can be accessed using a toolbar icon if you have the correct toolbar open.

- **Scene tabs:** A complex project can be broken up into several different scenes and each scene can have its own tab. These tabs appear at the top of the interface just under the toolbars. New tabs can be created and deleted using the Scenes Manager.

- **Right-click Pop-up Menus (Context Menus):** Right-clicking on an object or on a Scene tab reveals a pop-up menu. These pop-up menus offer context-sensitive commands based on the object or location being clicked and provide one of the quickest ways to access commands.

- **Feature dialog boxes:** Some commands open a separate window of controls. These dialog boxes may contain custom settings for controlling the behavior of the selected object or tool. Dialog boxes can also include their own sets of controls including tabbed panels, toolbar icons, and drop-down lists. A good example of this interface element type is the Materials dialog box, shown in Figure 2.2, which has enough controls to keep you busy for a while.

If there are any aspects of the interface that you don't like, SketchUp includes some customization features that make it possible to alter the interface to your liking.

FIGURE 2.1

SketchUp starts with several key interface elements visible.

Title Bar

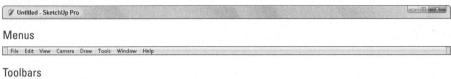

Menus

Toolbars

Drawing Area

Status Bar   Measurements Toolbar

Resize handle

CROSS-REF Customizing the SketchUp interface is covered later in this chapter.

FIGURE 2.2

The Materials dialog box includes its own set of controls.

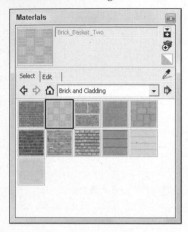

Using Menus

The main menus at the top of the SketchUp interface include most of the features available in SketchUp and are a great place for beginners to start. Several of the menu commands have corresponding toolbar buttons and keyboard shortcuts. To execute a menu command, you can choose it from the menu, click its corresponding toolbar button if it has one, or press its keyboard shortcut. You can also select commands using the keyboard arrows and press Enter to execute them.

The main menu includes the following options: File, Edit, View, Camera, Draw, Tools, Window, and Help. Unlike some other programs, these menu options do not disappear if not needed. The list is set, and they are always there when you need them.

If a keyboard command is available for a menu command, it is shown to the right of the menu item. If an ellipsis (three dots) appears after a menu item, that menu command causes a separate dialog box to open. A small black arrow to the right of a menu item indicates that a submenu exists. Clicking the menu item or holding the mouse over the top of a menu item makes the submenu appear. Toggle menu options (such as the Tools and Window menu options) change state each time they are selected. If a toggle menu option is enabled, a small check mark appears to its left; if disabled, no check mark appears.

CROSS-REF   A complete list of keyboard shortcuts can be found in Appendix C.

You can also navigate the menus using the keyboard by pressing Alt by itself. Doing so selects the File menu, and then you can use the arrow keys to move up and down and between menus. With a menu selected, you can press the keyboard letter that is underlined to select and execute a menu command. For example, pressing Alt and then F (for File) and N (for New) executes the File ⇨ New command; or you can press Alt, use the down arrow to select the New command, and press Enter.

TIP   By learning the underlined letters in the menu, you can use the keyboard to quickly access menu commands, even if the menu command doesn't have an assigned keyboard shortcut. And because you don't need to stretch for the Y key while holding down the Ctrl key, underlined menu letters can be faster. For example, by pressing Alt and T successively, you can access the Tools menu. From there you can use the arrow keys to navigate up and down the menu. The keyboard buffer remembers the order of the letters you type regardless of how fast they are keyed, making it possible to quickly access menu commands using the keyboard. Over time, you can learn patterns to help you remember how to access certain menu commands.

Not all menu commands are available at all times. If a menu command is unavailable, then it is grayed out, and you cannot select it. For example, the Hide command is available only when an object is selected, so if no objects are selected, the Hide command is grayed out and unavailable. After you select an object, this command becomes available. Figure 2.3 shows the visual clues for working with menus.

FIGURE 2.3

All menus feature visual clues for identifying keyboard shortcuts, submenus, and menus that open dialog boxes.

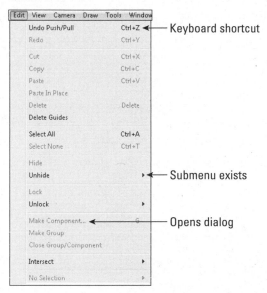

Accessing Toolbars

Now that you've learned the menu two-step (requiring two mouse clicks), it is time for the toolbar one-step (one click and done). The Getting Started toolbar appears by default directly under the menus at the top of the interface. Using toolbars is one of the most convenient ways to execute commands because most commands require only a single click.

By default, the Getting Started toolbar is docked along the top edge of the interface above the drawing area, but you can also stack up several additional toolbars by choosing View ⇨ Toolbars. These available toolbars include Getting Started, Large Tool Set, Camera, Construction, Drawing, Face Style, Google, Layers, Measurements, Modification, Principal, Sections, Shadows, Standard, Views, and Walkthrough. There are also two sets of default plug-in tools. Figure 2.4 shows the interface with all toolbars open. Notice that some icons are available on several different toolbars.

NEW FEATURE The Measurements toolbar is new to SketchUp 7. It allows you to move the Measurements toolbar or make it a floating toolbar. The Dynamic Components Toolbar is also new with SketchUp 7.

FIGURE 2.4

With all toolbars open, the drawing area is significantly reduced.

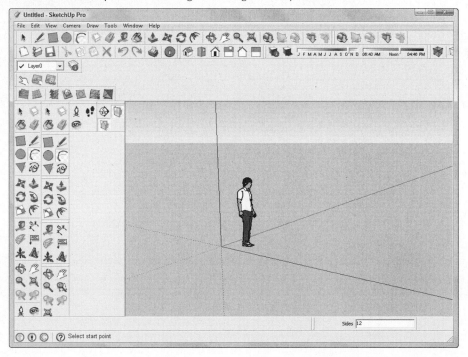

At the very bottom of the View⇨Toolbars menu is a toggle option to use Large Buttons. If this option is disabled, then all toolbar buttons are reduced, as shown in Figure 2.5.

NOTE The General panel of the System Preferences dialog box (opened by choosing Window⇨Preferences) includes an option to Use Large Tool Buttons. If this option is selected, then large icon buttons are used on all toolbars by default.

FIGURE 2.5

With the Large Buttons option disabled, the toolbar icons are smaller.

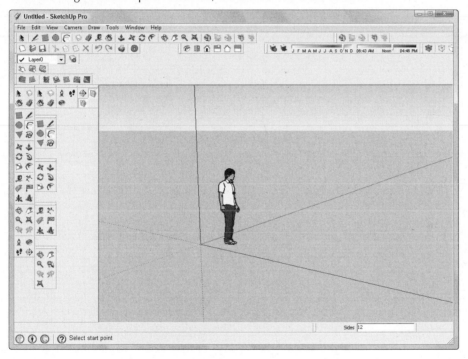

Docking and floating toolbars

All toolbars are automatically docked along the top or left side of the interface, but you can reposition any of the toolbars or even make the toolbars into a floating toolbar by clicking and dragging the two vertical lines on the left (or top) end of the toolbar away from the interface edge. After you separate it from the window, you can resize the floating toolbar by clicking and dragging on its edges or corners. You can then drag and dock it to any of the window edges or double-click the toolbar title bar to automatically dock the toolbar to its last docked location. Figure 2.6 shows the Large Tool Set Toolbar as a floating panel.

FIGURE 2.6

Floating toolbars can be positioned anywhere on the desktop.

Using tooltips

All icon buttons (including those found in toolbars and other dialog boxes) include tooltips, which are identifying text labels. If you hold the mouse cursor over an icon button, the tooltip label appears. This feature is useful for identifying buttons. If you can't remember a specific button's name, hold the cursor over the top of it and the tooltip gives you its name.

NOTE Another good way to learn the icon button names is the Quick Reference Card. You can open this PDF file by selecting it from the Help Center. Once open, you can print the file and hang it near your computer.

Using the toolbars

Most toolbar buttons offer access to tools. When a specific tool is selected, the toolbar button is indented. Other toolbar buttons, like the ones that open dialog boxes, require only a single click to access. These buttons don't stay indented when selected. Some toolbar buttons are disabled when they cannot be accessed. For example, the Paste command is disabled until an object is copied to the clipboard. Disabled toolbar buttons are light gray without any color.

Tables 2.1 through 2.16 list the controls found in the various toolbars. The keyboard shortcut for accessing a toolbar button is listed in the Name column in parenthesis next to the button's name. The Getting Started and Large Tool Set toolbars (shown in Tables 2.1 and 2.2, respectively) are compilations of buttons from the various toolbars. All the remaining toolbars are unique.

TABLE 2.1

Getting Started Toolbar Buttons

Toolbar Button	Name	Description
	Select tool (Spacebar)	Drag over an object to select it. Selected objects can have other commands applied to them.
	Line tool (L)	Draws lines by clicking at the line's beginning and ending points.

Toolbar Button	Name	Description
	Rectangle tool (R)	Create a rectangle shape by clicking at the first corner and clicking a second time to specify the opposite corner.
	Circle tool (C)	Creates a circle shape by clicking at the circle's center and dragging to specify the radius. Click a second time to create the circle.
	Arc tool (A)	Creates an arc shape by clicking twice to specify the arc's endpoints and then dragging to form the arc's radius.
	Make Component	Used to combine several objects into a single component. Moving a component also moves all the objects that are part of the component.
	Eraser tool (E)	Used to delete objects from the project.
	Tape Measure tool (T)	Used to measure distances. Distance values are displayed in the VCB.
	Paint Bucket tool (B)	Used to apply materials and colors to object surfaces.
	Push/Pull tool (P)	Used to extrude a surface forming a volume by moving the surface in a direction that is perpendicular to the surface.
	Move/Copy tool (M)	Drag to move the selected object or hold down the Ctrl key while moving to create and move a duplicate object.
	Rotate tool (Q)	Used to rotate individual objects and entities.
	Offset tool (F)	Creates copies of the selected object whose edges are offset from the original by a common value.
	Orbit tool (O)	Used to rotate the camera about the center of the drawing area while maintaining its distance from the object.
	Pan tool (H)	Used to move the camera vertically or horizontally while preserving the camera's orientation.
	Zoom tool (Z)	Used to zoom in and out of the scene.
	Zoom Extents tool (Shift+Z)	Zooms in or out of the current scene so that all objects are visible and centered within the drawing area.

(continued)

TABLE 2.1	(continued)	
Toolbar Button	**Name**	**Description**
	Get Current View	Captures the current view from Google Earth.
	Toggle Terrain	Toggles the Google Earth snapshot between a 2-D and 3-D view.
	Place Model	Places your current scene into Google Earth.
	Get Models	Provides access to 3D Warehouse where you can download models into your scene.
	Share Model	Used to upload your current model to 3D Warehouse.

TABLE 2.2		

Large Tool Set Toolbar Buttons

Toolbar Button	Name	Description
	Select tool (Spacebar)	Drag over an object to select it. Selected objects can have other commands applied to them.
	Make Component	Used to combine several objects into a single component. Moving a component also moves all the objects that are part of the component.
	Paint Bucket tool (B)	Used to apply materials and colors to object surfaces.
	Eraser tool (E)	Used to delete objects from the project.
	Rectangle tool (R)	Create a rectangle shape by clicking at the first corner and clicking a second time to specify the opposite corner.
	Line tool (L)	Draws lines by clicking at the line's beginning and ending points.
	Circle tool (C)	Creates a circle shape by clicking at the circle's center and dragging to specify the radius. Click a second time to create the circle.

Toolbar Button	Name	Description
	Arc tool (A)	Creates an arc shape by clicking twice to specify the arc's endpoints and then dragging to form the arc's radius.
	Polygon tool	Creates a polygon shape with six sides by clicking once at the shape's center and again to set the shape's radius. You can set the number of sides in the VCB.
	Freehand tool	Draws a freehand curve by dragging with the mouse cursor.
	Move/Copy tool (M)	Drag to move the selected object or hold down the Ctrl key while moving to create and move a duplicate object.
	Push/Pull tool (P)	Used to extrude a surface forming a volume by moving the surface in a direction that is perpendicular to the surface.
	Rotate tool (Q)	Used to rotate individual objects and entities.
	Follow Me tool	Extrudes a surface along a drawn path.
	Scale tool (S)	Used to scale the size of individual objects and entities.
	Offset tool (F)	Creates copies of the selected object whose edges are offset from the original by a common value.
	Tape Measure tool (T)	Used to measure distances. Distance values are displayed in the VCB.
	Dimension tool	Used to place dimension text for objects in your scene.
	Protractor tool	Used to measure angles. Angle values are displayed in the VCB.
	Text tool	Used to insert standard text into the scene.
	Axes tool	Used to specify and reorient the scene axes.
	3D Text tool	Creates extruded text in the scene.

(continued)

TABLE 2.2   *(continued)*

Toolbar Button	Name	Description
	Orbit tool (O)	Used to rotate the camera about the center of the drawing area while maintaining its distance from the object.
	Pan tool (H)	Used to move the camera vertically or horizontally while preserving the camera's orientation.
	Zoom tool (Z)	Used to zoom in and out of the scene.
	Zoom Extents tool (Shift+Z)	Zooms in or out of the current scene so that all objects are visible and centered within the drawing area.
	Previous View	Displays the last scene view.
	Next View	Displays the next scene view.
	Position Camera tool	Used to specify the camera's eye view when walkthrough mode is enabled.
	Look Around tool	Used to rotate the camera left, right, up, and down when walkthrough mode is enabled.
	Walk tool	Used to move through the current scene when walkthrough mode is enabled.
	Section Plane tool	Used to specify a cross-section plane allowing the inside of a model to be displayed.

TABLE 2.3

Camera Toolbar Buttons

Toolbar Button	Name	Description
	Orbit tool (O)	Used to rotate the camera about the center of the drawing area while maintaining its distance from the object.
	Pan tool (H)	Used to move the camera vertically or horizontally while preserving the camera's orientation.

Toolbar Button	Name	Description
	Zoom tool (Z)	Used to zoom in and out of the scene.
	Zoom Window tool	Used to zoom in on only that portion of the scene that you select by dragging.
	Previous View	Displays the last scene view.
	Next View	Displays the next scene view.
	Zoom Extents tool (Shift+Z)	Zooms in or out of the current scene so that all objects are visible and centered within the drawing area.

TABLE 2.4

Construction Toolbar Buttons

Toolbar Button	Name	Description
	Tape Measure tool (T)	Used to measure distances. Distance values are displayed in the VCB.
	Dimension tool	Used to place dimension text for objects in your scene.
	Protractor tool	Used to measure angles. Angle values are displayed in the VCB.
	Text tool	Used to insert standard text into the scene.
	Axes tool	Used to specify and reorient the scene axes.
	3D Text tool	Creates extruded text in the scene.

TABLE 2.5

Drawing Toolbar Buttons

Toolbar Button	Name	Description
	Rectangle tool (R)	Creates a rectangle shape by clicking at the first corner and clicking a second time to specify the opposite corner.
	Line tool (L)	Draws lines by clicking at the line's beginning and ending points.
	Circle tool (C)	Creates a circle shape by clicking at the circle's center and dragging to specify the radius. Click a second time to create the circle.
	Arc tool (A)	Creates an arc shape by clicking twice to specify the arc's endpoints and then dragging to form the arc's radius.
	Polygon tool	Creates a polygon shape with six sides by clicking once at the shape's center and again to set the shape's radius. You can set the number of sides in the VCB.
	Freehand tool	Draws a freehand curve by dragging with the mouse cursor.

TABLE 2.6

Face Style Toolbar Buttons

Toolbar Button	Name	Description
	X-Ray display style	Displays all objects as semitransparent so background objects are visible through foreground objects.
	Wireframe display style	Displays only the edges of all objects.
	Hidden Line display style	Displays only the edges of all objects, but hides those edges that are obscured by faces.
	Shaded display style	Displays all faces of objects using solid colors.
	Shaded with Textures display style	Displays all object faces including any applied textures.
	Monochrome display style	Displays all faces using solid grayscale colors.

TABLE 2.7

Google Toolbar Buttons

Toolbar Button	Name	Description
	Get Current View	Captures the current view from Google Earth.
	Toggle Terrain	Toggles the Google Earth snapshot between a 2-D and 3-D view.
	Place Model	Places your current scene into Google Earth.
	Get Models	Provides access to 3D Warehouse where you can download models into your scene.
	Share Model	Used to upload your current model to 3D Warehouse.

TABLE 2.8

Layers Toolbar Buttons

Toolbar Button	Name	Description
▶ Layer0 ▼	Layer drop-down list	A selection list that holds all the defined layers.
	Layer Manager	Opens the Layer Manager where you can create new layers and toggle their visibility.

TABLE 2.9

Measurements Toolbar

Toolbar Button	Name	Description
	Measurements field	Displays the value of the current measurement and allows that value to be changed.

TABLE 2.10

Modification (Edit) Toolbar Buttons

Toolbar Button	Name	Description
	Move/Copy tool (M)	Click and drag to move the selected object or hold down the Ctrl key while moving to create and move a duplicate object.
	Push/Pull tool (P)	Used to extrude a surface forming a volume by moving the surface in a direction that is perpendicular to the surface.
	Rotate tool (Q)	Used to rotate individual objects and entities.
	Follow Me tool	Extrudes a surface along a drawn path.
	Scale tool (S)	Used to scale the size of individual objects and entities.
	Offset tool (F)	Creates copies of the selected object whose edges are offset from the original by a common value.

 **CAUTION** The toolbar that is called the Modification Toolbar in the View ⇨ Toolbar menu is listed as the Edit Toolbar on its title bar.

TABLE 2.11

Principal Toolbar Buttons

Toolbar Button	Name	Description
	Select tool (Spacebar)	Click and drag over an object to select it. Selected objects can have other commands applied to them.
	Make Component	Used to combine several objects into a single component. Moving a component also moves all the objects that are part of the component.
	Paint Bucket tool (B)	Used to apply materials and colors to object surfaces.
	Eraser tool (E)	Used to delete objects from the project.

TABLE 2.12

Sections Toolbar Buttons

Toolbar Button	Name	Description
	Section Plane tool	Used to specify a cross-section plane allowing the inside of a model to be displayed.
	Display Section Planes	Displays the planes used to specify the cross-section cut.
	Display Section Cuts	Toggles the cross-section cuts on and off.

TABLE 2.13

Shadows Toolbar Buttons

Toolbar Button	Name	Description
	Shadow Settings	Opens the Shadow Settings dialog box for specifying the shadow's time, date, and brightness.
	Display Shadows	Toggles the shadows on and off in the scene.
J F M A M J J A S O N D	Date setting	Slider that sets the month for the shadows.
04:48 AM Noon 07:24 PM	Time setting	Slider that sets the time for the shadows.

TABLE 2.14

Standard Toolbar Buttons

Toolbar Button	Name	Description
	New (Ctrl+N)	Opens a new blank project.
	Open (Ctrl+O)	Opens an existing saved project.
	Save (Ctrl+S)	Saves the current project.

(continued)

TABLE 2.14 *(continued)*

Toolbar Button	Name	Description
	Cut (Ctrl+X)	Removes the current object and places it on the clipboard.
	Copy (Ctrl+C)	Copies the current object and places it on the clipboard.
	Paste (Ctrl+V)	Pastes the clipboard object into the scene.
	Erase (Delete)	Deletes the selected object.
	Undo (Ctrl+Z or Alt+Backspace)	Undoes the last command.
	Redo (Ctrl+Y)	Redoes the last undone command.
	Print (Ctrl+P)	Prints the current scene.
	Model Info	Opens the Model Info dialog box where you can set the preferences for the current model.

TABLE 2.15

Views Toolbar Buttons

Toolbar Button	Name	Description
	Iso view (Shift+1)	Displays the scene from an angled view above and to the side of the scene.
	Top view (Shift+2)	Displays the scene from a view above the scene.
	Front view (Shift+4)	Displays the scene from a view in front of the scene.
	Right view (Shift+6)	Displays the scene from a view to the right of the scene.

Toolbar Button	Name	Description
	Back view (Shift+5)	Displays the scene from a view behind the scene.
	Left view (Shift+7)	Displays the scene from a view to the left of the scene.

TABLE 2.16

Walkthrough Toolbar Buttons

Toolbar Button	Name	Description
	Position Camera tool	Used to specify the camera's eye view when Walkthrough mode is enabled.
	Walk tool	Used to move through the current scene when Walkthrough mode is enabled.
	Look Around tool	Used to rotate the camera left, right, up, and down when Walkthrough mode is enabled.

NOTE   At the bottom of the Views ➪ Toolbars menu, some additional toolbars may be available. These toolbars, such as the Dynamic Components and Sandbox toolbars, are included with installed sets of plug-ins. You can learn more about installing and using plug-in sets in Chapter 28.

Interacting with the Interface

Although the menus and the toolbar buttons are the main methods for accessing tools and executing commands, there are other helpful ways to work with the interface such as context menus, the status bar, and the Measurements Toolbar.

Using context menus

Although menus and toolbars are the default ways to execute commands in SketchUp, you can also access specific commands using the context menus. These menus appear when you right-click on an object and the command contained in these menus is specific to the object that you clicked. For example, if you click on a polygon object, you'll see commands to Erase, Hide, and Select its entities, but you won't see any commands to alter the scene's shadows, as shown in Figure 2.7. By limiting menu entries to options that are applicable, SketchUp keeps the menus to a reasonable size.

FIGURE 2.7

FIGURE 2.7

Context menus appear when you right-click on a scene object.

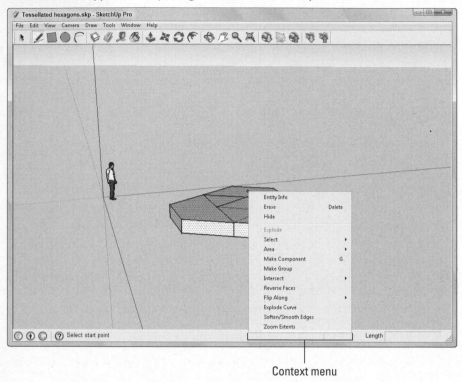

Context menu

Getting help from the status bar

The status bar shows the name of any toolbar button when you move the mouse over the top of the button. When a tool is selected, the status bar shows details on how to use the tool. For example, when the Arcs tool is selected, the status bar says, "Select Start Point," and after you click once in the drawing area, the status bar text changes to "Select end point or enter value." After clicking to specify the second point, the status bar says, "Select bulge distance or enter value."

This same process of walking you through the steps on how to use a tool works the same for all tools. The status bar also shows any additional features that are possible by holding down the keyboard keys. For example, when the Push/Pull tool is selected, the status bar says, "Pick face to push or pull. Ctrl = toggle create new starting face." The status bar reminds you that the Ctrl key has a special feature when this tool is selected.

Using the Measurements Toolbar

The Measurements Toolbar is a wonderful little control. It is located at the right end of the status bar and is always available. It also magically changes to show the current value that you are working with and lets you type a precise value without having to scroll through a long list of parameters.

The dimension label (which is the text that appears to the left of the toolbar) changes depending on the tool that is being used. For example, when you click the Circle tool, the label displays the number of Sides used to make the circle, but after you click to specify the center point, the label changes to Radius allowing you to type a precise Radius value.

NOTE **After typing a value in the Measurements Toolbar, you need to press Enter to accept the value.**

The Measurements Toolbar is ready to accept numerical values at any time, and you don't need to click on the toolbar before you can type a value. If a value is typed without any units, then the default units system is used, but you can also specify the units and SketchUp will automatically convert them to the entered units system. For example, if the system units are set to Feet and Inches and you type a value of 2.5m, the meters are converted to feet and inches.

Working with dialog boxes

Several SketchUp commands open up a dialog box of settings. You can identify the menu commands that open a dialog box by looking for the ellipsis (three dots) at the end of the menu command. Most of the SketchUp dialog boxes found in the Window menu are modeless, which means that they can stay open while you continue to work in the drawing area. Dialog boxes that aren't modeless require you to click OK before you can return to your work.

Because the SketchUp dialog boxes are modeless, you may want to keep them around while you are working. SketchUp allows you to dock dialog boxes to the outer interface edge while they are open. This helps free up some space and keeps the dialog boxes accessible, but out of the way. To dock an open dialog box to the outer edge of the interface, simply click and drag its title bar to the outer edge and the dialog box automatically snaps to the edge, as shown in Figure 2.8.

Dialog boxes can be docked to the outer edge of the interface.

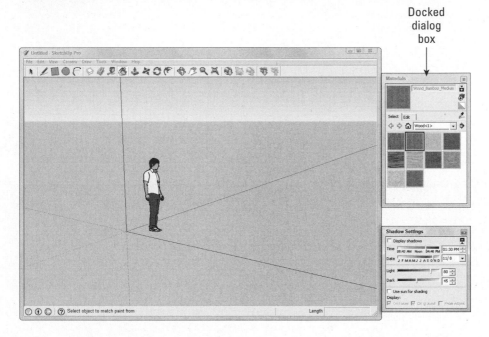

When a dialog box is open, you can collapse a dialog box so only its title bar is showing by clicking its title bar once. Clicking the title bar again expands the dialog box to its original size. Collapsed dialog boxes are marked in the Window menu with a small bar next to their names. Open dialog boxes have a check mark next to their menu names. Dialog boxes can be resized by clicking and dragging their edges or corners.

You can also snap dialog boxes to the top and bottom edge of any open dialog boxes to create a dialog box stack, as shown in Figure 2.9. All dialog boxes within the stack assume the width of the top dialog box. When you reposition the top dialog box, all dialog boxes in the stack move with it. Stacked dialog boxes can also be collapsed and expanded as needed.

The non-modeless dialog boxes in SketchUp include the File, Import, and Print dialog boxes that are accessed using the File menu. Other non-modeless dialog boxes include the Match New Photo, Preferences, and Ruby Console dialog boxes.

At the bottom of the Window menu is a command to Hide Dialogs. This command hides all open and collapsed dialog boxes and changes the command to Show Dialogs. When selected again, the hidden dialog boxes are made visible.

FIGURE 2.9

Multiple dialog boxes can be snapped together to form a stack.

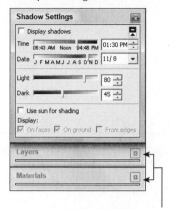

Collapsed dialog boxes

Learning the color clues

Colors play an important part of the interface. The axes that define the X, Y, and Z directions in the drawing area are colored red for the X-axis, green for the Y-axis, and blue for the Z-axis.

There are also colors associated with the various inference locations. These inferences are displayed as you move the mouse cursor over the top of an object and are displayed as a simple colored dot underneath the current tool, as shown in Figure 2.10. A tooltip also appears indicating the point's inference.

CROSS-REF You can learn more about inference in Chapter 6.

The available inference colors include the following:

- **Green:** A green inference point marks an endpoint.
- **Cyan:** A cyan inference point marks a midpoint of a line or edge.
- **Black:** A black inference point marks the place where a line intersects another line or a face.
- **Blue:** A blue inference point marks a point on the surface of a face.
- **Red:** A red inference point marks a point along an edge.
- **Magenta:** A magenta line indicates lines that are either perpendicular or parallel to the connected line.

FIGURE 2.10

Inference points are color coded to indicate different locations.

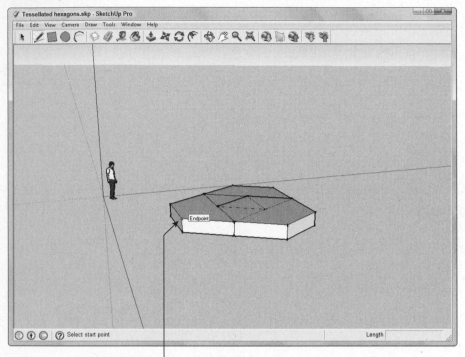

Inference point marking an endpoint

Customizing the Interface

There are a couple of ways to customize the current interface. One way is to move the toolbars around as described earlier. You can also resize the window by dragging on the edges or corners of the window. Within the System Preferences dialog box, the General panel, shown in Figure 2.11, holds an option to Use large tool buttons.

Customizing keyboard shortcuts

The System Preferences dialog box includes another key way to customize the interface by changing the keyboard shortcuts for the entire interface using the Shortcuts panel, shown in Figure 2.12.

FIGURE 2.11

The General panel in the System Preferences dialog box holds an option to Use large tool buttons.

FIGURE 2.12

The Shortcuts panel in the System Preferences dialog box lets you change keyboard shortcuts.

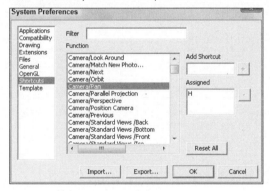

The Function pane in the center of the Shortcuts panel lists all the available commands. If you type in the Filter field, then you can focus the list of commands to a smaller set. If a selected command has a command currently assigned to it, it is listed in the Assigned field. If you click the minus sign button to the right of the Assigned field, then the current shortcut assignment is deleted.

To assign a new keyboard shortcut, simply select a command and type the new shortcut in the Add Shortcut field and click the plus sign button to the right of the Add Shortcut field. If the shortcut you've selected is already assigned to another command, then a dialog box, like the one in Figure 2.13, appears. This helps remind you when a shortcut is already assigned.

The Reset All button reassigns the default shortcuts. This eliminates any custom keyboard shortcuts that you've assigned.

FIGURE 2.13

A warning dialog box appears when you try to assign a shortcut that is already being used.

Summary

You should now be familiar with SketchUp's interface elements. Understanding the interface is one of the keys to success in using SketchUp. SketchUp includes a variety of different interface elements. Several ways to perform the same command exist, whether you use the menus, toolbars, or keyboard shortcuts. Discover the method that works best for you.

This chapter covered the following topics:

- Learning the interface elements
- Viewing and using the pull-down menus
- Working with toolbars
- Interacting with the SketchUp interface

This chapter skirted around the drawing area, covering all the other interface elements. The next chapter confronts the drawing area head-on and shows you how to configure the drawing area and how to navigate about it.

Chapter 3

Navigating and Configuring the Drawing Area

Although SketchUp consists of many different interface elements, such as toolbars, dialog boxes, and menus, the drawing area is the main element that will catch your attention because it makes up the bulk of the interface. You can think of the drawing area as looking at the television screen instead of the remote. Learning to control and use the drawing area can make a huge difference in your comfort level with SketchUp. Nothing is more frustrating than not being able to rotate, pan, and zoom the view.

The drawing area has numerous settings that you can use to provide thousands of different ways to look at your scene. This chapter includes all the details you need to make the drawing area reveal its secret.

IN THIS CHAPTER

Understanding 3-D space

Managing perspective

Using the drawing area camera controls

Walking through your model

Configuring the drawing area

Understanding 3-D Space

It seems silly to be talking about 3-D space because we live and move in 3-D space. If you stop and think about it, 3-D space is natural to us. For example, consider trying to locate your kids at the swimming pool. If you're standing poolside, the kids could be to your left or right, in front of you or behind you, or in the water below you or on the high dive above you. Each of these sets of directions represents a dimension in 3-D space.

Now imagine that you're drawing a map that pinpoints the kids' location at the swimming pool. Using the drawing (which is 2-D), you can describe the kids' position on the map as left, right, top, or bottom, but the descriptions of above and below have been lost. By moving from a 3-D reference to a 2-D reference, you lose a spatial coordinate, so the number of dimensions decreases.

The conundrum that 3-D computer artists face is how do you represent 3-D objects on a 2-D device such as a computer screen? The answer that SketchUp provides is to present a main view, called the *drawing area,* that can be switched between several different views and navigated to provide custom views. A drawing area is a window that displays the scene from one perspective and is the window into SketchUp's 3-D world.

Learning the Standard Views in SketchUp

Although SketchUp starts with a perspective view of the drawing area, you can change to view the scene from one of several standard views. These views are available in the Camera ⇨ Standard Views menu or in the Views toolbar. The available standard views in SketchUp include Top, Bottom, Front, Back, Left, Right, and Isometric (Iso). An Isometric view is one that views the scene from an angle above and to the right of the center.

Figure 3.1 shows a motorcycle file open in the default Iso view. Figure 3.2 shows the same motorcycle from the Top view, and Figure 3.3 shows the motorcycle from the Front view.

FIGURE 3.1

The default view displays all objects from an Isometric view.

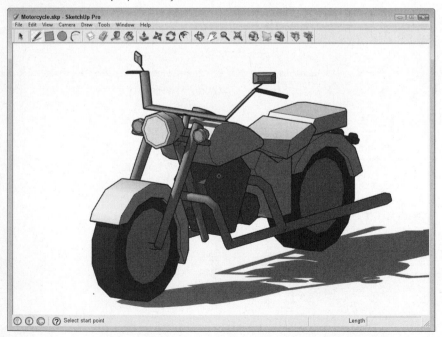

FIGURE 3.2

The Top view displays all objects from a position above the scene.

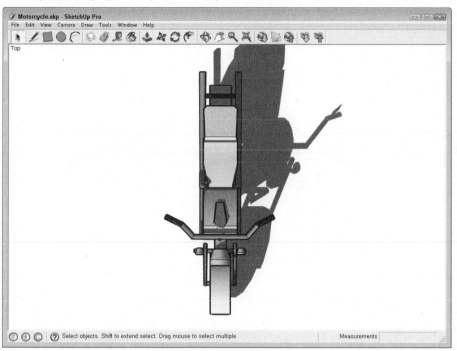

TIP   SketchUp includes several keyboard shortcuts for quickly changing between the different standard views in the drawing area including Shift+1 (Iso View), Shift+2 (Top view), Shift+3 (Bottom view), Shift+4 (Front view), Shift+5 (Back view), Shift+6 (Right view), and Shift+7 (Left view).

FIGURE 3.3

The Front view displays all objects from a position directly in front of the scene.

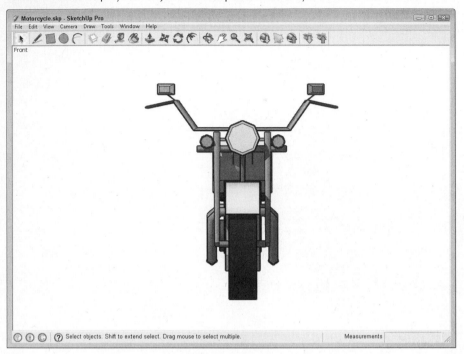

Managing Perspective

When you have the standard views figured out, you need to learn a thing or two about perspective. Perspective is an optical effect that causes objects to recede to a single point in the distance. Imagine looking down a long road lined with trees. The trees closest to you appear much larger than those in the distance. This is a natural effect of our eyes, but it makes it difficult to measure exact dimensions, which is a task that is important in SketchUp.

To get the actual dimensions of the scene objects, you can use a different type of view. An axonometric view represents objects using their actual dimensions without any distortion due to perspective.

Axonometric versus perspective

When it comes to views in the 3-D world, two different types exist — axonometric and perspective. Axonometric views are common in the CAD world where the viewer is set at an infinite distance from the object such that all parallel lines remain parallel. A perspective view simulates how our eyes actually work and converges all points to a single location off in the distance.

 Axonometric views are also referred to as paraline views.

You can see the difference between these two types of views clearly if you look at a long line of objects. For example, if you were to look down a long row of trees lining a road, the trees would gradually recede to a point on the horizon, as shown in Figure 3.4.

FIGURE 3.4

A perspective view causes objects to recede to a point in the distance.

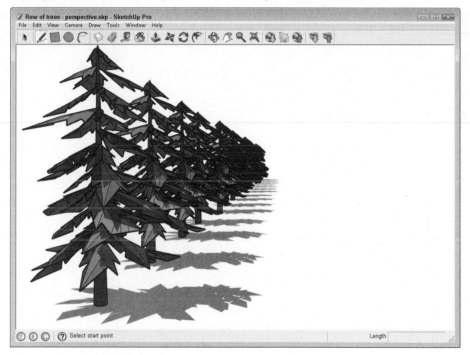

In axonometric views, lines stay parallel as they recede into the distance. Figure 3.5 shows the same row of trees with the axonometric view. Notice how the height of all the trees is the same.

To switch between perspective and axonometric views in SketchUp, simply choose Camera ⇨ Perspective to view the current scene using perspective, or choose Camera ⇨ Parallel Projection to view the scene using an axonometric view.

FIGURE 3.5

An axonometric view causes all dimensions to be accurate.

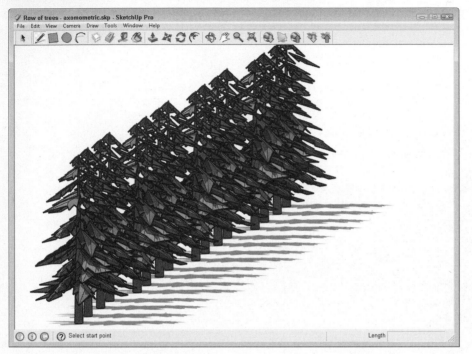

Orthographic and Isometric views

If you dig a little deeper into axonometric views, you find two different types — orthographic and isometric. Orthographic views are displayed from the perspective of looking straight down an axis at an object. This reveals a view in only one plane. Because orthographic viewports are constrained to one plane, they show the actual height and width of the object, which is why the CAD world uses orthographic views extensively. Isometric views are not constrained to a single axis and can view the scene from any location, but all dimensions are still maintained.

Orthographic views can be simulated in SketchUp by selecting any of the standard camera views except for the Iso view and turning on the Parallel Projection option. Isometric views are created using the Iso standard view.

> **TIP** If you need to measure the dimensions of an object such as the length of a boat from tip to tip, then switch to the Top view with the Parallel Projection option enabled to see the boat in accurate dimensions.

Two-Point Perspective

The Perspective option in SketchUp causes all horizontal lines to converge to a single point on the horizon, but this isn't the only perspective type. SketchUp also offers Two-Point Perspective that causes all horizontal lines to converge to not one, but two different points on the horizon. For example, if you're looking at the corner of a building, then one wall converges toward one point and the other wall converges toward a different point that is also on the horizon.

 **When a Two-Point Perspective view is enabled, a label in the upper-left corner of the drawing area says "Two-Point Perspective."**

Two-Point Perspective is common in the artistic and architectural industries. Many of the famous Renaissance drawings use this perspective method. You can display the current scene in Two-Point Perspective by choosing Camera ⇨ Two-Point Perspective. Figure 3.6 shows a large box in two-point perspective. Notice how the opposite edges along the top are not parallel and tend to converge toward opposite points on the horizon.

FIGURE 3.6

Two-Point Perspective causes parallel horizontal lines to converge to two different points.

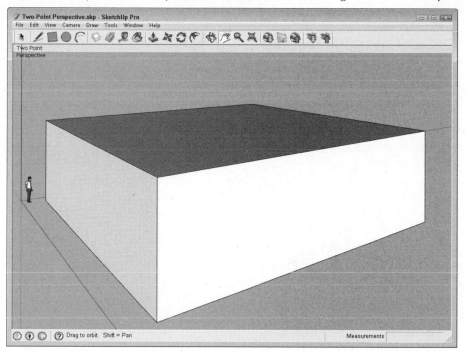

 In both Perspective and Two-Point Perspective views, vertical lines remain vertical.

Although not currently supported by SketchUp, there is also a three-point perspective that causes the vertical lines to also converge. It is used to represent tall buildings that tend to hover over an object.

Changing the Field of View

When working with a Perspective or a Two-Point Perspective view, you choose Camera ⇨ Field of View to alter the amount of perspective applied to the view. When the Field of View option is selected, the current Field of View is displayed in the Measurements ToolbarMeasurement Toolbar, and you can alter this value by typing a new value.

The Field of View value is an angular value that describes the width of the current scene that is visible to the camera lens. Telephoto lenses have a field-of-view value from 10 to 15 degrees, normal lenses have a field of view around 45 degrees, and wide-angle lenses range from 60 to 100 degrees. Panoramic scenes can be captured using a fisheye lens that has a field of view of 180 degrees.

Wide-angle lenses make a wider portion of the current landscape visible, but adjusting the field of view for a close-up object only distorts the object to a greater extent. Figure 3.7 shows a line of trees with an adjusted field of view set to 100. The before adjustment is shown in Figure 3.4.

FIGURE 3.7

By adjusting the Field of View value, you can make a wider portion of the landscape visible.

Using the Drawing Area Camera Controls

The drawing area shows you a single view of your current project. To orbit, pan, and zoom the drawing area, you need to use the camera tools. These tools can be selected from the Camera menu, from the Camera toolbar, or by pressing a keyboard shortcut.

Orbiting a view

Orbiting the view can be the most revealing of all the view changes. When the Orbit tool (O) is selected, you can click and drag in the drawing area to rotate the scene about its center. This provides an excellent way to view the scene objects from multiple angles. Figure 3.8 shows the motorcycle scene while being orbited.

 **When the Orbit tool is active, you can double-click to center the clicked-on location in the drawing area. This also works when the Pan and Zoom tools are selected.**

FIGURE 3.8

The Orbit tool lets you rotate about the scene objects.

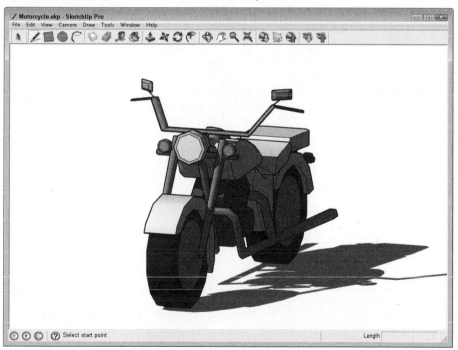

By default, the Orbit tool automatically constrains all Z-axis rotations so that all vertical lines remain vertical. This is like having the effect of gravity, and it keeps the model from rolling about the camera's axis line. You can suspend this gravity-imposed rotation by holding down the Ctrl key while dragging with the Orbit tool. Figure 3.9 shows the motorcycle model after dragging the Orbit tool with the Ctrl key held down.

FIGURE 3.9

Holding down the Ctrl key while dragging with the Orbit tool lets you spin the scene objects.

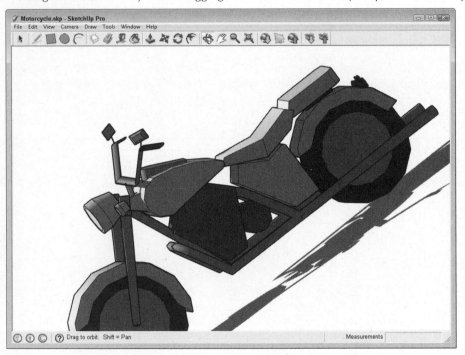

Panning a view

The Pan tool lets you reposition the camera view in the drawing area. With the Pan tool (H) selected, drag in the direction that you want the view moved. Note that this doesn't move the objects, only the view. Figure 3.10 shows the view of the motorcycle moved to the lower corner of the drawing area using the Pan tool.

FIGURE 3.10

The Pan tool lets you move the camera view within the drawing area.

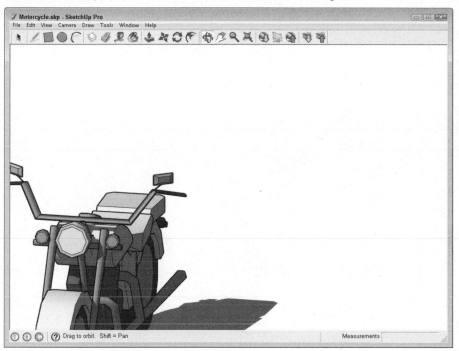

Zooming a view

You can zoom into and out of the scene in several ways. Selecting the Zoom (Z) tool enters Zoom mode where you can zoom into and out of a drawing area by dragging the mouse. Figure 3.11 shows the motorcycle model after zooming in on it.

You can also zoom in on a specific region of the drawing area using the Zoom Window command (Ctrl+Shift+W), which is found in the Camera menu. A button for this command is available in the Camera toolbar. Figure 3.12 shows the lights on the front of the motorcycle. This view was created by selecting the Zoom Window tool and dragging a rectangular region over the lights.

FIGURE 3.11

The Zoom tool lets you get close to the model.

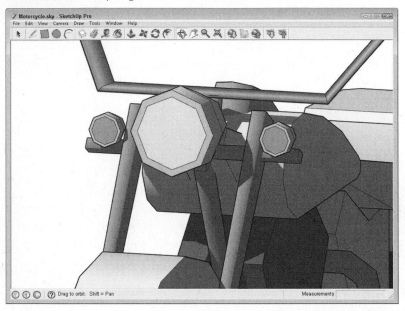

FIGURE 3.12

The Zoom Window tool lets you zoom in on a selected region.

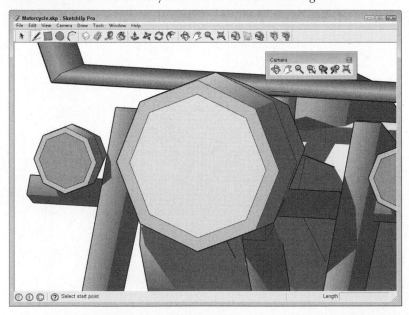

FIGURE 3.13

The Zoom Extents tool quickly centers and zooms the view to show all objects.

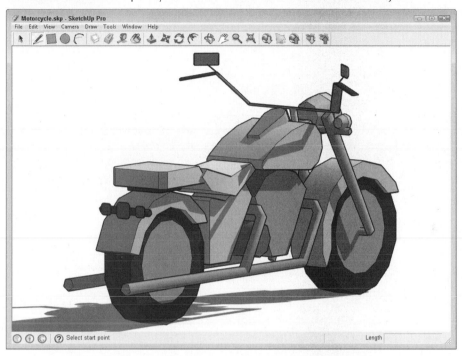

Controlling views with the mouse

Although you can navigate the view displayed in the drawing area using the various commands found in the Camera menu or the buttons found in the Camera toolbar, the quickest way to orbit, pan, and zoom the view is with the mouse. You can immediately access the Orbit tool by clicking and dragging with the middle mouse button (the scroll wheel). The Pan tool is accessed by holding down the Shift key while dragging with the middle mouse button. You can also zoom in and out of the scene by scrolling the scroll wheel.

> **TIP** You can also access the Pan tool by clicking and holding the middle mouse button and then clicking and holding the left mouse button instead of the Shift key.

When you release the middle mouse button, control is returned to whichever tool was selected before you clicked the middle mouse button.

> **CAUTION** The middle mouse button cannot control the view when the Walk tool is selected. This is the one exception.

Moving between views

If you make a change to a view and then realize that the last view was what you wanted, you can use the Camera ⇨ Previous menu command or the Previous button on the Camera toolbar to return the last view. The Previous button lets you move back through several views. Saved views are recorded every time a different view tool is used. SketchUp can remember up to five saved views.

The Camera ⇨ Next menu command or the Next button on the Camera toolbar can move forward to the next view in the opposite direction of the Previous button. These two buttons together work just like the similar buttons on a Web browser, allowing you to move back and forth through the views.

> **TIP** Because SketchUp only remembers the five most recent views, if you click the Previous button when you are viewing the oldest view, you'll actually wrap back around to the newest view. Both the Previous and the Next buttons let you scroll through the available saved views by repeated clicking.

Tutorial: Navigating the active drawing area

Over time, navigating with the drawing area will become second nature to you, but you need to practice to get to that point. In this tutorial, you get a chance to take the drawing area for a spin — literally.

To practice navigating a drawing area, follow these steps:

1. Open the `Armored truck.skp` file from the `Chap 03` directory on the CD or you can place the Armored truck component from the Components Browser.

   This file includes an armored truck model imported from the `Components` folder where SketchUp is installed. It provides a reference as you navigate the drawing area. The default view is the Iso view, as shown in Figure 3.14.

FIGURE 3.14

The file opens in the default Iso view.

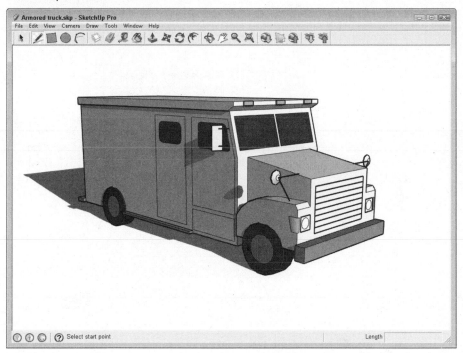

2. Click the Orbit button (or press O), and drag in the drawing area until the front of the truck is visible. Then click the Zoom button (or press Z), and drag in the drawing area until the truck fills the drawing area, as shown in Figure 3.15.

FIGURE 3.15

Using the Orbit and Zoom tools, you can get a close-up view of the front of the truck.

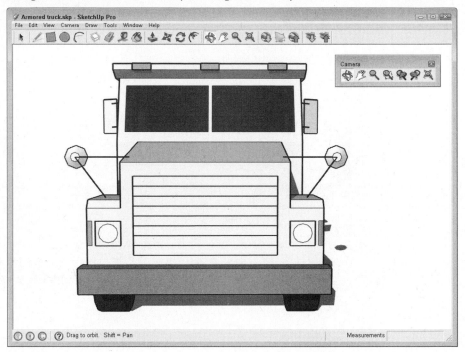

3. Click the Previous button in the Camera toolbar twice to return to the default Iso view. Then select the Zoom Window tool (or press Ctrl+Shift+W) and drag over the front grill of the truck. This zooms in on the selected area, as shown in Figure 3.16.

FIGURE 3.16

The Zoom Window tool lets you zoom in on a selected area.

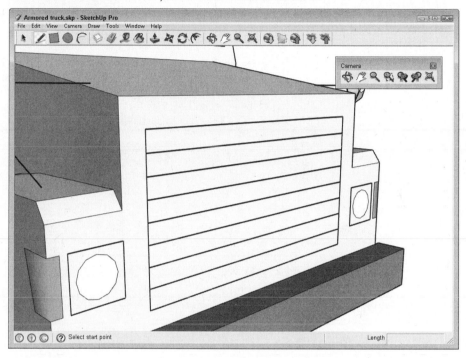

4. Click the Pan button (or press H) and drag downward in the drawing area to change the view so the front windshield is visible, as shown in Figure 3.17.

5. As a last step, click the Zoom Extents button (or press Ctrl+Shift+E) to zoom out so the entire truck is visible again.

If you tried this tutorial as outlined, try it again using the mouse's scroll wheel.

FIGURE 3.17

After panning the view, the front windshield is visible.

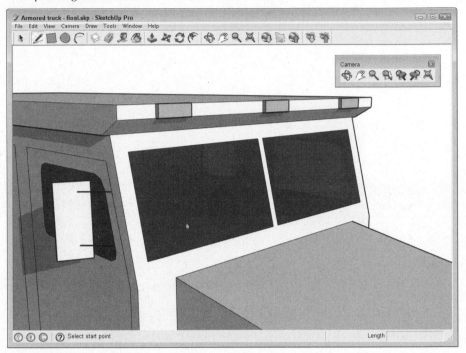

Walking Through Your Model

At the bottom of the Camera menu are three commands that allow you to walk through your model just as if you were playing a first-person shooter game. SketchUp even does collision detection, which prevents you from moving through walls.

Positioning the camera

The Position Camera tool, located in the Camera menu or on the Walkthrough toolbar, lets you place the camera in preparation to walk through the scene. When you click on a location in the scene with this tool, the camera is placed at exactly 5 feet, 6 inches above the point where you click, which is roughly eye level. While the Position Camera tool is selected, you can alter the eye-level height by typing a new value in the Measurements Toolbar.

After you click on a location in the scene with the Position Camera tool, the view is animated moving from its current location to the new specified location and the Look Around tool is automatically selected. Figure 3.18 shows the view from eye level after using the Position Camera tool.

 When you click in the scene with the Position Camera tool, the view is automatically set to look toward the top of the screen.

FIGURE 3.18

The Position Camera tool lets you place the camera at eye level in the scene.

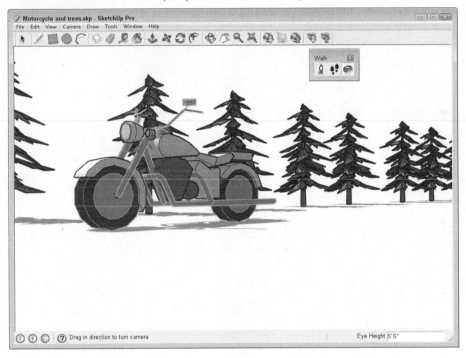

If you click and drag with the Position Camera tool, the camera is placed at ground level and oriented in the direction of the item that you dragged, as shown in Figure 3.19. You can then type an Eye Height value in the Measurements Toolbar to raise the camera off the ground level.

FIGURE 3.19

Clicking and dragging with the Position Camera tool places the camera at ground level and lets you control the camera's orientation by dragging to the item you want to see.

Looking around the scene

The Look Around tool can also be accessed from the Camera menu or from the Walkthrough toolbar. It allows you to change the camera's orientation by dragging in the drawing area. From a stationary position, you can tilt the camera to the left, right, or up and down. Figure 3.20 shows the motorcycle and trees scene after using the Look Around tool.

While the Look Around tool is selected, you can still change the Eye Height value in the Measurements Toolbar.

Walking around the scene

The Walk tool lets you interactively move around the scene by clicking and dragging the mouse. You can select the Walk tool by choosing Camera ➪ Walk, or from the Walkthrough toolbar. To move through the scene with the Walk tool selected, click and hold the mouse button down while you move the mouse. Moving the mouse forward moves the view forward as if you were walking through the scene. Moving the mouse backward moves the view back, or you could pan the camera to the left or right by moving the mouse in the same direction.

 **TIP** You can also use the arrow keys to walk about the scene when the Walk tool is selected.

When you first click in the scene with the Walk tool, a small plus mark (+) is positioned where you click. If you move the mouse cursor close to this plus mark the movements will be gradual and slow, but if you move the cursor far from the plus mark the movement speeds up. If you need to move even faster, hold down the Ctrl key and your view changes even more quickly.

With the Walk tool, you move about the scene at eye level, but you can interactively alter the Eye Height value by holding down the Shift key. With the Shift key held down, the camera moves up when you drag the mouse forward and down when you pull the mouse backward. This also changes the Eye Height value in the Measurements Toolbar.

FIGURE 3.20

The Look Around tool lets you tilt the camera from its stationary position.

**TIP** You can access the Look Around tool while the Walk tool is selected by dragging with the middle mouse button.

When moving through the scene with the Walk tool, collision detection is automatically enabled, which causes the camera to stop when it bumps into a wall. Collision detection also enables the camera to walk up and down stairs while maintaining its eye level. If you want to disable collision detection, simply hold down the Alt key and you'll be able to walk through the walls and other objects. Figure 3.21 shows how the camera has stopped when trying to walk through the base of a tree.

FIGURE 3.21

The camera cannot move through solid objects like this tree trunk when the Walk tool is enabled unless you hold down the Alt key.

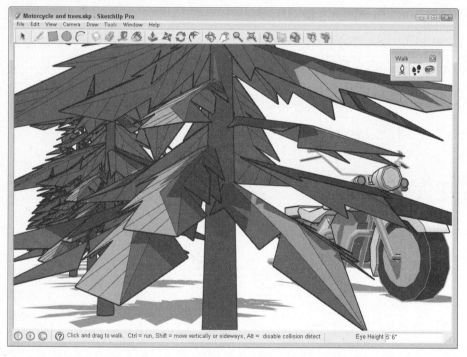

Tutorial: Walking through a scene

Viewing a scene from the perspective of a pedestrian has significant advantages. For example, such a perspective makes it possible to see where the shadows from a building are cast or how high the drinking fountains in a school are. In this simple tutorial, you practice moving through the scene using the Walkthrough tools.

To practice walking about a scene, follow these steps:

1. Open the `City street.skp` file from the `Chap 03` directory on the CD.

   This file includes a road lined with trees and several buildings. There is also a motorcycle on the road, as shown in an Iso view in Figure 3.22.

FIGURE 3.22

From the default Iso view, you can see all the scene objects.

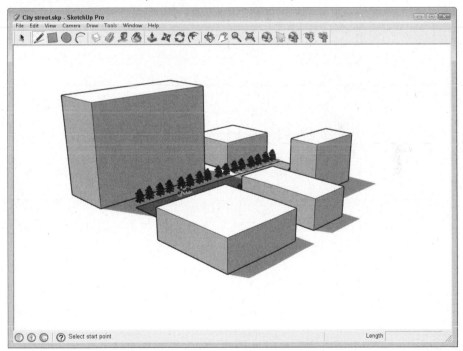

---

2. Choose View ➪ Toolbars ➪ Walkthrough to open the Walk toolbar. Move the toolbar to the upper-right corner of the interface.

3. Click the Place Camera button, and click in the drawing area on a location in the road in front of the motorcycle. The camera slowly moves until it is positioned at eye level at the location where you clicked, as shown in Figure 3.23.

FIGURE 3.23

The Place Camera tool lets you move the camera to eye level.

With the Look Around tool active, you can rotate the camera.

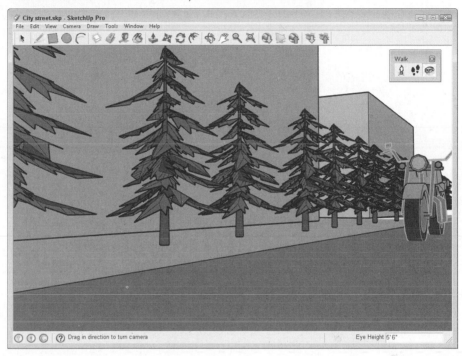

4. After clicking with the Position Camera tool, the Look Around tool is activated. Click and drag in the drawing area to the left to pan the camera's orientation, as shown in Figure 3.24.

5. Click the Walk tool and use the mouse to maneuver about the scene. Move between two buildings and look back at the road, as shown in Figure 3.25.

FIGURE 3.25

The Walk tool lets you move about the scene as if you were walking with the camera at eye level.

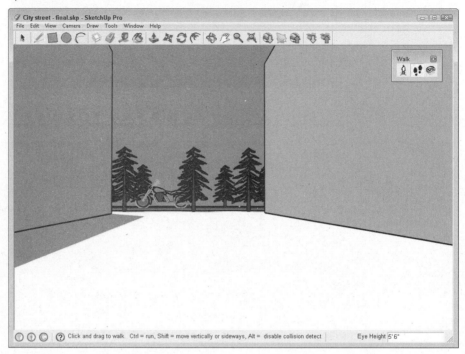

Configuring the Drawing Area

There are a number of ways to configure the drawing area, and each of the configuration options impacts the interface and how you work with models. For example, setting the system units impacts the type of values that are displayed in the Measurements Toolbar, and by changing the edge and face style, you can change how the objects appear in the drawing area.

Setting the drawing area style

Complex scenes take longer to display and render. The renderer used for the drawing area is highly optimized to be very quick, but if you're working on a huge model with lots of complex textures, then updating the drawing area can slow the program to a crawl. By altering the Edge and Face styles that are used, you can speed up a sluggish display.

CROSS-REF Using the Styles Browser, you can define and apply custom display styles. More on using styles and the Styles Browser is covered in Chapter 19.

Using the default Face styles

All of the default Face styles are located in the View ⇨ Face Style menu, but you can also access them from the Face Style toolbar. The default Face styles include the following:

NOTE Only one Face style may be selected at a time.

- **X-Ray:** Shows all faces as semitransparent
- **Wireframe:** Shows all polygon edges only
- **Hidden Line:** Shows only polygon edges facing the camera
- **Shaded:** Shows individual polygon faces as a solid color
- **Shaded with Textures:** Shows polygon faces as solid colors and displays any applied textures
- **Monochrome:** Shows all polygons faces as solid grayscale colors

The default display Face style is Shaded with Textures, as shown in Figure 3.26, but this is also the slowest of all the Face styles. By default, the Display Edges option in the Edge style is enabled also. This lets you see any applied textures and all edges.

FIGURE 3.26

The default Face style shows shaded surfaces, textures, and edges.

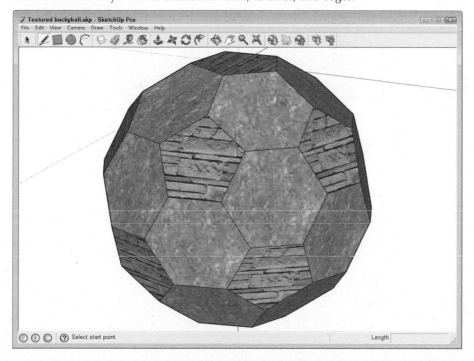

Depending on the size of the textures, you can speed up the display of a complex scene dramatically by switching to the Shaded Face style. This style replaces any textures with simple solid colors, as shown in Figure 3.27.

By hiding the textures, you can speed the display rate dramatically.

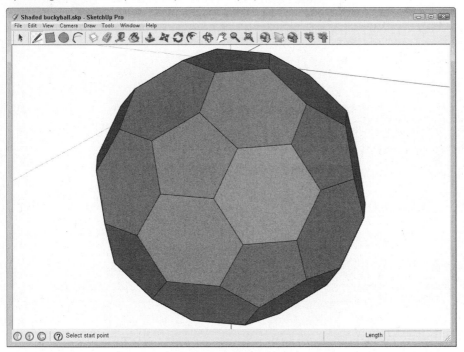

If you still want to see the face colors, but want to see the backside of the model also, then you can enable the X-Ray Face style. This style makes all faces semitransparent so you can see through it, as shown in Figure 3.28.

The Wireframe Face style is similar to the X-Ray option except it doesn't show any of the face colors. It does show all the edges, as shown in Figure 3.29. This is a very fast display style, but it can be confusing if you have a lot of edges.

If you find that the Wireframe Face style is too confusing, you can use the Hidden Line Face style. This Face style removes any edges that are on the backside of an object, but it still doesn't show any faces, as shown in Figure 3.30.

FIGURE 3.28

The X-Ray Face style lets you see through the faces.

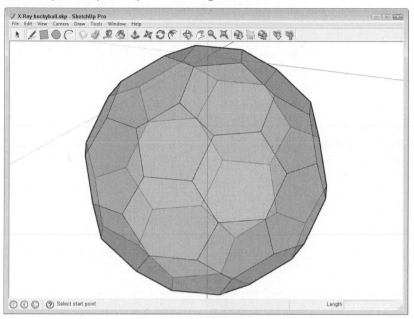

FIGURE 3.29

The Wireframe Face style is the fastest display method.

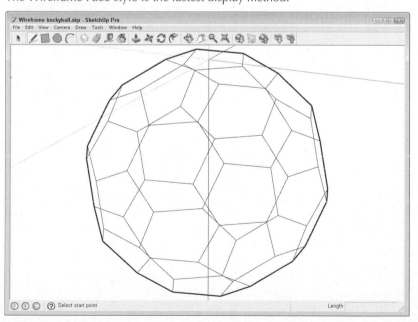

FIGURE 3.30

The Hidden Line Face style hides all edges on the backside of objects.

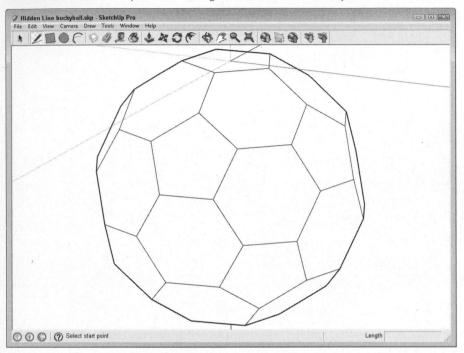

The final Face style is Monochrome. This face style is just like the Shaded Face style, except it displays all faces using standard grayscale shading, as shown in Figure 3.31.

Using the default Edge styles

After the Face style has been set, you can also set the Edge style to apply using the options found by choosing View ➪ Edge Style. Each of these options can be toggled on and off, and multiple Edge style options can be applied simultaneously. The available Edge style options include:

- **Display Edges:** Shows all edges as thin black lines
- **Profiles:** Shows a thicker line that defines the outline of the scene objects
- **Depth Cue:** Shows edges closest to the front as thicker lines and edges farther back as thinner lines
- **Extension:** Shows a short extension on the end of each line

The Display Edges option is enabled by default, but it can be disabled to give the object a more natural look, as shown in Figure 3.32.

The Profiles option adds a strong, thick line to the outer edge of the object, as shown in Figure 3.33. You can set the thickness in pixels in the Styles browser.

FIGURE 3.31

The Monochrome face style colors all faces using grayscale shading.

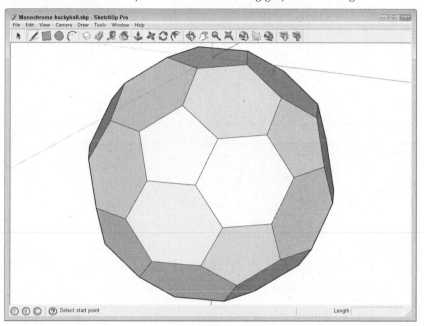

FIGURE 3.32

By disabling the edge display, the object has a more natural look.

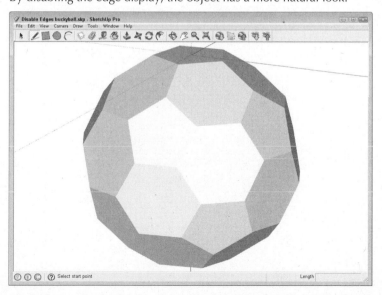

The Profiles Edge style highlights the objects by adding a thick line to their outer edge.

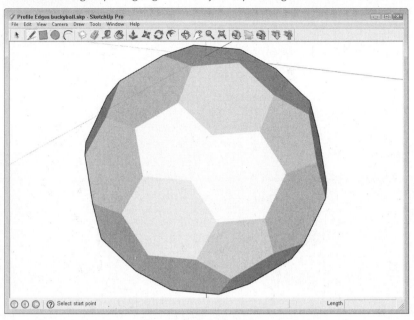

The Depth Cue Edge style option displays those edges nearest the camera as strong, thick lines and gradually decreases the line thickness as the edges get farther from the camera, as shown in Figure 3.34. You can set the thickness in pixels for the edges closest to the camera in the Styles browser. Making the closer edges thicker makes it easier to see the difference in depth.

 **The Depth Cue Edge style is often not apparent if the Profiles option is also enabled.**

The Extensions Edge style option adds a short extending line on the end of each edge, as shown in Figure 3.35. These lines make it easy to visually select and work with the various edges. You can set the amount in pixels that the lines extend in the Styles browser.

CAUTION **The Depth Cue and Extensions Edge styles are only visible if the Display Edges option is also enabled.**

FIGURE 3.34

The Depth Cue Edge style gives a sense of depth by gradually decreasing the line thickness as the edges get farther from the camera.

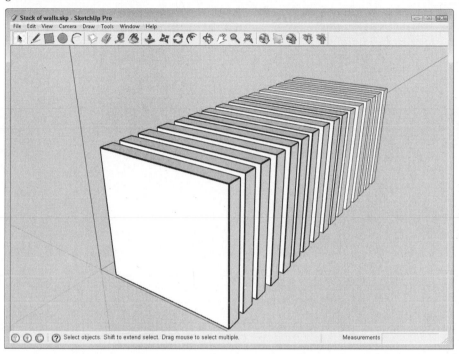

Displaying shadows and fog

One of the best ways to endow your model with a sense of depth is to enable shadows. Shadows can be configured to show based on a specific time and date using the Shadows Settings dialog box. Once shadows are configured, you can quickly turn them on and off by choosing View ⇨ Shadows or by clicking the Display Shadows button in the Shadows toolbar. Figure 3.36 shows a stack of wall planes with shadows enabled.

Fog adds an atmospheric effect to the current scene making it so objects farther from the camera aren't as clear. Using the Fog dialog box, you can set the distances where fog begins to appear and where the fog is at a maximum. You can also set the fog's color. Fog can be enabled and disabled by choosing View ⇨ Fog. Figure 3.37 shows the same scene with fog enabled. Notice how the shadows toward the back are faded.

FIGURE 3.35

The Extensions edge style adds a small extension onto the end of each line.

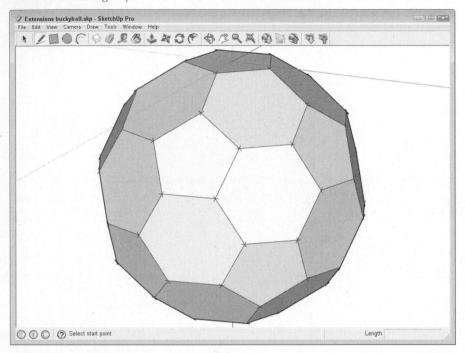

CROSS-REF   **The various shadow settings are covered in Chapter 21. Fog is covered in Chapter 20.**

Setting units

Although you can draw in SketchUp using generic units, there is a huge benefit in using real-world units as you draw. All the values in the Measurements Toolbar are displayed using the designated units, and when dimensions are added to a model, you can include the units.

Units are set using the Units panel of the Model Info dialog box, as shown in Figure 3.38. This dialog box can be displayed by choosing Window➪ Model Info, or by clicking the Model Info button in the Standard toolbar.

NOTE   **The Model Info dialog box is modeless, which means you can change units at any time causing all dimensions to be automatically updated when you begin working with the model again.**

FIGURE 3.36

Shadows add to the feeling of depth for a model.

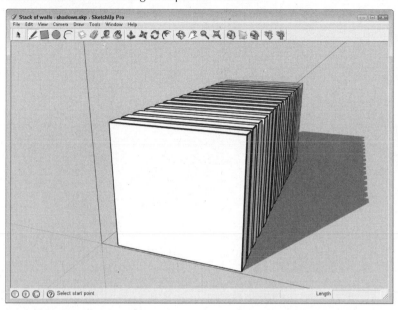

FIGURE 3.37

Fog gradually hides items far from the camera.

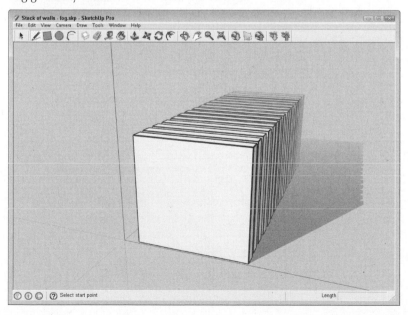

FIGURE 3.38

The Model Info dialog box includes a setting for changing the system units.

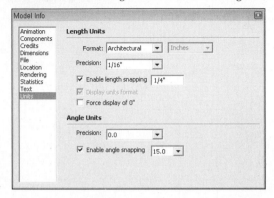

Setting Length units

At the top of the Units panel, you can choose from four different Formats including:

- **Architectural:** This unit format works in feet and inches and is common for building designs.

- **Decimal:** This unit format displays values using a decimal point and lets you choose from several different unit systems including Inches ("), Feet ('), Millimeters (mm), Centimeters (cm), and Meters (m).

- **Engineering:** This unit format measures objects in feet with a decimal point.

- **Fractional:** This unit format displays all measurements as fractional inches.

For each unit format, you can also set a Precision value. The Architectural and Fractional formats can set a precision value from 1/2" to 1/64" and the Decimal and Engineering formats can set a precision value from 0 to 6 digits beyond the decimal point.

The Enable length snapping option lets you specify a value. If the object is within this designated value, then it is automatically snapped to the nearest increment. This can be a great way to ensure precise alignment of objects.

CROSS-REF   For more on using object snapping, see Chapter 11.

If you select the Display units format option, the specified units are displayed after the value in the Measurements Toolbar and for any called-out dimensions. The unit designations for each unit type are listed in parenthesis: Inches ("), Feet ('), Millimeters (mm), Centimeters (cm), and Meters (m). This option is only available if the unit format is set to Decimal or Fractional.

The Force display of 0" option is only available when the Architectural format is selected. It causes the value of 0" to be displayed for dimensions of an even number of feet. For example, if a dimension measures 4 feet exactly, the value would be displayed as 4'0" instead of just 4' if this option is select.

Setting Angle units

All angles in SketchUp are measured in degrees. For dimensions, you can set the angle to have up to three digits after the decimal point. You can also enable Angle Snapping and set an angle value that is snapped to when enabled. If you set the Snap Angle to 15, then rotating an object will automatically snap to every 15 degrees.

Setting OpenGL preferences

SketchUp uses OpenGL to draw and render its graphics. OpenGL is an optimized set of system commands that works to produce graphic functions such as commands that cover everything from drawing straight lines to shading complex faces.

The OpenGL commands run as part of the software on typical computers, but if your system is using a graphics card that supports OpenGL, then the OpenGL commands are run on the graphics card's Graphics Processing Unit (GPU), which frees up the computer's Central Processing Unit (CPU) to accomplish other tasks. This can result in a significant speed increase when working with the software.

Enabling hardware acceleration

Within the System Preferences dialog box, which is displayed by choosing Window ➪ Preferences, is an OpenGL panel of settings, as shown in Figure 3.39. Selecting the Use hardware acceleration setting lets you specify that you want SketchUp to use the video card's GPU to speed the application.

 **CAUTION** Hardware acceleration is only possible if the video card on your system is 100 percent compatible with OpenGL.

FIGURE 3.39

The OpenGL panel in the System Preferences dialog box includes an option for enabling hardware acceleration.

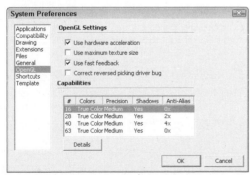

The OpenGL implementation on some video cards causes the Select tool to choose the reverse side of the clicked-on face. If you notice this behavior, you can select the Correct reversed picking driver bug option to fix the problem.

Selecting the Use Fast Feedback option enables the screen to be redrawn even faster than normal when working with large models. However, not all video cards support this feature. SketchUp tests your video card as it starts up and automatically enables this option if it is supported.

Enabling anti-aliasing

During the automatic video card test that happens when SketchUp is started, SketchUp compiles and lists the supported graphic modes that your video card supports in the Capabilities list. This list shows the number of colors that are supported, the precision of the lines, whether shadows are supported, and the anti-alias level. From this list, the current mode is highlighted or you can click to select a different graphics mode.

When diagonal lines are drawn, they can appear jagged due to pixilation that occurs when some pixels are fully colored and adjacent pixels are not. These jagged edges can be reduced by filtering the pixels using a process called *anti-aliasing*, which works by coloring the pixels on the edge of a line a lighter color. Anti-aliasing makes the lines smoother and eliminates the jagged rough edges, but it also comes at the expense of processing speed.

The Details button at the bottom of the OpenGL panel opens a simple dialog box that shows the details your system's video card, as shown in Figure 3.40.

FIGURE 3.40

Clicking the Details button presents a dialog box with information about your system's video card.

Troubleshooting hardware acceleration

The speed increase that you can get from hardware acceleration is significant enough that if you plan on using SketchUp extensively, you should really upgrade to a video card that enables hardware acceleration. If the video card isn't working properly, you'll notice a lot of artifacts (or random dots and lines) remaining as you move objects around and random lines and pixels scattered about the drawing area.

If you have a video card that supports OpenGL that you are having trouble with, there are a number of things you can try to improve its performance:

- Try disabling the Use hardware acceleration option in the OpenGL panel of the System Preferences dialog box. If the display is corrected by disabling this option, then the problem is with your video card.

- Using the video card settings, change the resolution and color depth settings. Some video cards only support OpenGL at specific resolutions and color depths. Generally, a color depth of 32-bit is accepted.

- Go to the Web site for your video card manufacturer and download and install the latest set of drivers. The manufacturers are always updating their video card drivers, and updating the drivers is sometimes all that is needed.

- As a final solution, try replacing your current video card with one that is compatible. Newer video cards made by ATI and NVIDIA are generally well supported and offer excellent results.

Summary

The goal of this chapter was to cover the large central drawing area in gritty detail. This was accomplished by showing you how to change the view, navigate, and walk about it with various camera tools. I also showed how the drawing area could be configured by changing its display style, setting units, and enabling hardware acceleration.

This chapter covered the following topics:

- Selecting from the standard views
- Changing perspective and field of view
- Orbiting, panning, and zooming the view
- Using the Walkthrough tools
- Choosing a face and edge display style
- Enabling shadows and fog
- Setting system units
- Enabling hardware acceleration

The next chapter covers everything you need to know about files — saving, opening, printing, importing, exporting, and backing them up.

Chapter 4

Working with Files

I f I ask what the hard drive is full of, the correct answer would be files. The same could be said for the Internet. Files come is all sizes, formats, and styles, and the files for SketchUp are no different.

SketchUp files provide a way to save your work and share that work with other users. However, files in SketchUp are more than just the project file; a project may include texture files, component files, and imported assets.

This chapter is all about files, including how to create and share them, how to import and export them, and how to configure the all-important Auto Save feature. The most important piece of advice I have for files is "save early, save often." If you can follow this advice, then you won't be as frustrated when your system crashes and you lose a bunch of work.

IN THIS CHAPTER

Opening and saving files

Setting file preferences

Importing files into SketchUp

Exporting SketchUp files

Printing scenes

Using SketchUp Viewer

Starting with a Template

When SketchUp starts, the first thing you see is the Welcome to SketchUp dialog box, shown in Figure 4.1. Using this dialog box, you can enter or view the license code, view a sample help video, or select a template. If you click on the Start using SketchUp button before selecting a template, a warning dialog box appears asking you to specify a template first.

From the Template Selection section in the Welcome to SketchUp dialog box are several different templates. Each of these templates defines the default units and the environment style. Sample default templates include Architectural Design, Google Earth Modeling, Engineering, and Plan View. Creating custom templates is covered later in this chapter.

FIGURE 4.1

The Welcome to SketchUp dialog box lets you select a template before starting.

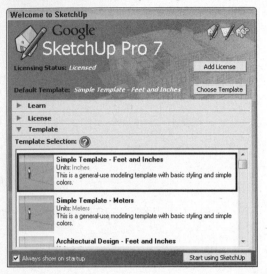

Opening and Saving Files

Of all the different file formats, there is one SketchUp file type that you probably will work with more than any other — the SKP format. This is Google's proprietary format for SketchUp project files. These files have the .skp extension, which allows you to save your work as a file and return to it at a later time.

After a template is selected, the Start using SketchUp button launches SketchUp using the new template as a new scene, as shown in Figure 4.2. You can start a new scene at any time by choosing File ➪ New (Ctrl+N) or by clicking the New button in the Standard toolbar. Although each instance of SketchUp can have only one scene open at a time, you can open multiple copies of SketchUp, each with its own scene instance.

Starting a new scene deletes the current scene, but SketchUp asks you whether you want to save the current scene if it has not been saved.

FIGURE 4.2

New scenes are blank and ready to be filled.

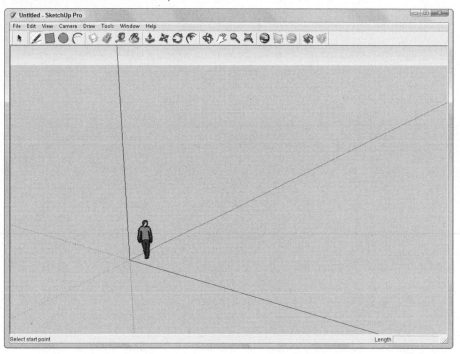

Saving files

After you start SketchUp, the first thing you should learn is how to save your work. After a scene changes, you can save it as a file. Before a file is saved, the word "Untitled" appears in the title bar; after you save the file, its new name appears in the title bar. Choose File ➪ Save (Ctrl+S) to save the scene. If the scene hasn't been saved yet, a Save As dialog box appears, as shown in Figure 4.3. You can also make this dialog box appear by choosing File ➪ Save As. After you save a file, choosing File ➪ Save saves the file without opening the file dialog box. Pretty simple — just remember to do it often.

The actual look of the Save As dialog box depends on the operating system you are using. For example, the Windows Vista dialog box that is shown in Figure 4.2 includes several buttons to go to the last folder visited, go up one directory, create a new folder, and to view a pop-up menu of file view options. The View Menu options include Extra Large Icons, Large Icons, Medium Icons, Small Icons, List, Details, and Tiles. The various icon options display an image of the drawing area as it looks when the file is saved, as shown in Figure 4.4. This view option is especially useful when you open files.

 If you try to save a scene over the top of an existing scene, SketchUp presents a dialog box confirming this action.

FIGURE 4.3

Use the Save As dialog box to save a scene as a file.

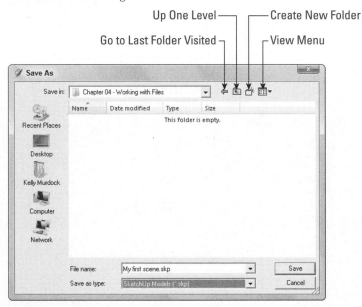

FIGURE 4.4

Setting the Views menu to Medium Icons shows the drawing area for each saved file.

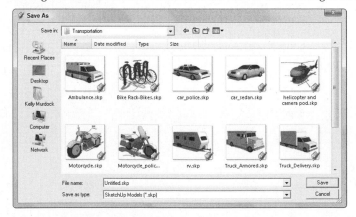

The Name, Date Modified, Type, and Size tabs at the top of the Save As dialog box let you sort the folder's files in different ways.

If you click the File name down arrow, the drop-down list displays the paths and names of the recently saved files in the order they were saved. This lets you quickly jump to a recent path when saving the current file.

In the Save As Type drop-down list, there are options for saving the current file using a different format of SketchUp. The default setting saves the file using the SketchUp 7 format, but you can choose to save the file using the SketchUp 6, 5, 4, or 3 versions. If you know that the file needs to be opened in one of these earlier versions, then save the file using the correct format.

> **CAUTION** Although files saved in earlier version of SketchUp can be opened within SketchUp 7, files created in SketchUp 7 cannot be opened in earlier versions of SketchUp unless saved using the earlier format.

> **TIP** Because all versions of SketchUp have the same .skp extension, it is a good idea to include the file version in the name if you save a file using an earlier format. For example, "Helicopter saved for SketchUp 3."

The File menu also includes an option to Save Copy As. This command lets you save the current scene to a different name without changing its current name. For example, you could create a temporary backup of the current scene using this command.

If you've made some changes to a file that you don't want to keep, you can choose File ⇨ Revert to discard the last round of changes and automatically reopen the file in its state when it was last saved.

Another useful feature for saving files is to enable the Auto Backup feature in the General panel of the System Preferences dialog box. This dialog box can be accessed by choosing Window ⇨ Preferences. Configuring and using this feature is covered later in this chapter.

Saving templates

Any SketchUp scene can be saved as a template using the File ⇨ Save As Template menu command. This command opens the Save As Template dialog box, shown in Figure 4.5. Using this dialog box, you can name the custom template, provide a description and a filename. There is also an option to make this template the default.

Saved templates will appear in the Welcome to SketchUp dialog box and within the Template panel in the System Preferences dialog box.

FIGURE 4.5

The Save As Template dialog box lets you name the custom template.

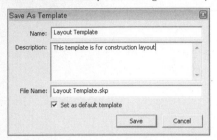

Opening files

When you want to open a file you've saved, you can choose File ⇨ Open (Ctrl+O) or click the Open button in the Standard Toolbar, which opens a file dialog box that is similar to the one used to save files. The one big difference is the inclusion of the Preview pane.

The Preview pane shows the drawing area for the selected file regardless of the view selection, so if you keep the View Menu set to List, the Preview pane still shows the drawing area of the selected file, as shown in Figure 4.6.

 The Open dialog box allows you to select only one file at a time.

The most recently opened scenes are listed at the bottom of the File menu. Selecting these scenes from the list opens the scene file.

Adding objects to the current scene

If you happen to create the perfect model in one scene and want to integrate that model into another scene, you can drag and drop the saved model from Windows Explorer or Macintosh's Finder directly onto the drawing area. When a saved file is dropped onto the drawing area, the dropped model is added to the current scene without removing any of the existing objects.

You can also add saved SKP files to the current project by choosing File ⇨ Import. Simply select the SketchUp file type, and the saved file is added to the existing file without removing any of the existing objects.

Getting out

As you can probably guess, you can choose File ⇨ Exit to exit the program, but only after it gives you a chance to save your work. Clicking the Close button (X) in the upper-right corner has the same effect (but I'm sure you knew that).

FIGURE 4.6

The Preview pane in the Open dialog box helps ensure that you are opening the right file.

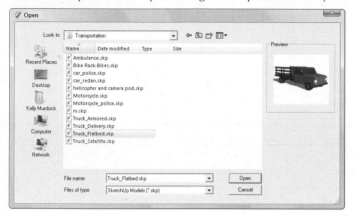

Setting File Preferences

Within the System Preferences dialog box are several settings that can save you some time and can save your sanity. The settings that deal with files are found in both the Files panel and in the General panel.

Setting default folders

By default, SketchUp opens to the Documents directory for the logged-in user, which is handy if you plan on saving all your work there. However, if you plan on saving a lot of files to a different directory, then you will need to navigate to that directory every time you save a file.

Using the Files panel in the System Preferences dialog box, shown in Figure 4.7, you can specify the folder that is opened when opening and saving several different file types, including the following:

- **Models:** Defines the default folder where all SketchUp models and scenes are opened from and saved to
- **Components:** Defines the default folder where all components listed with the Component Browser are opened from and saved to
- **Materials:** Defines the default folder where all defined materials listed with the Materials Browser are opened from and saved to
- **Styles:** Defines the default folder where all defined styles listed with the Styles Browser are opened from and saved to

- **Texture Images:** Defines the default folder where all texture bitmap images are opened from when the Choose Image button in the Materials Browser is clicked
- **Watermark Images:** Defines the default folder where all watermark images are opened
- **Export Models:** Defines the default folder where all exported models are saved

To change any of the default folders, simply click the Browse for Folder icons to the right of the folder path and locate the new folder. The new folder path then appears in the Files panel. All file dialog boxes will then open to the new folder automatically.

FIGURE 4.7

The Files panel in the System Preferences dialog box lets you define the default folders for SketchUp resources.

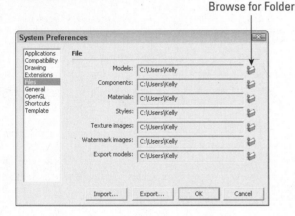

After the folders for a project are defined, you can save the file preferences to an external file with the .dat extension using the Export button at the bottom of the dialog box. These definitions can then be recalled using the Import button.

Backing up a project

You can also find some file settings in the General panel of the System Preferences dialog box, as shown in Figure 4.8. The Create backup option is a good one to keep enabled. This option causes a backup of the current file to be made whenever the current file is saved. When a save command is issued, the existing file is saved with an .skb extension and the new file is then saved in its place using the .skp extension.

FIGURE 4.8

The General panel in the System Preferences dialog box includes settings for enabling backups and Auto-Save.

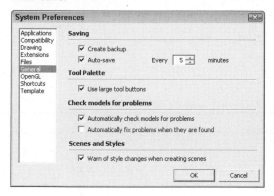

Backup files can be dragged and dropped into the current scene, or you can recover them by simply renaming the file with the .skp extension and opening it by choosing File ⇨ Open.

Enabling Auto-Save

Another great feature is Auto-Save. When enabled, it causes SketchUp to automatically save the current file every so often. You can specify how often by setting the number of minutes to the right of the Auto-save check box. If you enable Auto-Save to save the file every 15 minutes, then every 15 minutes the current model is saved using the name `Autosave_filename.skp`. In the next 15 minutes, the file is overwritten with a new file in the same directory where the file is saved.

TIP By keeping the Auto-Save option set to 15 minutes, you can ensure that the most you will ever lose is 15 minutes of work due to a system crash, power failure, or some other unexpected event.

Checking for problems

Sometimes when drawing, you can inadvertently add a problem to your model. The General panel of the System Preferences dialog box includes a setting to have SketchUp automatically look for potential problems every time the file is opened and/or saved. If a problem is found, a dialog box appears with options to Always Fix my model, Fix it Now, or Fix It Later.

NOTE If you disable the Automatically check models for problems option, then you can manually check for problems using the Statistics panel of the Model Info dialog box.

If you select the Automatically fix problems when they are found option, then the dialog box does not appear when a problem is found.

Setting a default template

All of the templates listed in the Welcome to SketchUp dialog box are available for selection in the Template panel of the Preferences dialog box, as shown in Figure 4.9. The template that is selected is used by default whenever a new scene is opened using the File ⇨ New menu command.

FIGURE 4.9

The Template panel in the System Preferences dialog box lets you select the default template.

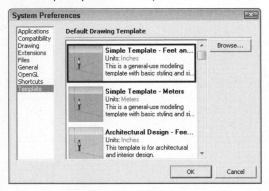

Importing Files into SketchUp

If you haven't noticed, SketchUp isn't the only game in town. A number of different 3-D packages exist, and exchanging files between them is where the importing and exporting menu commands come in. The File ⇨ Import menu command opens a file dialog box that looks just like the Open dialog box, except the Files of type drop-down list offers several additional 2-D and 3-D formats that you can select.

Importing 3-D files

SketchUp can import several 3-D file formats, including the following:

- **SketchUp (SKP):** When SketchUp files are imported, they are added to the current model.

- **AutoCAD (DWG, DXF):** These formats are used by Autodesk's AutoCAD.

- **3D Studio (3DS):** This format is an older format used by the DOS version of 3D Studio, but 3ds Max can export to this format.

- **Digital Elevation Model (DEM, DDF):** These formats are created by the United States Geographical Society (USGS) to represent terrain contours.

For each of these 3-D file formats, a dialog box of import options can be opened by clicking Options located under the Preview pane, as shown in Figure 4.10. Using these options you can define what types of objects are imported and how units are handled. The settings in these Options dialog boxes are different for each of the various format types.

FIGURE 4.10

When a 3-D file format is selected, the Options button is available.

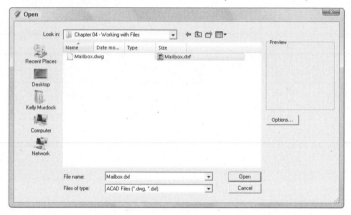

Importing SketchUp files

The first and most obvious import type is to import SketchUp files. This is different from the File ⇨ Open menu command in that it adds the imported SketchUp objects to the current scene. This works great for combining objects that have already been created into the current scene. By contrast, the File ⇨ Open menu command causes the file that is being opened to replace the current scene, although it does give you a chance to save the current scene before replacing it.

 Be aware that importing a SketchUp file into the current scene opens all of the objects in the imported file.

 The Component Browser provides another way to import objects into the current scene. The Component Browser is covered in more detail in Chapter 15.

 You can also add objects to the current scene by dragging and dropping the SketchUp file from Windows Explorer or Mac Finder.

Importing AutoCAD files

If you select the AutoCAD file format in the Import dialog box and click Options, the Import AutoCAD DWG/DXF Options dialog box, shown in Figure 4.11, appears. This dialog box lets you specify some settings about how the geometry is imported.

 Only the most basic AutoCAD elements can be imported into SketchUp. SketchUp cannot import complex elements like regions, XRefs, hatching, text, and dimensions.

When polygon faces are imported into SketchUp, they are imported as triangulated faces even if the surface exists on the same plane (is coplanar). If you select the Merge coplanar faces option, then coplanar surfaces are not triangulated and are imported as polygon faces.

Another common headache during the importing process is that sometimes the surface normal vector gets flipped, causing some polygons to appear inside out. Selecting the Orient faces consistently option causes all surface normal vectors to point in the same direction, thereby eliminating the inside-out problem.

FIGURE 4.11

The Import AutoCAD DWG/DXF Options dialog box lets you set the units of the imported file.

The Import AutoCAD DWG/DXF Options dialog box also lets you set the units used on the imported objects. This impacts the scale of the imported objects. If you can match the units for the imported object to the current scene units, then the object is scaled correctly. The Units options include Inches, Feet, Millimeters, Centimeters, and Meters.

 Even if you import objects at the wrong units, you can always use SketchUp's own Scale tool to change the object's size relative to the scene.

When objects are created in either AutoCAD or SketchUp, their position relative to the scene's origin is saved with the file. If you want to import the AutoCAD object using the same relative position used in AutoCAD, then you can select the Preserve drawing origin option. If this option is not selected, the object is simply imported to SketchUp's origin.

 If you import an object into a blank scene, you can use the Zoom Extents button to zoom in on the imported object regardless of its size.

Importing 3DS files

If you select the 3DS file format in the import dialog box and click Options, the 3DS Import Options dialog box, shown in Figure 4.12, appears. This dialog box includes only the Merge coplanar faces option and a setting for specifying units. Both of these options work the same as the similar options for the AutoCAD files.

FIGURE 4.12

The 3DS Import Options dialog box includes options similar to the AutoCAD import options.

Importing DEM files

If you select the DEM file format in the import dialog box and click Options, the DEM Import Options dialog box, shown in Figure 4.13, appears. These options are different than the other two 3-D formats. The TIN options let you specify the number of points used to represent the imported contours. Specifying a large number of points results in a more detailed model, but larger models take longer to load and cause the SketchUp display to slow down. As you change the number of points, the number of faces also changes.

FIGURE 4.13

The DEM Import Options dialog box lets you specify the number of points to use to create the model.

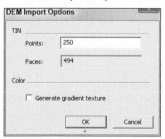

The Generate gradient texture option causes a gradient texture to be created for the imported terrain. This gradient displays the lower areas as darker areas and lighter areas in a lighter color.

CROSS-REF   You can learn more about working with terrains and TIN surfaces in Chapter 9.

Importing 2-D files

SketchUp can also import several 2-D file formats, including the following:

- **JPEG images (JPEG):** This image format is common on the Web for representing 16.7 million color images. It also allows images to be compressed.

- **Portable Network Graphics (PNG):** A newer Web format that allows compression and support for alpha channel transparency.

- **Tagged Image Files (TIF):** An older format that is quite popular offering a lossless form of compression.

- **Targa Files (TGA):** Another older format that also offers support for alpha channel transparency.

- **Windows Bitmap (BMP):** The default Windows image format.

When importing a 2-D image format using the import dialog box, the Options button is disabled, but a set of radio buttons lets you choose to load the image as an image, as a texture, or as a New Matched Photo, as shown in Figure 4.14. A preview of the selected image is also shown in the Preview pane.

FIGURE 4.14

When a 2-D file format is selected, options are available for choosing how the image is used.

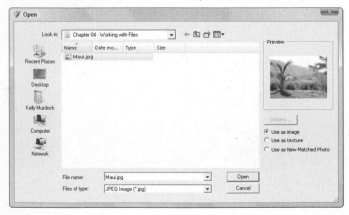

Exporting SketchUp Files

Models generated in SketchUp can be exported to other 3-D packages. You can also export 2-D images of the model that can be printed or used in other presentations.

 **The ability to export SketchUp files to most 3-D formats is only available in the Pro version.**

Exporting 3-D content

When you choose File ⇨ Export, there is a submenu with several different options. If you select to export to a 3D Model, then the Export Model dialog box appears. This dialog box is similar to the Save As dialog box, except in the Export Type list, you can choose from several different 3D formats. The available 3-D file formats that you can export to using the Pro version of SketchUp include the following:

- **3D Studio (3DS):** This format is an older format used by the DOS version of 3D Studio, but 3ds Max can export to this format.

- **AutoCAD (DWG):** This format is used by Autodesk's AutoCAD.

- **AutoCAD (DXF):** This is an older AutoCAD file format, but still widely used.

- **Google Earth 4 (KMZ):** This format is the latest version that is compatible with Google Earth.

- **Collada (DAE):** This format is a broadly supported new format that allows data interchange across a huge number of 3-D packages.

- **FilmBox (FBX):** This format is supported by Autodesk and used by both 3ds Max and Maya.

- **Google Earth (KMZ):** This format is an older version used by Google Earth.

- **Wavefront OBJ (OBJ):** This format was originally developed for the Wavefront 3-D package, but it is still supported by many programs.

- **VRML (WRL):** This format is for the Virtual Reality Modeling Language and lets 3-D models be displayed on the Web using a player.

- **SoftImage XSI (XSI):** This format is supported by the SoftImage XSI 3-D modeling package.

For each of these 3-D file formats, a dialog box of options can be opened by clicking Options, as shown in Figure 4.15. Using these options you can define what types of objects are exported and how units are handled. The settings in these Options dialog boxes are different for each of the various format types.

FIGURE 4.15

Clicking Options opens a dialog of export options for the selected format.

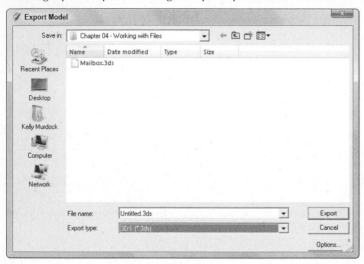

Exporting 3DS files

If you select the 3DS file format in the Export dialog box and click Options, the 3DS Export Options dialog box, shown in Figure 4.16, appears. This dialog box includes options for exporting the Geometry, the Materials, the Cameras, and setting the Scale.

The Export drop-down list at the top of the 3DS Export Options dialog box lets you specify how to split the SketchUp model as it is exported. The options include Full hierarchy, By layer, By material, and Single object. The Full hierarchy option retains any hierarchy that is established in SketchUp including groups and components. The By layer and By material options split the model based on the layers that the object is on or based on the applied material. So, each connected set of polygons that are on the same layer or have the same material applied are combined into a single object when exported. The Single object option exports the entire model as a single entity.

CAUTION The 3DS format has a limitation on the size of individual objects. If a single object has more than 65,536 vertices and faces, then the object is split into two mesh objects.

You can specify to only export the selected part of the model if the Export only current selection option is selected.

FIGURE 4.16

The 3DS Export Options dialog box includes options for exporting materials and even cameras.

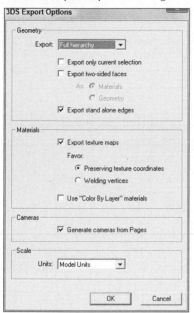

To save on the total number of polygons, most 3-D programs only show one side of each polygon as determined by the normal vector. However, if your model has a hole in the surface, then the interior of the mesh is not visible. To fix this, you can have the program make both polygon sides visible. Doing so doubles the number of polygons, but it ensures that the backsides of polygons are visible. You can enable this by selecting the Export two-sided faces option. You can further choose to have any materials that are applied to the front of the polygon also be applied to the backside or to leave it as just geometry.

SketchUp supports edges by themselves, but other formats, including the 3DS format, have trouble when an edge is by itself. If the Export stand-alone edges option is selected, any edges in SketchUp are exported as thin rectangular faces. Be aware that this may throw off your texture coordinates, which may make the scene nonrenderable.

You can select to export any applied texture maps to the 3DS format by selecting the Export texture maps option. The 3DS format only allows one UV mapping coordinate per vertex, so if you have different mapping coordinates on adjacent polygon faces, then one of the textures will be lost. If it is more important to maintain the applied textures, then choose the Preserving texture coordinates option. However, if the geometry — most notably the smoothing between faces — is more important, then select the Welding vertices option. The Preserving texture coordinates option actually breaks up the geometry and adds more vertices so the textures are preserved, but this can eliminate the smoothing between adjacent faces. The Welding vertices option keeps the smoothing of faces, but eliminates a texture if two faces share a vertex.

Although the 3DS format doesn't support layers, you can simulate layers by having each SketchUp layer be given a different material. Select the Use "Color By Layer" materials option to do this.

Selecting the Generate cameras from Pages option automatically creates a camera for the default view. It also creates cameras for any defined Pages that you have.

The Scale Units settings let you select the units used for the exported model. The options include Model Units (which is a generic unit value), Inches, Feet, Yards, Miles, Millimeters, Centimeters, Meters, and Kilometers.

Exporting AutoCAD files

If you select the AutoCAD DWG or the AutoCAD DXF file formats in the Export dialog box and click Options, the AutoCAD Export Options dialog box, shown in Figure 4.17, appears. This dialog box includes options for selecting the AutoCAD format to use and which object types to export.

The AutoCAD Export Options dialog box lets you choose to which AutoCAD version to export.

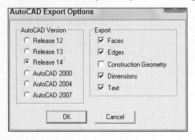

Both the DWG and DXF formats use the same Options dialog box. Using this dialog box, you can choose the AutoCAD version to export to. Each version of AutoCAD has features that are unique, and typically older versions of AutoCAD cannot open files saved in the newer version, so make sure that you export your model using the format that matches the version of AutoCAD that you are using or you won't be able to open the file.

The AutoCAD Export Options dialog box also lets you specify the objects that are exported with the file, which can be Faces, Edges, Construction Geometry (such as the grid and guides), Dimensions, and Text.

 When exporting to the AutoCAD format, the exporter is smart enough to retrieve and use the current unit settings.

Exporting to Google Earth

The export dialog box has the ability to export the current model to either the Google Earth 4 format or to the original Google Earth format. Neither of these formats has an options dialog box.

CROSS-REF You can learn more about exporting to Google Earth in Chapter 24.

Exporting Collada files

The Collada format is the work of an independent team that was tired of the interoperability issues involved in trying to move 3-D data between different programs. With broad industry support, they have defined a 3-D format that provides an easy way to transport data.

If you select the Collada file format in the Export dialog box and click Options, the Collada Export Options dialog box, shown in Figure 4.18, appears. This dialog box, like the same dialog box for the 3DS format, includes options for exporting geometry, materials, cameras, and scale.

FIGURE 4.18

The Collada Export Options dialog box lets you define how to export geometry, materials, and cameras.

The Export only current selection option allows only the selected object to be exported. The Triangulate all faces option causes all polygons to be divided into triangles by adding a crossing edge between the vertices of any polygons that have more than three vertices. By triangulating the model, you can ensure that all polygon faces are coplanar. There is also an option to export two-sided faces to ensure that the backsides of polygons are visible.

Texture maps can also be saved with the exported model as well as a camera generated from any defined Pages. The available units are the same as those for the 3DS format.

Exporting FBX files

The FBX format is the preferred format for exporting files to the popular 3ds Max and Maya products. Most of the settings in the FBX Export Options dialog box, shown in Figure 4.19, are the same as those for the Collada format. The one difference is the additional Swap YZ coordinates option, which changes the coordinate system for the model making the Y-axis point upward. If the exported model appears displayed on its side, you can select this option to make it stand up straight.

FIGURE 4.19

The FBX Export Options dialog box lets you define how to export geometry and materials.

Exporting OBJ files

The OBJ format was developed by Wavefront, an older 3-D package that has since been rolled into other products, but the format is quite common and used by many other 3-D packages. The settings in the OBJ Export Options dialog box, shown in Figure 4.20, are similar to the other formats, except that the OBJ format can support edges and includes an option to Export edges. The edges appear in the OBJ file as simple lines.

Exporting VRML files

The VRML format is a text-based format that lets 3-D objects be viewed on the Web. This requires a VRML Player in order to see the model. If you select the VRML file format in the Import dialog box and click Options, the VRML Export Options dialog box, shown in Figure 4.21, appears. This dialog box includes several unique settings that only apply to the VRML format.

FIGURE 4.20

The OBJ Export Options dialog box lets you define how to export geometry and materials.

FIGURE 4.21

The VRML Export Options dialog box lets you define the appearance of the exported model.

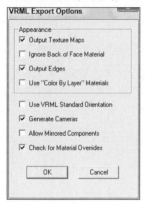

VRML allows texture maps to be output along with the model by selecting the Output Texture Maps option. If this option is not selected, only the colors are displayed. If the Ignore Back of Face Material option is selected, the texture map is only applied to the front face of the polygon. If disabled, the same material is applied to both sides of the polygon.

The VRML format supports edges, so you can export edges if the Output Edges option is selected. You can also output the SketchUp defined layers as separate materials with the Use "Color by Layer" Materials option.

The standard coordinate system for VRML models defines the XZ plane as the horizontal ground plane. This is different from SketchUp, which defines the XY plane as the ground plane. If you select the Use VRML Standard Orientation option, the XZ plane is considered the ground plane in the exported file; if disabled, the XY plane is the ground plane. By changing this setting, you can control the orientation of the exported model.

Selecting the Generate Cameras option creates a camera for the default view and for any defined pages. The default view is named Default Camera when exported.

When components are mirrored in SketchUp, they maintain a link to the original. Selecting the Allow Mirrored Components option exports these mirrored components as opposites of the originals.

Finally, selecting the Check for Material Overrides option does a quick check to see if any of the faces, edges, or components contain references to the default material.

Exporting XSI files

The XSI format is the default format for the SoftImage XSI product and its settings, shown in Figure 4.22, are the same as those for the OBJ format.

FIGURE 4.22

The XSI Export Options dialog box lets you define the appearance of the exported model.

Exporting 2-D graphics

If you don't plan on opening your model in a different 3-D package, you might want to consider exporting the model to a 2-D graphic. After you have the 2-D graphic, you can place it on a Web site, in a presentation, or you can print it.

To export a SketchUp model to a 2-D image format, choose File ➪ Export ➪ 2D Graphic. This opens the Export 2D Graphic dialog box, where you can specify a location and a filename. The dialog box also includes a drop-down list of several different available formats including:

- **Portable Document Format (PDF):** This format was created by Adobe. It is a layout format that is common on the Web for representing printed documents and requires Adobe Reader to be viewed.

- **Encapsulated PostScript Format (EPS):** Another Adobe format used to save vector-based images that can be edited or spooled to a printer.

- **Windows Bitmap (BMP):** The default Windows image format.

- **JPEG Images (JPEG):** This image format is common on the Web for representing 16.7 million color images. It also allows images to be compressed.

- **Tagged Image Files (TIF):** An older format that is quite popular offering a lossless form of compression.

- **Portable Network Graphics (PNG):** A newer Web format that allows compression and support for alpha channel transparency.

- **Piranesi Epix (EPX):** This format is the proprietary format for the Piranesi software package. This package enables SketchUp models to be rendered.

- **AutoCAD (DWG):** This format is used by Autodesk's AutoCAD. It can save 3-D data as well as 2-D images.

- **AutoCAD (DXF):** This is an older AutoCAD file format, but is still widely used. It can save 3-D data as well as 2-D images.

 The ability to export SketchUp files to PDF, EPS, EPX, DWG, and DXF is only available in the Pro version.

Exporting PDF and EPS files

If you select the PDF file format in the export dialog box and click Options, the Portable Document Format (PDF) Hidden Line Options dialog box, shown in Figure 4.23, appears. This dialog box includes options for setting how the various line widths are displayed in the exported PDF file.

At the top of the dialog box are settings for scaling and sizing the model. Selecting the Full Scale option saves the PDF file at a 1 to 1 ratio. Using the Width and Height values, you can set the page size for the document. There is a drawing size limit of 100 inches. If you change either value, the other value automatically changes to maintain the set aspect ratio of the current model:

The Scale settings show the In hidden line output value, which is the measured dimensions in the exported file as compared to the actual dimension in the SketchUp file. These two values together give a ratio of the exported document compared to the actual dimensions. For example, if the Scale is set to 1/10, then 1 inch in SketchUp is displayed as 1/10 of an inch in the exported PDF.

The other settings in this dialog box let you define how the Profile, Section, and Extension Lines are displayed. If you select the Show profiles option, any profile lines are drawn with thicker lines just as they are if the View➪Edge Styles➪Profiles menu command is enabled. If the Show profiles option is enabled, you can set the line width of the profile lines or you can have the width set automatically using the Match screen display (auto width) option. The width value is only available if the Match screen display (auto width) option is not selected.

FIGURE 4.23

The Portable Document Format (PDF) Hidden Line Options dialog box includes options for setting the dimensions of the PDF document.

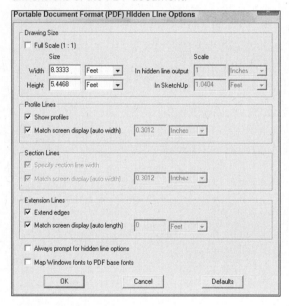

 The Section Lines options are only available in the DWG/DXF Export Options dialog box.

The same settings are available for Extension Lines. These lines can confuse some AutoCAD packages that rely on the endpoint to determine intersections. To hide extension lines, deselect the Extend edges option.

If you select the Always prompt for hidden line options option, a dialog box with these settings appears automatically when you export to the PDF format. Selecting the Map Windows fonts to PDF base fonts option opens a dialog box where you can select the PDF fonts to use to represent any text in the SketchUp model.

The EPS format uses the same options dialog box as the PDF format.

Exporting BMP, TIF, and PNG files

If you select the BMP file format in the Export dialog box and click Options, the Export Image Options dialog box, shown in Figure 4.24, appears. This dialog box includes options for setting the dimensions of the exported BMP file.

If the Use view size option is selected, the model is exported at a 1-to-1 ratio with the drawing area. You can also set the dimensions in pixels for the exported image using the Width and Height values. Selecting the Anti-alias option causes the exported image to be smoothed to eliminate any jagged edges. Enabling anti-aliasing can increase the time to export the file.

The options for exporting to the TIF and PNG image formats are exactly the same.

FIGURE 4.24

The Export Image Options dialog box includes options for setting the dimensions of the BMP file.

Exporting JPEG files

If you select the JPEG file format in the Export dialog box and click Options, the Export JPG Options dialog box, shown in Figure 4.25, appears. This dialog box includes the same options for setting the dimensions of the exported file as the other formats, but it also includes a setting for compressing the image. The higher the compression setting, the smaller the file size, but the image quality is also reduced.

Figure 4.26 shows the mailbox model exported to the JPEG image format with the maximum compression turned on. Notice how there are lots of artifacts around the lines that hurt the image quality. The file size for this image file is 24K, and the same image saved with minimal compression is 68K.

EPX files can be opened and rendered within the Piranesi software. You can find more information on this software at the Piranesi Web site at www.informatix.co.uk/piranesi.htm.

FIGURE 4.25

The Export JPG Options dialog box includes an option for compressing the image.

FIGURE 4.26

JPEG images with a high level of compression cause artifacts to appear in the image.

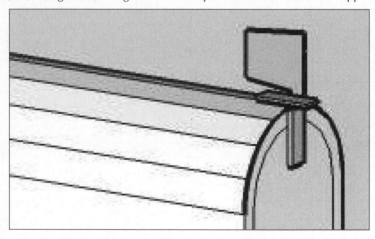

Exporting EPX files

If you select the EPX file format in the Export dialog box and click Options, the Export Epx Options dialog box, shown in Figure 4.27, appears. This dialog box includes many of the same options for setting the dimensions of the exported file as the other formats, but it also includes settings that are unique to this format including the ability to export edges, textures, and the ground plane.

Exporting DWG and DXF files

If you select either the DWG or the DXF file formats in the Export dialog box and click Options, the DWG/DXF Hidden Line Options dialog box, shown in Figure 4.28, appears. This dialog box includes options for setting how the various line widths are displayed and is very similar to the PDF options.

FIGURE 4.27

The Export Epx Options dialog box includes options for exporting edges, textures, and the ground plane.

FIGURE 4.28

The DWG/DXF Hidden Line Options dialog box includes options for setting which lines are visible in the exported image.

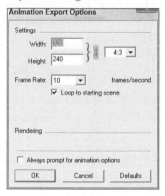

At the top of the dialog box are settings for scaling and sizing the model. Selecting the Full Scale option saves the image file at a 1-to-1 ratio. If the Full Scale option is disabled, you can change the dimensions using the Width and Height values. There are also values that show the scaling relationships between the drawing and the model.

Just like in the 3-D export options, you can also select the AutoCAD version to use. Remember that files saved in newer versions of the software cannot be opened in older versions of AutoCAD.

For Profile and Section lines, you can set these lines to be exported as Polylines in AutoCAD. You can also set the line width or have the width set automatically. If you don't want to export these lines as Polylines, you can select to export the lines as a different line type, such as the Wide line entity. The Wide line entity is only supported in AutoCAD 2000 and later. You also have the option to separate these lines to a different layer.

For Extension Lines, you can choose to show them or hide them. You can also set their length or let the length be set automatically.

Selecting the Always Prompt for Hidden Line Options option causes this dialog box to appear automatically when a file is exported to one of these formats.

Exporting section slices

SketchUp also offers the ability to export just the section slice using the DWG or DXF formats. To do so, choose File ⇨ Export ⇨ Section Slice. This opens the Export 2D Section Slice dialog box. From this dialog box, you can select either the DWG or the DXF format. Clicking Options opens the 2D Section Slice Options dialog box, as shown in Figure 4.29.

FIGURE 4.29

The 2D Section Slice Options dialog box lets you export sections to a 2-D DWG or DXF file.

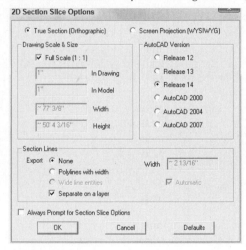

 If the model doesn't include a section plane, this option is disabled.

At the top of the 2D Section Slice Options dialog box are options to export the section slice as a True Section taken from an Orthographic view or to export the section slice as a Screen Projection (WYSIWYG). The WYSIWYG acronym stands for What You See Is What You Get. Selecting the True Section option shows the model in its actual dimensions, but selecting the Screen Projection option shows the model using perspective.

The remaining settings in this dialog box are the same as those for a standard 2-D export using the DWG and DXF formats.

Exporting animations

By dividing a model into several different scenes, you can move between the different scenes to create a rough animation sequence. These animated sequences can be exported to the AVI video format or to a series of sequenced images using the JPEG, PNG, TIF, or BMP image formats.

 **If the model doesn't include any scenes, this option is disabled.**

To export an animated sequence, choose File ⇨ Export ⇨ Animation. This opens the Export Animation dialog box where you can name the file, choose a location, and select a format. The only video format available is AVI for Windows and QuickTime for Mac, but you can also export the animation to a series of sequenced image files.

If you select the AVI option in the Export Animation dialog box and click Options, the Animation Export Options dialog box, shown in Figure 4.30, appears. Using this dialog box, you can set the dimensions of the exported file. If the little link icon is displayed, the length and width ratio is maintained. The Frame Rate defines the number of images that are shown per second. Standard television runs at 30 frames per second (fps) and film runs at 24 fps. Web animations can run as low as 12 fps.

Selecting the Loop to starting scene option adds a command to continually run the animation until it is stopped. Selecting the Play when finished option causes the animation to be loaded and played within the system's default video player when the export is completed.

The Codec button displays the codec driver that is used to compress the video sequence. Many different codecs are available and each has its own settings. Figure 4.31 shows the settings dialog box for the Cinepak Codec. Most codec settings have an option for setting the amount of compression to apply to the video sequence. More compression generally reduces file size and decreases image quality.

Animation sequences can be anti-aliased just as images can, and selecting the Always Prompt for Animation Option causes this dialog box to open every time a file is exported.

For sequenced images using one of the image formats, the same Animation Export Options dialog box is used, except the Codec and anti-aliasing options are removed, as shown in Figure 4.30.

FIGURE 4.30

The Animation Export Options dialog box lets you specify the size of the final animation.

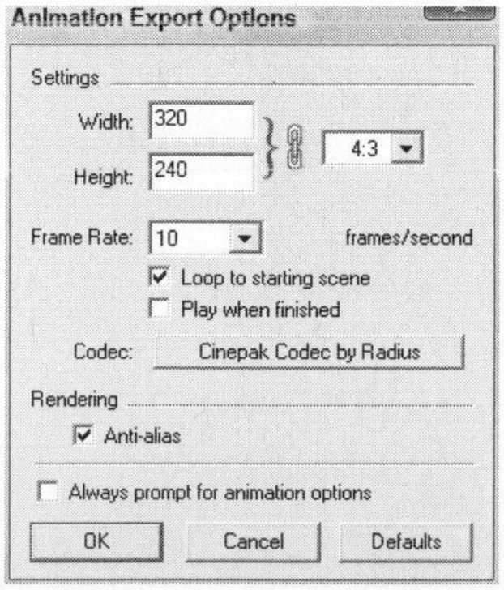

121

FIGURE 4.31

The Video Compression dialog box lets you choose a codec to use to compress the animation file.

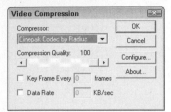

Printing Scenes

To send your current scene to the printer directly from within SketchUp, you can choose File ⇨ Print (Ctrl+P). If you need to configure the printer, choose File ⇨ Print Setup to display the Print Setup dialog box, as shown in Figure 4.32. From this dialog box you can choose from any of the online printers and change the paper size, source, and orientation.

FIGURE 4.32

The Print Setup dialog box lets you configure the printer.

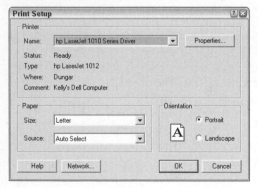

After you configure the printer you want to use, you can choose File ⇨ Print Preview to view how the model will look on the printed page before it is actually printed. Finally, choose File ⇨ Print to open the Print dialog box, as shown in Figure 4.33. Using this dialog box you can set the number of copies and the print quality among other settings.

FIGURE 4.33

The Print dialog box is the final step before printing a document.

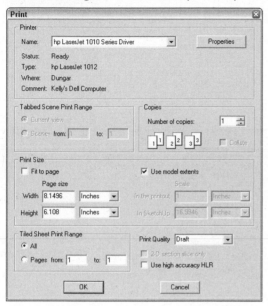

Using SketchUp Viewer

If you want to share your drawing with a client who isn't familiar with SketchUp and who doesn't have the software, then you can have him download and install the SketchUp Viewer application, shown in Figure 4.34. This application is a subset of SketchUp that gives the user the ability to open, view, navigate, and even print SketchUp documents, but it does not have the ability to edit SketchUp files. The SketchUp Viewer application can be downloaded for free from the SketchUp Web site at `sketchup.google.com/download/gsuviewer.html`. SketchUp Viewer is available for Windows 2000, XP, Vista, and Mac OS X.

FIGURE 4.34

The SketchUp Viewer application is a simple version of SketchUp.

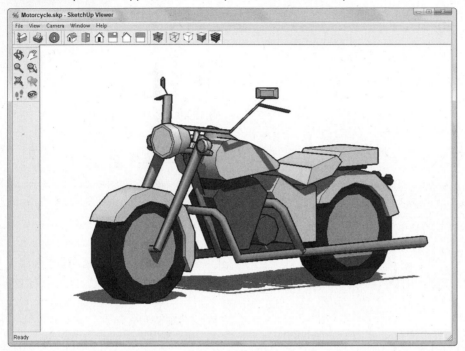

Summary

Now that you know how to work with files, let me repeat the advice to "save early, save often." Even with safeguards such as backups and Auto-Save, remembering to save your work on your own will save you the headache of losing data.

This chapter covered the following topics:

- Opening and saving files
- Setting file preferences and default folders
- Importing 3-D and 2-D images into SketchUp
- Exporting 3-D models, 2-D images, and animations
- Printing in SketchUp
- Using SketchUp Viewer

The next chapter concludes the first part of this book with a look at the different ways to customize the interface.

Part II

Working with Objects

Chapter 5

Selecting Objects

Before you can edit or work with any objects, you need to know how to select objects and components. And before you can select any objects, you need some basic objects in the scene to select. You can add objects to the scene by opening an existing model or one of the tutorial models, or you can add a component to the scene using the Component browser.

SketchUp offers several different ways to select exactly the object or objects you want. After selecting a group of objects, you can create a selection set. Selection sets let you instantly recall a specific selection. For example, if you are drawing a car, you could create a selection set of all the windows. Then when you go to apply materials, you simply choose the selection set and apply the glass material.

Another way to select objects is with the Outliner. This dialog box lists all the objects in the scene and lets you choose an object by name. This is especially helpful when you have small objects in the scene. So, let's get going. There are objects to select.

Selecting Objects with the Select Tool

Objects can be selected using the Select tool. You can select this tool by choosing Tools ⇨ Select, by pressing the Spacebar, or by clicking the Select button in the Getting Started toolbar. This is the default tool that is selected when no other tools are selected.

When the Select tool is active, you can select individual objects by simply clicking on them. When an object is selected, it is highlighted in blue and surrounded with a blue bounding box, as shown for the park bench in Figure 5.1.

To select multiple objects, click and drag with the Select tool. A rectangular selection area is displayed. When you release the mouse, all the objects that are completely contained within this rectangular selection area are selected. This provides a way to select multiple objects at once.

If you drag with the Select tool from left to right to create a rectangular selection area, objects are only selected when they are completely within the rectangular selection area, but if you drag from right to left, items are selected if any part of them is contained within the selection area. Dragging with the Select tool from left to right is called a Window selection and dragging from right to left is called a Crossing selection.

Another way to select multiple objects is to hold down the Ctrl key while clicking on or dragging over multiple objects. Each new object that you click on is added to the selection set and is highlighted in blue. When the Ctrl key is held down, a small plus sign appears next to the mouse cursor.

FIGURE 5.1

The selected object is highlighted and surrounded with a bounding box.

You can also select multiple objects by holding down the Shift key, but the Shift key acts a little different in that it lets you add unselected objects to the selection set or remove selected objects from the selection set. If you click on a selected object with the Shift key held down, the selected object becomes unselected. When the Shift key is held down, a small plus and minus sign appears next to the mouse cursor. Figure 5.2 shows two objects selected — the park bench and the trash can.

To remove an object from the selection set, you can use the Shift key or hold down the Shift and Ctrl keys together and click on the objects you want to remove. A small negative sign appears next to the mouse cursor when these keys are held down.

 **TIP**   **If you need to remember all the selected objects, simply make all the objects into a group by choosing Edit ⇨ Make Group.**

FIGURE 5.2

Holding down the Ctrl or Shift keys lets you quickly select multiple objects.

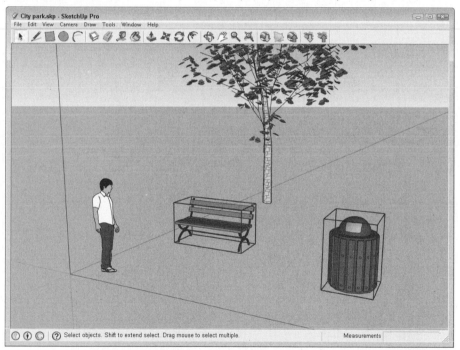

Selecting Objects with Menu Commands

If you want to select all of the objects in the scene, you can drag over all the objects with the Selection tool, or you can simply choose Edit ➪ Select All (Ctrl+A). You can also deselect all objects in the scene by clicking in an open space away from all other objects or by choosing Edit ➪ Select None (Ctrl+T).

Viewing Object Info

When an object is selected, specific commands can be issued that impact the selected object. One of these commands is to view the information about the selected object in the Entity Info palette, as shown in Figure 5.3. This palette can be opened for the selected object by choosing Window ➪ Entity Info or by right-clicking on the object and selecting Entity Info from the pop-up menu.

FIGURE 5.3

The Entity Info palette holds information about the selected object.

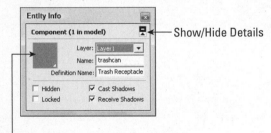

Paint thumbnail

In the upper-left corner of the Entity Info palette is a thumbnail showing the current paint selection. The Entity Info palette also lists the selected item's assigned layer, name, and a definition. Clicking on the Show Details button in the upper-right corner reveals several object properties that you can set including Hidden, Locked, Cast Shadows, and Receive Shadows.

CROSS-REF Applying paint and materials to a selection is covered in Chapter 18.

If multiple objects are selected, the number of selected components is listed at the top of the palette. The Entity Info palette contains different types of information depending on the type of subobject that is selected. For example, if an object's face is selected, then the Entity Info palette includes a field that lists its Area, as shown in Figure 5.4.

FIGURE 5.4

The Entity Info palette holds different types of information depending on the selected part.

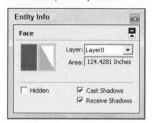

Selecting Objects with the Outliner Palette

Another way to select objects in the scene is in the Outliner palette, as shown in Figure 5.5. Open this palette by choosing Window ➪ Outliner. This palette is especially helpful when trying to select small objects.

FIGURE 5.5

The Outliner palette lists all objects in the current scene.

Objects are displayed in the Outliner palette in hierarchical order with subobjects listed underneath their object. Each object is listed by its name with its descriptive name in brackets. Whichever objects are selected in the scene are also selected in the Outliner palette. If multiple objects are selected in a scene, then the names for each of these objects are also selected in the Outliner palette.

CROSS-REF The Outliner can also be used to edit the object hierarchy. More on this is presented in Chapter 8.

If you hold down the Ctrl key, you can select multiple names in the Outliner palette by clicking on each; by holding down the Shift key, you can select a range of Outliner objects.

Selecting Entities

Every object is made of several different parts, also know as entities. For a simple cube, the entities include faces, vertices, and edges. Being able to select these individual entities is the key to editing objects. Entities can be selected just like selecting objects by clicking on them with the Selection tool.

Multiple entities can also be selected in the same manner using the Shift and Ctrl keys. When a line entity is selected, it is highlighted in blue; face entities are highlighted with a dotted pattern, as shown in Figure 5.6.

 **TIP** If you keep the Entity Info palette open, it confirms which entity of the number of entities that are selected.

Selecting surrounding entities

When a single entity is selected, you can expand its selection to include the surrounding entities such as the bounding edges or connected faces using the Select submenu in the right-click pop-up menu. The available options depend on the type of entity that is selected, but some available commands include the following:

- **Bounding Edges:** This command is available when a face entity is selected and lets you select all the adjacent edges.

- **Connected Faces:** This command selects all the adjacent faces to the currently selected face.

- **All Connected:** This command quickly selects all the entities that make up the current object.

- **All on Same Layer:** This command selects all the objects that are on the same layer as the current selection.

- **All with Same Material:** This command is used to select all entities with the same material applied to it such as the windows in a building.

FIGURE 5.6

Face entities are filled with a dotted pattern when selected.

Selected face

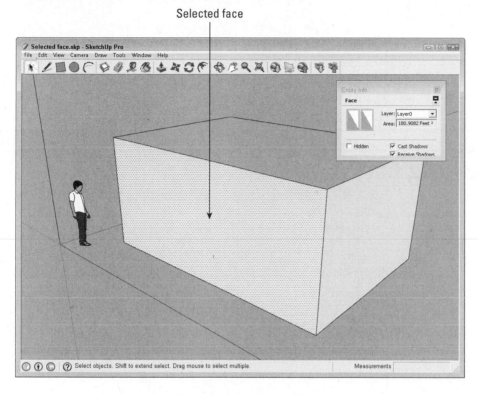

Expanding a selection

In addition to the right-click pop-up menu, you can also expand the current selection by double- or triple-clicking on an object or entity. For example, if you double-click on a face entity, the face along with its bounding edges are selected and if you triple-click on the face, then all face and edge entities in the cube are selected.

Tutorial: Practicing selecting objects

The best way to figure out how the selection features work is to practice using them. For this example, you'll practice selecting objects in a simple maze scene. Follow these steps:

1. **Open the** `Friends in maze.skp` **file from the Chap 05 folder on the CD-ROM.** This scene includes a simple maze with several people positioned around.

2. **Select all the people.** Hold down the Ctrl key and click on each of the people. Each is highlighted blue when selected.

3. **You can also select all people by dragging from right to left with the Select tool or by choosing Edit ➪ Select All (Ctrl+A).** Hold down the Ctrl and Shift keys and drag over the edges that make up the maze to deselect them from the selection set.

4. **Finally, you can select all the people using the Outliner palette.** Choose Window ➪ Outliner to open the Outliner palette, and click on each of the people objects. Figure 5.7 shows the selection of people.

FIGURE 5.7

Using the selection tools you can select just the people in this scene.

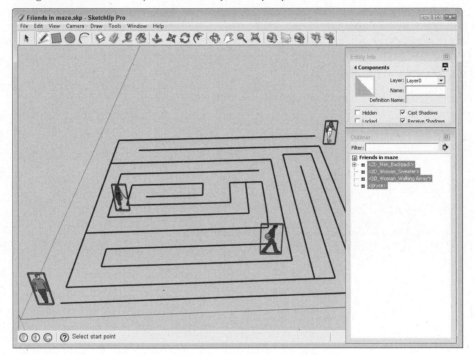

Summary

Before you can use the various commands to work with the various objects and entities, you first need to learn how to select them. This chapter covered the various ways to select objects and entities using the Select tool, the Edit menu, the Outliner, and the right-click pop-up menu.

This chapter covered the following topics:

- Selecting objects
- Selecting with menus
- Viewing object info
- Selecting with the Outliner palette
- Selecting entities

In the next chapter, we'll get things moving. With the various transform tools, you can move objects about the scene.

Chapter 6

Transforming Objects

I f you begin to add objects to the scene and realize that one of your objects isn't positioned right, you could delete the object and place the new one in the correct position, or you could simply use the Move tool to move it into the right place.

The transform tools provide the first and most general way to edit objects. There are three basic transformations including Move, Rotate, and Scale, and each tool can be used in unique ways.

IN THIS CHAPTER

Using the Move tool

Using the Rotate tool

Using the Scale tool

NOTE Don't confuse the transform tools with the Zoom, Pan, and Orbit tools that are used to change the view.

Using the Move Tool

The Move tool lets you change the position of the selected object. It can be selected by choosing Tools ➪ Move, selecting it from the Edit or Getting Started Toolbar, or by pressing the M hotkey. After you select the object, you can move it by simply clicking and dragging in the main window. The mouse cursor changes to four arrows when the Move tool is active.

TIP If you get lost as you transform an object, you can press Esc to exit the transformation at any time.

Moving along a straight line

When the selected object is being dragged with the Move tool, a line extends from the location where you first click with the Move tool to the location where you drag the object. This line is known as the inference line. If the direction is along the X-axis, then this inference line is red; if the direction is in the Y-axis, then the inference line is green; and if the direction is in the Z-axis, then the inference line is blue. If you release the mouse when this inference line is red, green, or blue, then you are confirmed that the object has been moved along a straight line. Figure 6.1 shows a simple brick component that is being moved along the X-axis.

If you press the Shift key while dragging along the X, Y, or Z-axes, the axis becomes locked so that the object can only be moved along the dragging axis. You can also lock the axis by pressing one of the arrow keys.

FIGURE 6.1

A red axis line confirms that the object is moved in a straight line.

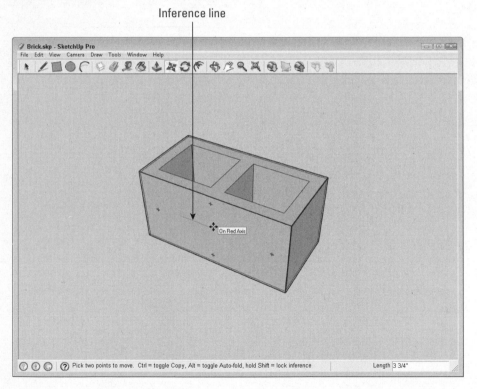

Moving a precise distance

If you want to move the selected object a precise amount, select the object you want to move and start dragging in the direction that you want the object to move. This causes the amount that is dragged to be displayed in the Measurements Toolbar in the lower-right corner of the interface. When a value appears in the Measurements Toolbar, you can type a precise value and the object is moved this entered distance.

Stretching entities

If you select an entity and drag with the Move tool, the connected entities will stretch as the selected entity is moved, as shown in Figure 6.2.

FIGURE 6.2

Connected entities stretch when selected entities are moved.

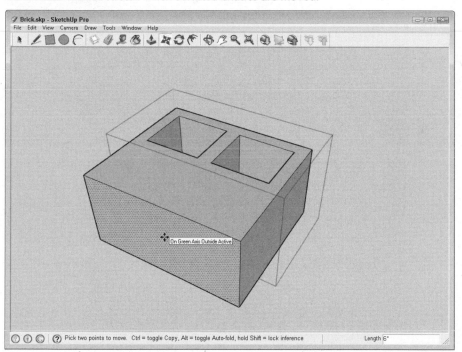

Using the Rotate Tool

Another way to transform an object or an entity is to rotate it. Rotation always takes place around a pivot point, and the resulting rotation depends on the location of this pivot point. The pivot point is determined by where you click with the Rotate tool.

The Rotate tool lets you change the orientation of the selected object. Select it by choosing Tools ⇨ Rotate, or from the Edit or Getting Started Toolbar, or by pressing the Q hotkey. Once selected, the pivot point is placed by clicking on its location. This places a protractor guide where you place the pivot point. You then need to click to set the starting point of the rotation and then drag to rotate the object. The selected object is moved by simply clicking and dragging in the main window. The mouse cursor changes to four arrows when the Move tool is active.

Rotating to regular intervals

The protractor guide is divided into 15-degree increments. If you align the inference line to one of these increments, then you can control the rotation amount. Figure 6.3 shows an object being rotated.

FIGURE 6.3

The protractor guide marks the pivot point and the rotation amount.

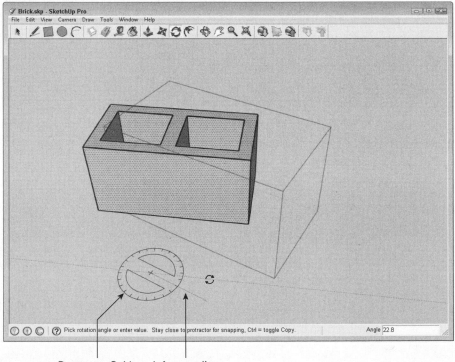

Protractor Guide   Inference line

If you press the Shift key while dragging along the X, Y, or Z-axes, the axis becomes locked so that the object can only be moved along the dragging axis. You can also lock the axis by pressing one of the arrow keys.

Rotating to a precise angle

If you want to rotate the selected object a precise amount, select the object to rotate and start dragging in the direction that you want the object to move. This causes the amount that is dragged to be displayed in the Measurements Toolbar in the lower-right corner of the interface. When the value appears in the Measurements Toolbar, you can type the precise value you want and the object rotates this entered amount.

Stretching entities

If you select an entity and rotate with the Rotate tool, the connected entities stretch as the selected entity is moved, as shown in Figure 6.4.

FIGURE 6.4

Connected entities stretch when selected entities are rotated.

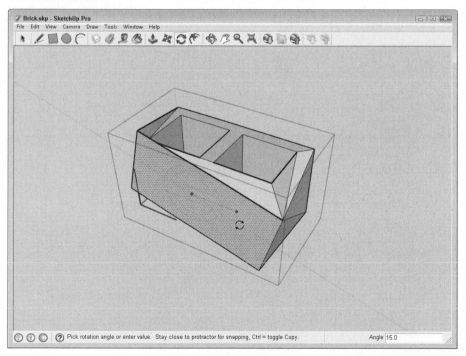

Using the Scale Tool

The third big transformation tool is the Scale tool. Scaling, like rotation, also depends on the pivot point, which is the point about which the object is scaled. When the Scale tool is made active, the object or entity is surrounded by grip handles that make it easy to constrain the scaling to a specific axis.

The Scale tool lets you change the size of the selected object. To select it, choose Tools ⇨ Scale, or select it from the Edit or Getting Started Toolbar, or by pressing the S hotkey. Once selected, the grip handles appear at each corner, face center, and edge midpoint on the selected object.

Scaling along a single axis

Dragging on one of the corner grip handles scales the object uniformly in all axes, but if you drag on an edge, you can scale the object within a single plane. If you click and drag a face center grip handle, scaling is constrained to a single axis, as shown in Figure 6.5.

FIGURE 6.5

Grip handles appear when the Scale tool is selected.

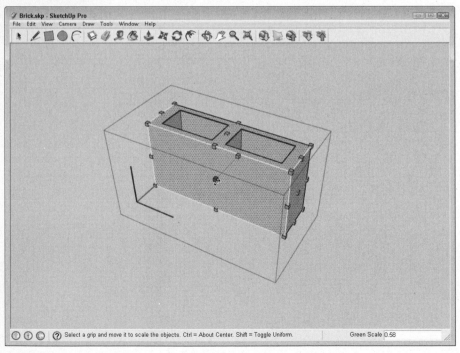

If you press and hold the Shift key while dragging any of the grip handles, the entire object is scaled uniformly along all axes.

Scaling to a precise value

If you want to scale the selected object a precise amount, select the object to scale and start dragging in the direction that you want the object to move. This causes the amount that is dragged to be displayed in the Measurements Toolbar in the lower-right corner of the interface. When a value appears in the Measurements Toolbar, you can type a precise value and the object will be scaled to this value. Scale values are measured as a percent of the current size with 1.0 reflecting the current size. Scale values less than 1 make the object smaller; values larger than 1 make the object larger. For example, a scale value of 2.0 results in an object that is twice as big as the original.

Stretching entities

If you select an entity and rotate with the Scale tool, the connected entities stretch as the selected entity is moved, as shown in Figure 6.6.

FIGURE 6.6

Connected entities stretch when selected entities are scaled.

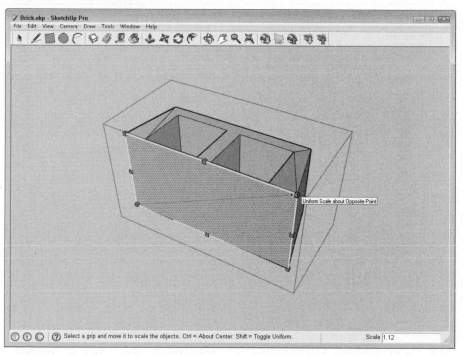

Tutorial: Rearranging the furniture

One real-world use for SketchUp is to visualize how stage productions are laid out, but this same idea can be used to rearrange the living room furniture using the transform tools, which you do in this example.

To rearrange the living room furniture, follow these steps:

1. **Open the** `Living room.skp` **file from the Chap 06 folder on the CD-ROM.** This file contains a simple set of furniture components from the Components library.

2. **The first problem to fix is that the room is much too large.** Click on the back wall with the Select tool to select it. Then choose the Move tool (M), and click and drag the wall forward toward the other furniture pieces. Drag until the green inference line is visible and release the mouse.

3. **Select the couch with the Select tool and select the Rotate tool (Q).** Click on the floor to place the protractor guide, and click to set the initial rotation point. Then drag the mouse cursor until the couch is rotated 90 degrees. Use the Move tool to move the couch back against the wall.

4. **Repeat step 3 for the coffee table and position it in front of the couch.** Figure 6.7 shows the resulting layout.

FIGURE 6.7

Furniture repositioned compliments of the transform tools.

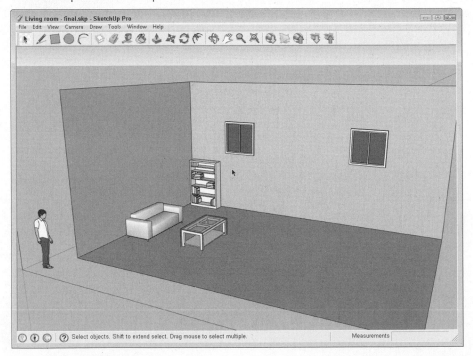

Summary

Using the transform tools, you can move, rotate, and scale objects and entities in the scene. These tools include multiple guides and helpers that make transforming objects easy.

This chapter covered the following topics:

- Accessing the transform tools
- Using the transformation guides
- Entering precise transformation values

The next chapter looks into how you can clone and copy objects.

Chapter 7

Cloning Objects

Cloning objects and entities is easy and can be done in a number of ways including the Cut, Copy, and Paste commands. You can also clone objects using the Move/Copy tool.

IN THIS CHAPTER

Using Cut, Copy, and Paste commands

Cloning with the transform tools

Creating linear and radial arrays

Using the Cut, Copy, and Paste Commands

Perhaps the most intuitive way to clone an object is with the Cut, Copy, and Paste commands. These commands are found in the Edit menu. Choose Edit ➪ Cut (Ctrl+X) to place a copy of the selected object on the clipboard and remove the object from the scene. You can choose Edit ➪ Copy (Ctrl+C) to do the same thing but leave a copy in the scene.

After copying an object to the clipboard, choose Edit ➪ Paste (Ctrl+V) to place the object back in the scene. When the Paste command is selected, the object appears attached to the cursor where you can drag it around the scene and drop it by releasing the mouse button. When using the Paste command, you can place copied objects in the same scene or you can open a different scene and place the object there.

There is also a Paste in Place command that you can use to place the copied object in the exact place from where it was copied.

Cut, Copy, and Paste entities

In addition to objects, the Cut, Copy, and Paste commands can also be used to duplicate entities. To duplicate an entity, simply select the entity and use the commands just as you would for duplicating an object.

Tutorial: Creating a row of sunflowers

The Cut, Copy, and Paste commands make it easy to create a row of objects. For this tutorial, you'll create a row of sunflowers. Follow these steps:

1. **Open the** `Sunflower.skp` **file from the Chapter 07 folder on the CD.** This file includes a single sunflower component.

2. **Select the sunflower by clicking on it.** Choose Edit ⇨ Copy (Ctrl+C) to copy the object to the clipboard.

3. **Choose Edit ⇨ Paste (Ctrl+V).** Position the cloned sunflower next to the existing one and click to place it.

4. **Select both sunflowers and repeat the Copy and Paste commands.** Repeat one more time until there are eight sunflowers. Figure 7.1 shows the resulting line of sunflowers.

FIGURE 7.1

Use the Copy and Paste commands to create a row of objects.

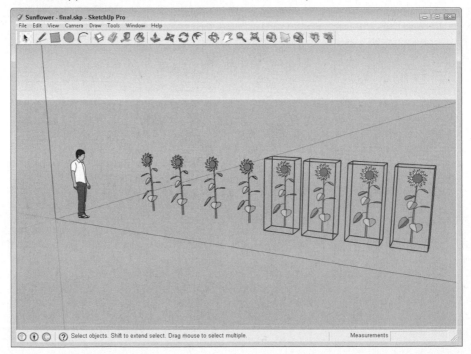

Cloning with the Transform Tools

You can also clone objects using the transform tools. The Move/Copy tool is the easiest to use, but you can also clone objects with the Rotate and Offset tools.

CROSS-REF Cloning objects with the Offset tool is covered in Chapter 10.

Cloning with the Move/Copy tool

To clone an object with the Move/Copy tool, hold down the Ctrl key before you release the object that is being dragged with the Move tool and a copy is made. The Ctrl key can be pressed before the object is first moved or after it has started to move. The cursor appears as a small plus sign when the Ctrl key is pressed to indicate that the object being moved will be cloned.

Creating a linear array of objects

When you clone an object with the Move/Copy tool, you can add a multiplier value in the Measurements Toolbar to indicate the number of duplicate copies to create. For example, if you clone a telephone pole by holding down the Ctrl key while dragging with the Move/Copy tool, a single duplicate pole is created. After creating a single cloned pole, you can type a value followed by "x" in the Measurements Toolbar to indicate the number of duplicates to create; for example, a value of 4x creates four additional poles. You can also create duplicates by typing an * (asterisk) and a number, such as *6.

TIP If you make a mistake in the number of copies to create, you can alter the number (even if it is less) by simply typing a new multiplier value before selecting another command.

When creating duplicate objects this way, each object is spaced the same distance as the first moved object, causing all objects in the array to be equally spaced.

Using the multiplier value repeats the move and clone operation, but you can also distribute the cloned objects over a specified distance using the divide operator in the Measurements Toolbar. For example, if you move and clone one slat of a white picket fence to the end of the property line and type the 25/ value in the Measurements Toolbar, then 25 slats will be equally spaced between the starting and ending slats, as shown in Figure 7.2.

FIGURE 7.2

Cloned objects can be distributed between two placed objects.

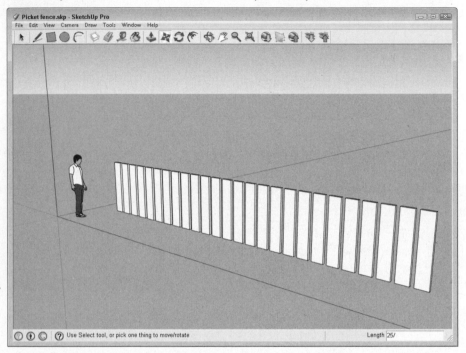

Creating a radial array of objects

All of the commands used to clone and duplicate objects that are available for the Move/Copy tool are also available for the Rotate tool. The key difference is that when creating an array of objects with a multiplier value it creates a radial array of objects instead of a linear array.

To clone an object with the Rotate tool, simply hold down the Ctrl key when rotating an object; and after rotating an object, you can type a multiplier value like 4x to repeat the cloning effect or a divisor value like 12/ to distribute objects between the clone and its original object. Figure 7.3 shows a simple wheel with spokes created using this method. The key is to position the rotation gizmo at the center of the disc.

FIGURE 7.3

The Rotate tool can be used to create radial arrays of objects.

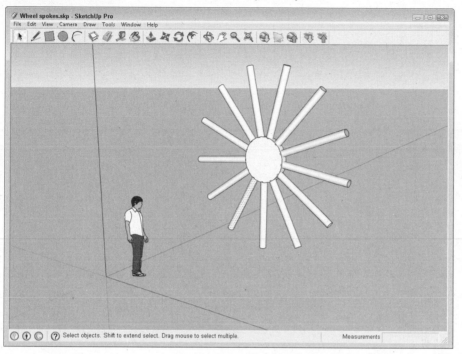

Tutorial: Adding bolts to a flange

After placing an object where it needs to be, you can use the cloning operations to quickly place other objects around a center point, such as bolts in a flange.

To add several bolts to a flange, follow these steps:

1. **Open the** `Bolts and flange.skp` **file from the Chapter 07 folder on the CD.** This file includes flange and bolt components.

2. **Select the placed bolt and choose the Rotate tool (Q).** Click to place the rotation gizmo on the center of the flange, then hold down the Ctrl key and drag the bolt to the second hole that is 90 degrees from the first.

3. **Immediately after placing the second bolt, type 3x in the Measurements Toolbar and press Enter.** The cloned bolts are placed where they need to be, as shown in Figure 7.4.

FIGURE 7.4

After placing the first bolt, the others are easily copied in place.

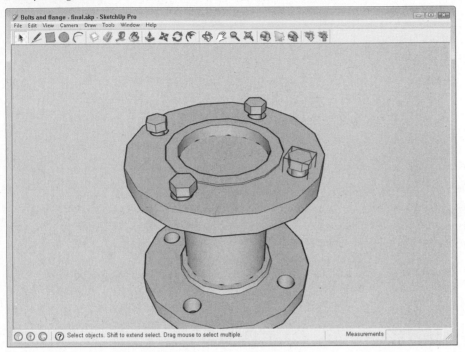

Summary

Learning to clone objects helps as you add more objects to the current scene. Cloned objects are easily placed relative and inline with the original. SketchUp offers several ways to clone objects including the common Cut, Copy, and Paste commands along with holding down the Ctrl key while dragging with the Move/Copy and Rotate tools. Using multipliers, you can create linear and radial arrays of objects by typing a multiplier in the Measurements Toolbar. Objects can also be distributed using a divisor value.

This chapter covered the following topics:

■ Using the Cut, Copy, and Paste commands

■ Cloning objects with the transform tools

■ Creating linear and radial arrays of objects

Now that you've figured out how to create multiple objects, the next chapter covers how to organize these objects using the Group, Hide, and Lock options.

Chapter 8

Grouping, Hiding, and Locking Objects

As you create more and more objects, the scene can get pretty complicated, making it difficult to select and maneuver the exact objects you want, but SketchUp includes several commands that help with this problem.

By grouping objects together, you can move them all as one object. This is convenient and organizes objects into logical groups. The grouping command can also be undone if you still need to move an individual object.

Once objects are in their correct position, you can hide or lock them so they cannot be selected. This helps eliminate them from the list of objects that can be selected, making it easier to select and work with the objects that aren't quite done.

IN THIS CHAPTER

Creating a group

Working with groups

Hiding and unhiding objects

Locking and unlocking objects

Creating a Group

If more than one object is selected, the Edit ⇨ Make Group menu command becomes active. With this command, all selected objects become grouped together. When selecting a group, a bounding box that surrounds the entire selection set is highlighted, as shown in Figure 8.1.

> **TIP** You can also access the Make Group command from the right-click pop-up menu.

If you need to access a subject in the group, simply double-click on the group.

FIGURE 8.1

All objects within a group are included in the bounding box.

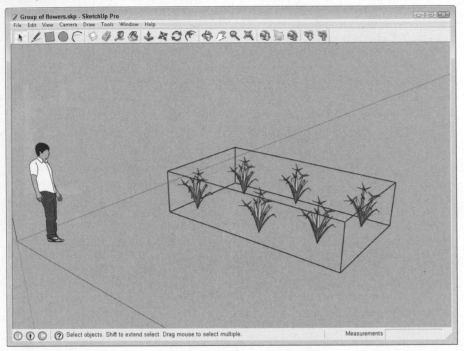

> **CROSS-REF** Components are similar to groups and are also helpful for organizing objects, but they have many more features. Components are discussed in Chapter 15.

Groups can also be nested within other groups. To nest a group within a group, select a grouped object along with other objects and use the Make Group command.

All objects contained within a group can be identified as subobjects of the group when viewed in the Outliner panel, as shown in Figure 8.2. The Outliner panel also provides a way to select a group's subobject. If you click on a group subobject, the group is opened and the subobject is selected.

FIGURE 8.2

Objects within a group are listed in the Outliner panel.

Working with Groups

When a group is selected, a new menu named Group appears at the bottom of the Edit menu. This menu includes commands that let you edit the selected group. There is also a command to explode (or dissolve) the group.

Editing a group

To get access to a group's subobject, simply select the group and choose Edit ⇨ Group (*name of group*) ⇨ Edit Group, or you can double-click on the group and the subobjects within the group can be selected. When a group is opened, the group's bounding box becomes a dashed line, as shown in Figure 8.3.

 When a group is opened, all scene objects that are not part of the group are dimmed.

With access to the group's subobjects, you can transform and edit them normally. When you are finished editing the group, choose Edit ⇨ Close Group/Component, or you can simply click outside of the group's bounding box to close the group.

Exploding a group

To ungroup all objects that make up a group, select the group and choose Edit ⇨ Group ⇨ Explode. The Explode command undoes only the current selected group; all nested subgroups remain intact.

FIGURE 8.3

When a group is opened, you can select its subobjects.

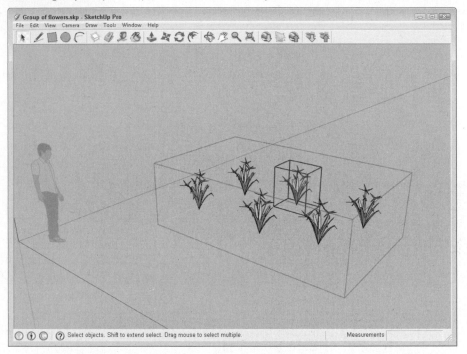

Hiding and Unhiding Objects

If you want to eliminate an object from the scene without deleting it, you can choose Edit ⇨ Hide. This causes the selected object to be hidden from the scene. Hidden objects cannot be selected from the interface, which keeps them from being accidentally moved. Hidden objects still appear in the Outliner panel, but they are dimmed, as shown in Figure 8.4.

Not only can objects be hidden, but SketchUp also allows individual entities to be hidden. This gives you the chance to see inside an object. Figure 8.5 shows a mailbox component with the front panel hidden, allowing the viewer to see inside.

FIGURE 8.4

Hidden objects appear dimmed in the Outliner panel.

FIGURE 8.5

Individual entities can also be hidden, revealing the interior.

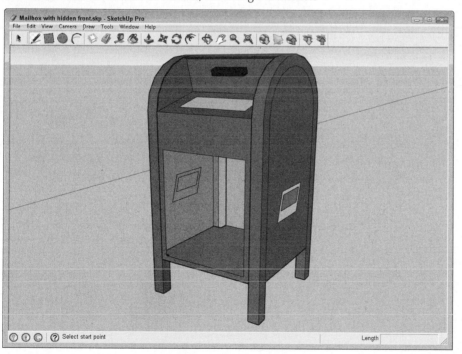

Hidden objects are not visible, but if you want to quickly see all the items that are hidden without unhiding them, simply toggle the View ⇨ Hidden Geometry menu command. This makes all hidden objects visible and selectable. If an entity is hidden, then the Hidden Geometry toggle shows the hidden face as a grid, as shown in Figure 8.6.

One nice aspect of hiding objects is that it is reversible. However, deleted objects can only be recovered by choosing Edit ⇨ Undo. To unhide an object, you have three options. Choosing Edit ⇨ Unhide ⇨ Selected is only available if the View ⇨ Hidden Geometry toggle is enabled. With this toggle selected, you can select hidden objects and unhide them by choosing Unhide ⇨ Selected.

Choosing Edit ⇨ Unhide ⇨ Last causes the last hidden object to reappear. If this command is used multiple times, the objects reappear in the reverse order in which they were hidden. Choosing Edit ⇨ Unhide ⇨ All causes all hidden objects to reappear.

FIGURE 8.6

Hidden faces are shown as grids with the View ⇨ Hidden Geometry toggle enabled.

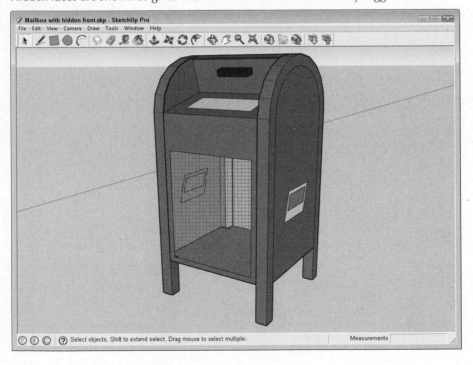

Locking and Unlocking Objects

If you want to prevent an object from moving, but you need the object to be visible as you place other objects in the scene, you can choose Edit ⇨ Lock to make an object so it cannot be moved, rotated, or scaled. When an object is locked, it is highlighted with a red bounding box, as shown in Figure 8.7.

Locked objects can be selected, but you cannot transform them. To unlock a selected object, choose Edit ⇨ Unlock ⇨ Selected, or you can choose Edit ⇨ Unlock ⇨ All to unlock all locked objects.

Locked objects are highlighted in red.

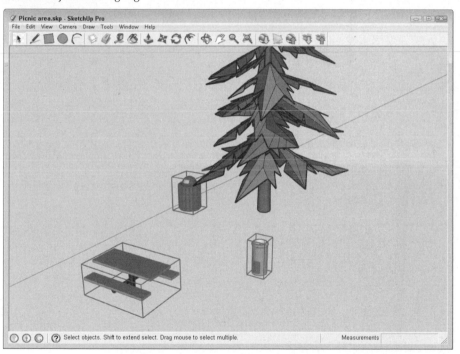

Tutorial: Locking multiple objects

When working on models, sometimes you can have all the objects lined up and looking good only to discover that one object is way out of line. Sometimes you can inadvertently select an object or an entity on the backside of an object and accidentally move it out of place. Using the lock feature, you can quickly fix such a mistake and ensure that nothing else gets moved.

To lock multiple selected objects, follow these steps:

1. **Open the** `Misaligned window.skp` **file from the Chapter 8 folder on the CD.** This file includes a simple building with four rows of windows. One window has been moved out of line.

2. **Choose Edit ➪ Select All (Ctrl+A) to select all the items in the scene.** Then hold down the Shift and Ctrl keys and click on the misaligned window. This selects all scene objects except for the misaligned window.

3. **Choose Edit ➪ Lock to lock all objects except for the misaligned window, as shown in Figure 8.8.**

4. **Select the misaligned window with the Select tool.** Use the Move/Copy tool to align the window where it needs to be.

5. **Choose Edit ➪ Unlock ➪ All to unlock all objects.**

FIGURE 8.8

All objects are locked except for the one that needs to be moved.

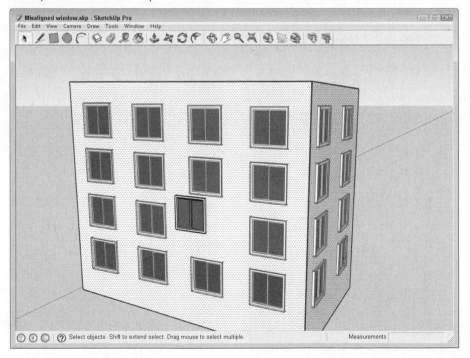

Summary

Complex scenes will have some small detailed pieces that can easily be lost when the larger objects are moved. Using groups, you can combine these smaller objects with the larger pieces that they need to move with. Another common headache is being able to select and move objects when the scene has multiple overlapping objects. To help overcome this, SketchUp includes the ability to hide and lock objects.

This chapter covered the following topics:

- Grouping objects and entities
- Editing and exploding groups
- Hiding and unhiding objects and entities
- Locking and unlocking objects

This chapter concludes the basic working with objects section, and you're ready to start drawing custom objects with the Drawing tools, which is covered in the next chapter.

Part III

Modeling Basics

Chapter 9

Drawing in SketchUp

S ketchUp is designed to let you turn simple sketches into 3-D scenes. This chapter presents the tools used to create many of the simple basic elements that make up a project.

SketchUp includes a number of tools (which happen to be called drawing tools) that help you sketch perfect circles, arcs, and straight lines. Using these tools, your sketches can become drawings.

Understanding the Drawing Axes

The key to working in 3-D is to keep track of the axes. The standard axes are located at the origin of the drawing area, as shown in Figure 9.1. These axes are color coordinated with red denoting the X-axis, green marking the Y-axis, and blue indicating the Z-axis.

If you find that the axes are in the way when you print the model, you can turn them off by choosing View ⇨ Axes. This is a toggle command that simply hides and unhides the axes.

FIGURE 9.1

The default axes help keep the correct orientation.

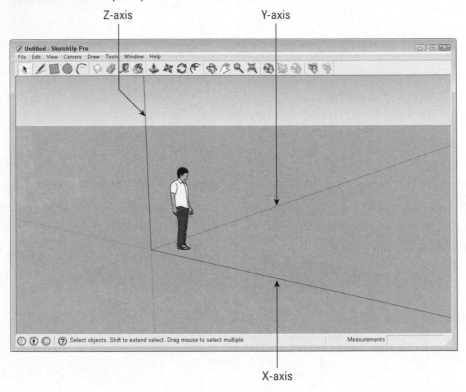

Z-axis

Y-axis

X-axis

Drawing Lines and Faces

Drawing is accomplished by dragging in the drawing area with one of the various drawing tools. The simplest drawing tool is the Line tool, which looks like a pencil in the Getting Started toolbar. You can select this tool from the Draw⇨ Line menu command (L) or by selecting it from the Getting Started Toolbar. You can draw straight lines from point to point with this tool.

When dragging with the Line tool, the line turns red, green, or blue when the line is aligned with one of the axes. This makes it easy to sketch and connect lines together to form faces.

Three or more lines that are connected and that exist in the same plane form a face. When a face is created, it is automatically shaded gray, as illustrated by the triangle in Figure 9.2.

FIGURE 9.2

A minimum of three edges are required to define a face.

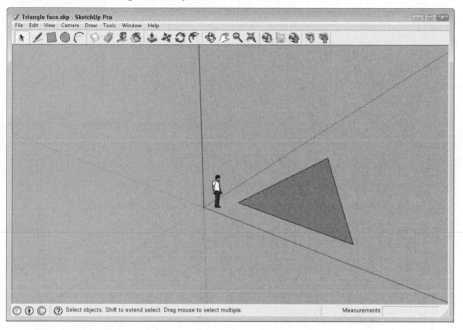

CROSS-REF If you need some help drawing lines, you can set some guidelines using the Tape
Measure tool, which is covered in Chapter 12.

When drawing a line, the line's length is displayed in the Measurements Toolbar. If you type a
value in the Measurements Toolbar while drawing a line, then a line of that length is drawn.
Alternatively, you can type three coordinates in the Measurements Toolbar and a line is drawn
from the starting point to the specified coordinate position.

Understanding inference positions

When you drag over the top of objects within the drawing area, you may have noticed that the point
located at the tip of the Line tool changes color based on where the mouse cursor is located. These
points identify specific locations and are used to help you draw accurately by giving you a visual
clue as to where the cursor is located. This feature is called inference and the key to using inference
is to learn what the different colors indicate. SketchUp identifies the following inference points:

TIP If you hover with the mouse cursor over an inference point, a tooltip appears identifying the inference point.

- **Endpoints:** Endpoints appear at each end of a line entity and are identified by a green point.

- **Midpoints:** Midpoints appear directly in the middle of a line entity and are identified by a cyan point.

- **Intersections:** Intersections appear where one line entity crosses another line entity and are identified by a black point.

- **On Edge:** On Edge points appear anywhere along the edge of a line entity and are identified by a red point.

- **On Face:** On Face points appear anywhere on the surface of a face entity and are identified by a blue point.

Figure 9.3 shows each of these various inference points along with their tooltips.

FIGURE 9.3

Inference points are identified by colored points and tooltips.

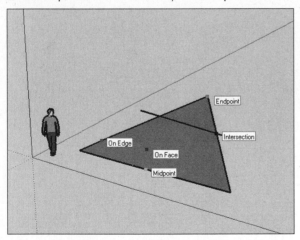

In addition to specific points, lines can also be lined up using inference. Lines that use inference are displayed as solid colored lines or as dashed colored lines, depending on the inference type. Tooltips also appear above the various inference lines if you hold the mouse still. Inference can recognize the following lines:

- **On Red Axis, On Green Axis, On Blue Axis:** Lines that are aligned to a specific axis are displayed in the color of the axis that it is aligned with: red for the X-axis, green for the Y-axis, and blue for the Z-axis.

- **From Point:** If the endpoint of a line is positioned so that it has the same X, Y, or Z-axis value as another point in the scene, then a dashed line connecting the two points is displayed.

- **Perpendicular to Edge:** When a line is perpendicular to another line, a magenta line is displayed. Perpendicular lines have a 90-degree angle between them.

- **Parallel to Edge:** When a drawn line is parallel to an existing line, the line is also displayed in magenta.

Figure 9.4 shows each of these various inference lines along with their tooltips.

FIGURE 9.4

Inference lines are also identified by colored lines and tooltips.

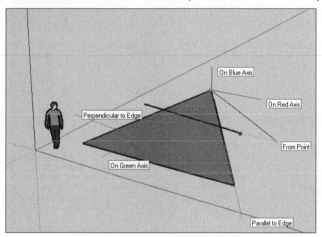

Constraining inference

As a model gets more and more complex, getting the right inference can be tricky. If you find the right inference, you can constrain the line to the selected inference using the Shift key. For example, if you are creating a line that is perpendicular to the midpoint of an edge, then drag out from the midpoint until the Perpendicular to Edge inference is identified and press and hold the Shift key. The line remains constrained to be perpendicular as you continue to drag with the Line tool.

Tutorial: Building a hexagon tower

For this example, I created three hexagon shapes that are vertically aligned. The goal is to draw lines between the corner points of these hexagons using inference. The result will be a nice hexagon tower.

To connect three vertically aligned shapes, follow these steps:

1. **Open the** Hexagon tower.skp **file from the Chapter 09 folder on the CD.** This file includes three vertically aligned hexagons.

2. **Select the Line tool (L).** Move the mouse cursor over one of the corner points on the bottom polygon shape. Notice how a green point appears indicating that the point is an endpoint. Click on the highlighted endpoint and move the mouse cursor to the corner point above and to the right of the clicked point. Click again on the corner point above on the third polygon, then press L to deselect and reselect the Line tool.

3. **Repeat Step 2 for each set of corner points around the polygon.** Figure 9.5 shows the resulting tower.

FIGURE 9.5

Using inference makes it easy to draw lines between specific points.

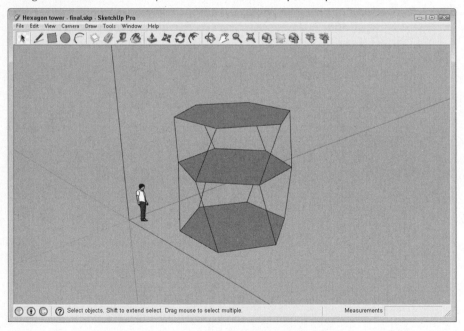

Drawing Arcs

Arcs are drawn with the Arc tool. This tool is located in the Draw ➪ Arc menu (A) or on the Getting Started Toolbar. It works by clicking to specify where the two endpoints of the arc are located and then dragging to curve the arc between the two endpoints.

While the Arc tool is active, you can specify the chord length, the distance of the bulge, the radius of the arc, or the number of segments in the Measurements Toolbar. The chord length is the distance between the arc endpoints. The bulge distance is the distance from the chord length midpoint to the highest point of the arc. The arc radius only applies when the arc is a perfect half circle where the radius equals the chord length. The number of segments defines how many lines are used to create the arc. Specifying a higher number of segments results in a smoother curve. Each of these values is displayed in Figure 9.6.

The chord length can be specified after clicking to locate the first arc point. The Measurements Toolbar lists this value as Length. After clicking to place the arc endpoint, the Measurements Toolbar reads Bulge, and typing a value specifies the bulge distance. If you add an "r" to the end of the bulge distance, the value is interpreted as a radius value and the arc becomes a half circle. Adding an "s" to the end of the value typed in the Measurements Toolbar indicates the number of segments, or lines, that are used to draw the arc.

FIGURE 9.6

These terms define an arc.

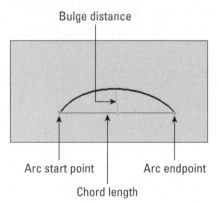

Arc inference

There are two inference points that apply specifically to arcs. When dragging to specify the bulge of an arc, the arc snaps at the location where the arc is a perfect half circle and the tooltip indicates this location. When the arc is a half circle, a tooltip appears, as shown in Figure 9.7.

FIGURE 9.7

A half circle is where the chord length equals the radius.

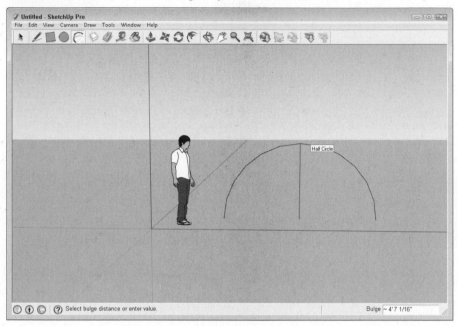

When two arcs share an endpoint, a cyan inference line is displayed to indicate where the arc is positioned that the tangents at the shared vertex are equal. When the tangents for these arcs are equal, the two arcs form a smooth transition if the arcs are opposite or they leave a same angle to form similar shaped peaks. Both of these conditions are shown in Figure 9.8.

FIGURE 9.8

Cyan inference lines are displayed from adjacent arcs whose tangents are equal.

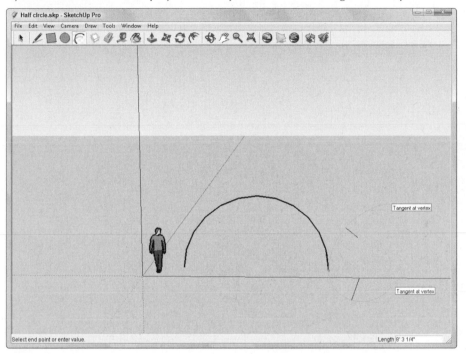

Tutorial: Drawing arcs within a hexagon

Using the inference engine, you can quickly draw arcs based on an existing shape, such as a hexagon.

To draw arcs within a hexagon, follow these steps:

1. **Open the** Hexagon.skp **file from the Chapter 09 folder on the CD.** This file includes a single hexagon.

2. **Select the Arc tool (A).** Move the mouse cursor over one of the corner points on the hexagon shape. Notice how a green point appears indicating that the point is an end-point. Click on the highlighted endpoint and move the mouse cursor to an adjacent

corner point. Click again to specify the chord length, and drag toward the center of the hexagon until the arc snaps to where a half circle is created. Click to create the arc.

3. **Repeat Step 2 for each edge around the hexagon.** Figure 9.9 shows the resulting pattern.

FIGURE 9.9

A pattern is created by adding arcs to all edges of a hexagon.

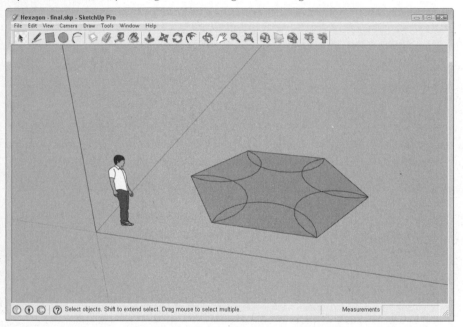

Using the Freehand Tool

If you've had enough with regular-shaped objects, you can use the Freehand tool to draw shapes without any inference or alignment. This tool is located in the Draw ⇨ Freehand menu or on the Drawing Toolbar. When this tool is selected, the cursor changes to a pencil; wherever you drag with the mouse, line segments are created. If you return to the beginning location, a closed shape is created. Figure 9.10 shows two shapes created with the Freehand tool: one open and one closed. Closed shapes are filled with a gray surface.

Dragging across an existing shape with the Freehand tool divides the shape. However, if you hold down the Shift key while dragging with the Freehand tool, a 3-D polyline object is created. 3-D polylines do not divide any shapes that they cross. If you later want to convert a 3-D polyline to a regular curve, simply select the line and choose Edit ⇨ 3D Polyline ⇨ Explode.

FIGURE 9.10

The Freehand tool can create open and closed shapes.

Open shape   Closed shape

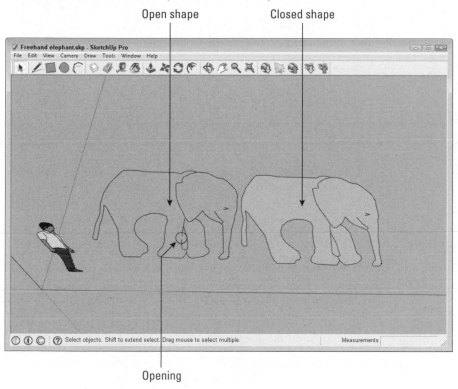

Opening

Using the Eraser Tool

To fix any errant curves that you've drawn, you can use the Eraser tool (E). This tool is located in the Tools ⇨ Eraser menu (E) or on the Getting Started toolbar. With the Eraser tool selected, you can drag over specific line segments to erase. When you drag over a line segment with the Eraser tool, the line segment is colored blue; when you release the mouse button, the line is deleted. If you drag over multiple line segments, they are all erased.

Dragging over lines with the Eraser tool when the Shift key is held down causes the lines to be hidden instead of deleted. This is handy to reduce the visual complexity of a scene without deleting the lines.

The Eraser tool can also be used to soften and smooth specific lines by holding down the Ctrl key while dragging over lines. This action can also be undone if you drag over the lines with the Ctrl and Shift keys held down together.

Drawing Shapes

Drawing regular shapes with the Freehand tool can be difficult, but SketchUp includes several tools that make drawing regular shapes easy. These tools include the Rectangle, Circle, and Polygon tools, which are found in the Draw menu.

Creating rectangles and squares

The Rectangle tool (R) lets you draw rectangles and squares by dragging from one corner to the opposite corner. The Rectangle tool automatically creates a face entity.

As you drag with the Rectangle tool, a diagonal dashed line appears within the center of the face when a perfect square or a Golden Rectangle (Golden Section) is sized. If you release the mouse button when either of these dashed lines is showing, the Square or the Golden Section is created, as shown in Figure 9.11. A tooltip appears identifying it as a Square or a Golden Section.

> **NOTE** A Golden Rectangle is a common shape found in classic architecture such as the Parthenon. It has a ratio where the distance of the length and height is proportionate to the longer length just as the length is proportionate to the height — a value known as the Golden Ratio, which equals 1.618034.

FIGURE 9.11

A dashed line appears between opposite corners when a square or a Golden Section is created.

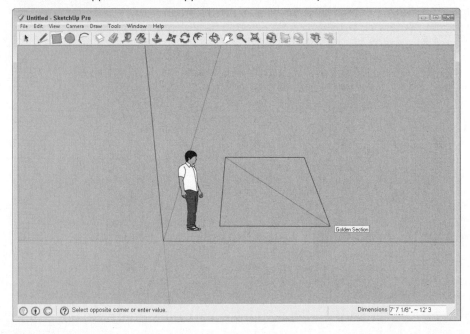

When drawing a rectangle, its dimensions appear within the Measurements Toolbar. If you type new values for the Length and Height separated by a comma, a new rectangle with those dimensions is created.

Circles

The Circle tool (C) lets you draw perfect circles by clicking at the location of the circle's center and dragging outward to define the circle's radius. The Circle tool also automatically creates a face entity. Figure 9.12 shows several circles drawn with the Circle tool.

FIGURE 9.12

Circles are drawn with the Circle tool.

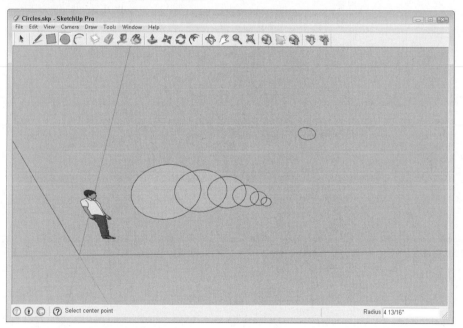

 The default value of 24 sides is enough to make most circles appear round.

When drawing a circle, its radius appears within the Measurements Toolbar. If you type a new radius value, a new circle with the specified radius is drawn. You can also change the number of sides used to create a circle when the Circle tool is first selected. The Measurements Toolbar reads Sides when first selected. If you type a number followed by the letter "s" after a circle is created, you can change the number of sides of a circle. Figure 9.13 shows several circles that have a gradually decreasing number of sides.

FIGURE 9.13

For circles, you can specify the number of sides.

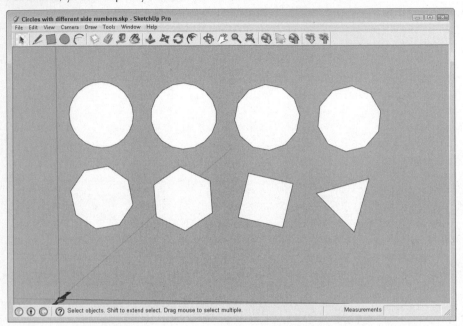

Polygons

Although polygons can be created by changing the number of sides of a circle, you can also create them using the Polygon tool. This tool is found in the Draw⟳Polygon menu or on the Drawing toolbar. Drawing polygons works the same way as drawing a circle. Simply click at the center point and then drag to set the polygon's radius. If you rotate about the center point before releasing the mouse button, you can orient the polygon.

When the Polygon tool is first selected, the Measurements Toolbar shows the number of sides that make up the polygon. After you click to set the center point, the Measurements Toolbar shows the radius value for the polygon. Typing a value for the number of sides or the radius changes the current polygon.

Drawing Preferences

Within the System Preferences dialog box is a panel of Drawing options that are used to control how the mouse works when drawing lines with the Line tool. This panel, shown in Figure 9.14, is opened by choosing Window⟳Preferences.

FIGURE 9.14

The Drawing options in the System Preferences dialog box let you define how the mouse works when drawing lines.

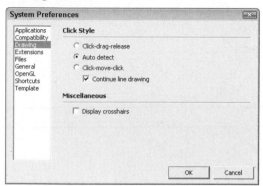

Within the System Preferences dialog box is a panel of Drawing options that are used to control how the mouse works when drawing lines with the Line tool. This panel, shown in Figure 9.14, is opened by choosing Window ⇨ Preferences.

The Drawing Preferences let you switch between two options. The Click-drag-release option only draws a line when you click on the first point and drag to form a line. If you click and release the mouse button, a line isn't created. This option is good if you want to draw several disconnected lines.

The Click-move-click option lets you draw lines by simply clicking at the start point and again at the endpoint without having to worry about dragging the mouse. If you select the Continue line drawing option, you can draw several connected lines. This is more efficient for creating shapes. After forming a closed shape, the tool is released from the last line and lets you start a new shape.

The Auto detect option combines both options and lets you create continuous lines if you drag from the endpoint of a line, but if you move the mouse away from the endpoint, the new line isn't connected.

Selecting the Display crosshairs option causes a set of coordinate crosshairs to appear as you drag with the Line tool. Figure 9.15 shows these crosshairs, which consist of a different color line for each axis.

FIGURE 9.15

The Display Crosshairs option causes coordinate crosshairs to follow the cursor around.

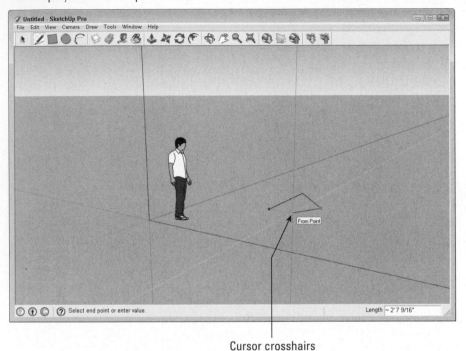

Cursor crosshairs

Using a Graphics Tablet

SketchUp includes support for graphics tablets, which is helpful for sketching. A graphics tablet is an input device that consists of a rectangular tablet that detects when a stylus pen is drawn on top of it. It works as a replacement to a mouse to enter in strokes. When using a tablet, it can be tough to select the small buttons, but you can increase the button size by choosing View ➪ Toolbars ➪ Large Buttons.

Summary

With coverage of the basic drawing tools, you can create objects using lines and shapes. SketchUp includes several tools to make drawing perfect shapes easy. For each of these tools, you can use values in the Measurements Toolbar to make the lines and shapes precise.

This chapter covered the following topics:

- Working with the drawing axes
- Drawing lines and faces
- Drawing arcs and shapes
- Drawing freehand curves and using the Eraser tool
- Setting drawing preferences

Now that a number of lines and shapes dot the scene, the next chapter shows how you can modify these objects using tools like the Push/Pull and Follow Me tools.

Chapter 10

Modifying Objects

O nce you have simple shapes in the scene, SketchUp includes multiple tools for modifying those shapes and curves. Some of these tools
can extrude the shape and others can divide and intersect the
curves to create new shapes. Learning to use these tools enables you to create
unique models.

Using the Push/Pull Tool

The Push/Pull tool is used to extrude the selected face. Extruding is the process of moving the shape in a perpendicular direction, adding faces at each
side. The result is to make a 2-D shape into a 3-D volume. The Push/Pull
tool is selected from the Tools ⇨ Push/Pull menu (P) or from the Getting
Started Toolbar.

Creating 3-D objects

The Push/Pull tool can only be used on face entities. Extruding a rectangular
face creates a box object and extruding a circle creates a cylinder object. To
use the Push/Pull tool, simply select a face and drag it upward with the tool
to add depth to the face, as shown for the hexagon in Figure 10.1.

Dragging on a face with the Push/Pull tool increases the height that the face
is extruded. If you release the mouse button and then click and drag on the
same face again, you can continue to increase or decrease the extrusion
height. If you stop dragging with the Push/Pull tool and then double-click on
the face, the extrusion height is repeated again. For example, if you drag a
face upward with the Push/Pull tool 1 foot and then release the mouse button and double-click on the face again, the extrusion height changes to

2 feet; if you double-click again, the extrusion height changes to 3 feet. This height extrusion can be applied to any face that you double-click on.

FIGURE 10.1

Faces are extruded using the Push/Pull tool.

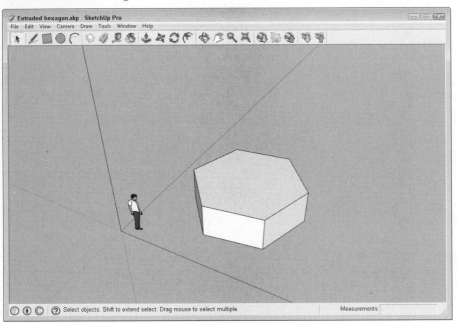

Tutorial: Extruding faces of a column

Using the Push/Pull tool, you can quickly extrude multiple faces to the same extent.

To extrude all the faces of a column, follow these steps:

1. **With the Polygon tool, create a simple hexagon shape.**
2. **Select the Push/Pull tool from the Getting Started toolbar.** Drag upward on the hexagon face to extrude it into a column.
3. **Drag on one of the side faces to move it a short distance from the column center.**
4. **Double-click on the adjacent face to extrude it the same distance as the first side face.**

5. Hold down the Alt key and drag with the scroll mouse button to rotate the view so you can see the next adjacent side face and double-click on it.

6. Continue to double-click on all the side faces around the column.

Figure 10.2 shows the resulting column with equally extruded side faces.

FIGURE 10.2

By double-clicking on each side face, you can extrude each an equal amount.

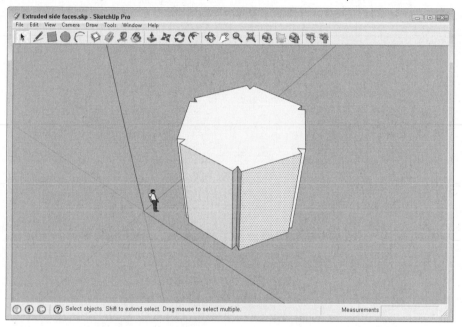

Creating holes

Not only can the Push/Pull tool be used to extrude faces, but if you push in on a face that is already part of a 3-D volume, the face is removed from the volume, and if you push it far enough, it creates a hole through the 3-D object, as shown in Figure 10.3. This provides a great way to create doors and windows in walls.

If you hold down the Ctrl key while pushing or pulling a face, the top row of specified edges remains, allowing you to create another extrusion level. If you don't hold down the Ctrl key, the previous extrusion continues without a break. Figure 10.4 shows multiple levels of the top face after extruding with the Ctrl key held down.

FIGURE 10.3

Hole pushed through an extruded face

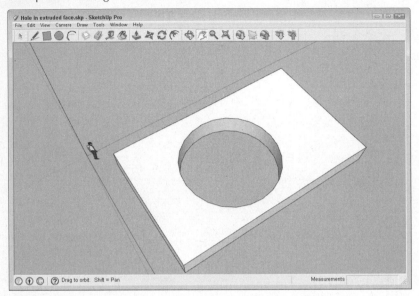

FIGURE 10.4

Holding down the Ctrl key while extruding creates different levels.

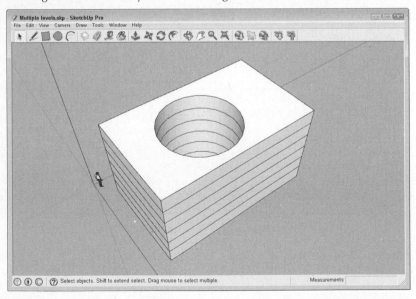

The amount of the extruded distance is displayed in the Measurements Toolbar. If you type a new value, the extrusion height changes to this new value.

Using the Follow Me Tool

The Follow Me tool is used to make a cross-sectional area follow the length of a path that is positioned perpendicular to the shape. This is called lofting in other packages. The Follow Me tool is found in the Tools ⇨ Follow Me menu and also in the Edit Toolbar.

To use the Follow Me tool, you need to create a face entity to be the cross-section area and a path that the face follows. The face entity should be approximately perpendicular to the path. With these two items created, choose the Follow Me tool and click on the face to loft along the path. You can then drag along the path to follow. The path turns red as the shape is extruded. When the Follow Me tool comes to a corner, you can continue around the corner and the cross-section continues to follow the path, as shown in Figure 10.5.

FIGURE 10.5

The Follow Me tool can follow the edge of a shape like this rectangle.

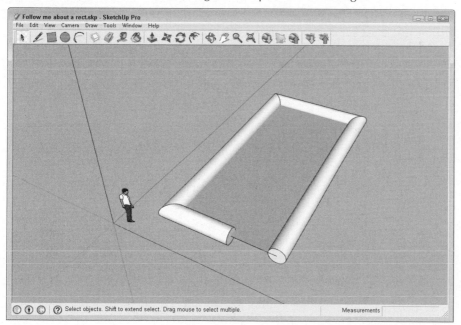

Following the exact path can be tricky if you have a lot of detail, but you can make sure to get the exact path if you select the path with the Select tool prior to selecting the Follow Me tool. If the Follow Me tool detects a selected set of edges, it automatically applies the Follow Me tool to the selected edges.

Following a path

Another way to use the Follow Me tool is to have a cross-section face follow the length of an open curve. This is useful for creating longer curved surfaces that follow a specific path like the trunk of a tree or a bending straw.

> **TIP** The easiest way to make sure that the path is perpendicular is to draw the face in a specific view like the Top view and the path in a perpendicular view like the Front view. These views are selected by choosing Camera ⇨ Standard Views.

Tutorial: Creating a sink drain pipe

The Follow Me tool can be used to create all sorts of pipes, even if they follow a strange path. A sink drain pipe follows a unique path to create a trap with two bends. It's also a perfect chance to practice using the Follow Me tool.

To create a sink drain pipe, follow these steps:

1. **Choose Camera ⇨ Standard Views ⇨ Front to switch to the Front view.**

2. **Select the Line tool and draw a straight line from the base upward.** Use the Arc tool to create two half circles that are opposite of each other, and conclude the path with another straight line.

3. **Choose Camera ⇨ Standard Views ⇨ Top to switch to the Top view.**

4. **Use the Circle tool to create a small circle that is perpendicular to the top of the path.**

5. **Choose Camera ⇨ Standard Views ⇨ Iso to switch back to the Isometric view.**

6. **With the Select tool, click on all the segments that make up the path.** Select the Follow Me tool and click on the top circle face.

Figure 10.6 shows the resulting pipe.

FIGURE 10.6

The Follow Me tool can make a cross-section follow an odd path.

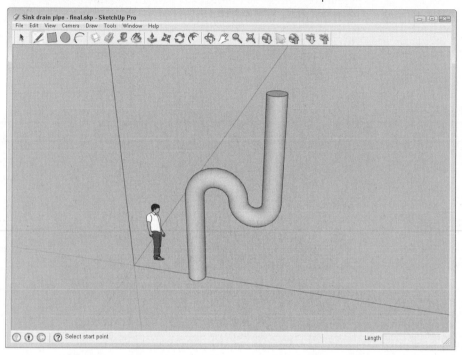

Beveling an edge

The Follow Me tool can also be used to add a bevel to the edge of an object. The bevel profile can be cut into the existing face. The face can then be selected normally with the Follow Me tool and the edge selected as a path. Figure 10.7 shows a long extruded rectangle turned into a unique bookshelf by drawing some connected arcs on the end of the object and using the Follow Me tool to bevel the lower edge.

FIGURE 10.7

The Follow Me tool can bevel object edges.

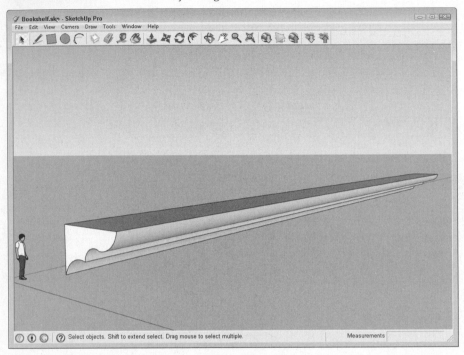

Lathing about a circle

If you construct the cross-section path to be the interior of an object and then make the path a simple circle, you can use the Follow Me tool to lathe 3-D objects. Figure 10.8 shows a baseball bat created by drawing the outline of the bat's interior and then using the Follow Me tool to follow the shape about a circular path.

> **TIP** Although SketchUp doesn't have a spherical primitive object, you can quickly create a sphere by using the Follow Me tool on two circles of equal size that are oriented 90 degrees to each other.

FIGURE 10.8

The Follow Me tool can also be used to lathe circular objects.

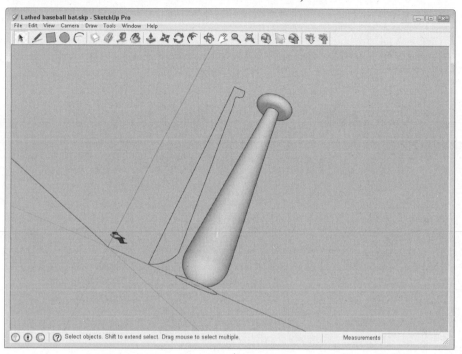

Using the Offset Tool

One of the easiest ways to create a room of four walls is to draw a rectangle and then subtract away an inset rectangle that is only smaller by the thickness of the intended walls. If you manually create a rectangle and try to exactly match the drawn rectangle, one of the walls may be thicker if you don't exactly match the outer rectangle. An easier way to match the outer rectangle is with the Offset tool. The Offset tool (F) is found by choosing Tools ➪ Offset and in the Getting Started and Edit toolbars.

To use the Offset tool, simply click on the face or curve that you want to offset and drag to set the distance from the original. When you release the mouse, a new copy of the original face is created. You can also type a specific distance value in the Measurements Toolbar.

If an offset distance is set by dragging, you can duplicate the offset distance again by double-clicking on the new face. The target in Figure 10.9 was created by dragging to create the first offset ring and then double-clicking within the interior face to create more offsets.

FIGURE 10.9

The Offset tool creates faces that are inset or outset from the original.

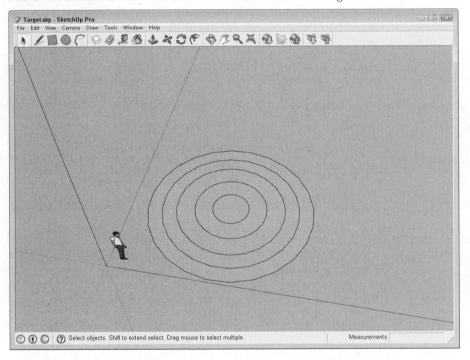

The Offset tool can also be used to clone and offset lines and curves. It can only be used on two or more selected co-planar lines. To offset a selection of lines, simply select them and then click and drag on the selected lines. Figure 10.10 shows a set of zigzag lines that are duplicated using the Offset tool.

FIGURE 10.10

The Offset tool can also offset selected lines.

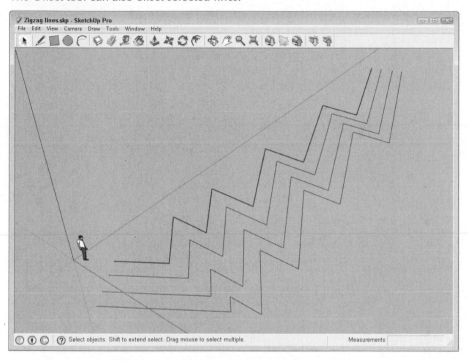

Detecting Intersections

When two 3-D objects overlap, SketchUp continues to recognize them as whole objects, making it so you cannot select and remove specific parts. For example, in Figure 10.11, portions of the sphere and the cube's surfaces are overlapping, but in the leftmost instance, selecting any part of the sphere selects the entire sphere. This makes it difficult to work with the intersecting pieces.

You can have SketchUp identify and mark the intersecting lines by choosing Edit ⇨ Intersect ⇨ Intersect with Model. This command causes the intersecting portions of the volumes to be identified with edges that you can select and edit, as shown in the middle of Figure 10.11. The rightmost volume shows how the individual parts can then be removed to show the interior.

If you need more control over the precise faces that are intersected, you can choose Edit ⇨ Intersect ⇨ Intersect Selected Only. This adds intersecting lines only to the selected faces. Or you can choose Edit ⇨ Intersect ⇨ Intersect With Context to cause the intersection between two entities in the current context, which ignores all faces outside of the current selection.

FIGURE 10.11

The Intersect with Model menu command shows the intersecting portion of overlapping objects.

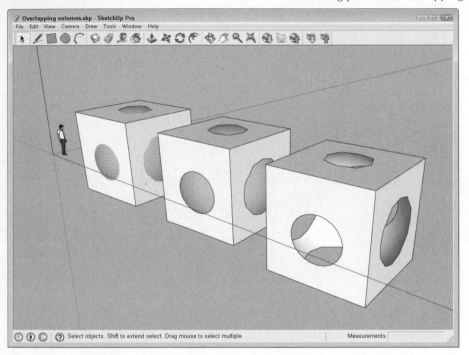

Summary

Along with the transform tools, you now have knowledge of the various tools used to edit shapes and lines. The editing possibilities that these tools make available enable you to create some interesting models.

This chapter covered the following topics:

- Extruding faces and creating holes with the Push/Pull tool
- Lofting, lathing, and beveling edges with the Follow Me tool
- Insetting and outsetting faces and curves with the Offset tool
- Defining intersections between two overlapping objects

The next chapter covers how text and dimensions can easily be added to a scene to label and highlight specifics. For flare, you can use the 3D Text tool.

Chapter 11

Adding Text

A dding text to a drawing is a helpful way to add information such as the scene's title, callouts, and dimensions. SketchUp includes a couple of ways to add text to a scene. Using the Text tool, you can add Leader text, which points to a specific location and is used to identify dimensions. The Text tool can also add Screen text for titles and labels.

If you want to extrude text to give it a 3-D look, you can use the 3D Text tool. This tool creates text that can be manipulated just like other objects using the transform tools.

After text is added to the scene using either the Text tool or the 3D Text tool, you can edit the text, and change its font, size, color, and position.

Creating 2-D Text

There are actually two types of 2-D text in SketchUp: Leader text and Screen text. Leader text has an arrow that points to an object and is used to identify positions or dimensions for scene objects. Screen text is free-floating text that can be used for titles or information.

Creating Leader text

Leader text is created with the Text tool. You can select the Text tool from the Construction Toolbar or by choosing Tools ⇨ Text. After the tool is selected, the cursor changes and all inference points are recognized. The place where you click with the Text tool becomes the location of the leader arrow.

If the point where you click is an endpoint, the text label lists the dimension of the point's location. If you click on the center of a face entity, the text label lists the area dimensions of the selected face. Clicking on a named component reveals the name of the component in the text label.

If you click and drag with the Text tool, you can position the text label within the scene. The text label stays wherever it is when you release the mouse button. Releasing the mouse button also selects the text and lets you edit the text by typing a new label, as shown in Figure 11.1. Pressing Enter twice or clicking away from the text label exits Text Edit mode.

FIGURE 11.1

Leader text points to an object in the scene.

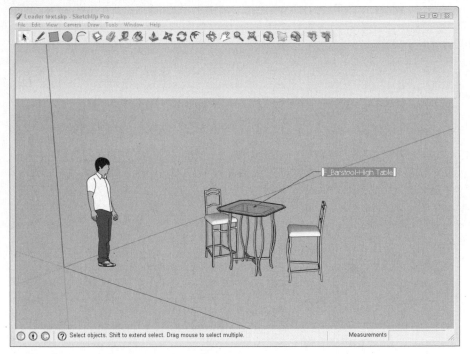

Creating Screen text

Screen text is different from Leader text in that it doesn't have an arrow pointing to something. Screen text is created by clicking with the Text tool on a blank area of the screen. If the cursor isn't over any object when clicked, a simple text box is created where you can type your own text, as shown in Figure 11.2.

FIGURE 11.2

Screen text is used for labels and information.

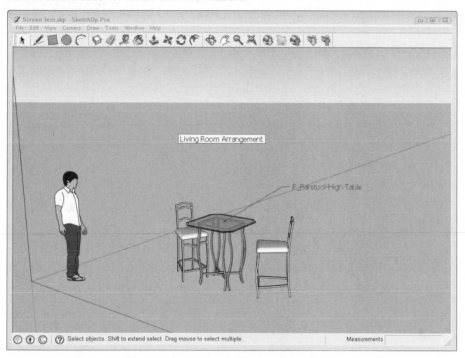

Editing text

After placing text in the scene, you can edit it later by clicking on it with the Text tool. Click once to move it to a new location, or you can double-click on the text to select it for editing.

Clicking on the text (either Leader or Screen text) with the Select Object tool causes the text to be highlighted in blue. When highlighted, you can choose Edit ➪ Text to make the text editable, to change the arrow, or to change the leader style.

These same settings are also available in the Entity Info dialog box shown in Figure 11.3. This dialog box is opened by choosing Window ➪ Entity Info or by right-clicking on the text and selecting Entity Info from the pop-up menu.

FIGURE 11.3

Text settings are available in the Entity Info dialog box.

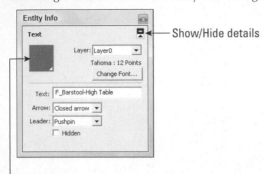

Show/Hide details

Text color swatch

Clicking on the text color swatch opens the Choose Paint dialog box, as shown in Figure 11.4. Using this dialog box, you can select from a list of available paint colors, or you can click Edit to access the Edit Material dialog box, as shown in Figure 11.5.

CROSS-REF More on creating custom materials is covered in Chapter 18.

FIGURE 11.4

The Choose Paint dialog box lets you select a material to use for the selected text.

The Layer drop-down list in the Entity Info dialog box lets you specify the layer that the text is on. The list has all defined layers that you can choose from.

Beneath the Layer list, the current font and font size are listed. Clicking Change Font opens the Font dialog box, as shown in Figure 11.6, where you can select any of the available system fonts, the font style, and size. The Sample pane shows an example of what the selected font looks like.

FIGURE 11.5

The Edit Material dialog box lets you change the text color, texture, and opacity.

FIGURE 11.6

The Font dialog box lets you change the text font, style, and size.

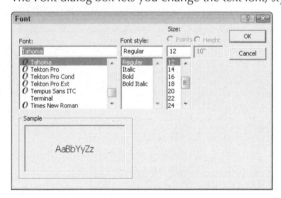

The Text field in the Entity Info dialog box lists the current text string. You can edit the text here, also.

Within the Arrow drop-down list in the Entity Info dialog box are several options for defining how the arrow looks at the end of the Leader text. The available options include the following:

- **None:** This option displays only a line with no arrow at its end.
- **Dot:** This option places a dot at the end of the leader.

■ **Closed Arrow:** This option displays a single solid arrow at the end of the leader.

■ **Open Arrow:** This option displays an arrow as two angle lines receding back from the end of the leader.

Each of these arrow options is shown in Figure 11.7.

 The Arrow and Leader settings are only available when Leader text is selected.

FIGURE 11.7 ·

You can change the arrowhead at the end of the leader line.

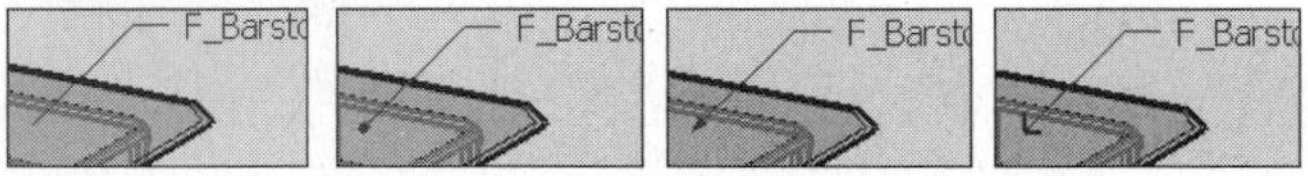

The Leader setting controls the orientation of the leader. There is also an option to hide the leader. The Leader drop-down list has the following options:

■ **View based:** This option maintains the position of the leader line locked to the view when the scene is rotated so a line that is positioned at a 45-degree angle to the surface remains at this angle when the scene is rotated.

■ **Pushpin:** This option positions the leader line in 3-D space, which causes the leader to change its orientation when the scene is rotated. A leader line positioned at a 45-degree angle to the surface changes as the scene is rotated, but the text remains flat.

■ **Hidden:** This option hides the leader line.

The Hidden option in the Entity Info dialog box causes the leader and its text to be hidden from the scene. You can view hidden objects by choosing View ➪ Hidden Geometry.

Tutorial: Labeling the height of a vehicle

When labeling objects with leader text, the leader typically identifies a single point, but if you draw a couple of straight lines off an object, you can have the leader text point to the line to get the height of the total object, such as for a vehicle, as shown in this example.

To label the total height of a vehicle, follow these steps:

1. **Open the** `Camper.skp` **file from the Chapter 11 folder on the CD.** This file includes a camper component taken from the default library.

2. **Use the Line tool to draw a straight line from the bottom of the wheel to the back of the camper.** Make sure the line is parallel to the red X-axis.

3. Draw another straight line from the top of the camper to the back that extends out as far as the first line.

4. Draw a line that connects the endpoints of these two lines.

5. Select the Text tool from the Construction toolbar or by choosing Tools⇨Text. Then click on the center of the height line and drag to position the text.

6. Repeat the previous Steps 2 through 5 to label the length of the camper.

7. Click above the camper with the Text tool, and type a title for the scene.

8. Choose the Select tool and click on the title text. Choose Window⇨Entity Info to open the Entity Info dialog box. Click Change Font.

9. In the Font dialog box, set the Font to Arial with a point size of 24. Click OK.

Figure 11.8 shows the resulting camper with its dimensions labeled.

FIGURE 11.8

Adding lines lets you identify the dimensions of an object.

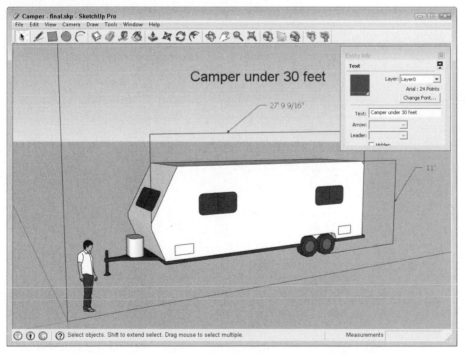

201

Creating 3-D Text

As an alternate to the standard 2-D text, SketchUp also includes the ability to add 3-D extruded text to the scene using the 3D Text tool. This tool is located on the Construction Toolbar or by choosing Tools⇨3D Text.

Once selected, this tool lets you click at the location where you want the 3-D text object to be placed. After clicking on a location, the Place 3D Text dialog box, shown in Figure 11.9, opens. Using this dialog box, you can adjust the text settings, including the extrusion depth.

 **3D Text tool can handle multiple lines of text while the Text tool only allows a single line at a time.**

FIGURE 11.9

The Place 3D Text dialog box lets you configure the settings for the 3-D text.

Once placed in the current scene, the 3-D text object can be selected and transformed just like other objects using the Move, Rotate, and Scale tools.

Within the Place 3D Text dialog box, you can choose a font from the available system fonts. You can also select the Font style as Regular or Bold; the Alignment at Left, Center, or Right; the Height value; and the Extrusion depth value. The Filled option lets you create 3-D text that is filled when enabled, or text that is just the outlines when disabled, as shown in Figure 11.10.

The Place 3D Text dialog box also includes an Extrusion value that you can set. The Height value determines how long the text is and the Extrusion value sets the height of the text. If you disable this option, the text appears as flat text that is similar to 2-D text. Figure 11.11 shows several different extrusion depths.

 **The Extrusion value can also be set to a negative value, which causes the depth to move in the opposite direction.**

FIGURE 11.10

3-D text can be filled or unfilled.

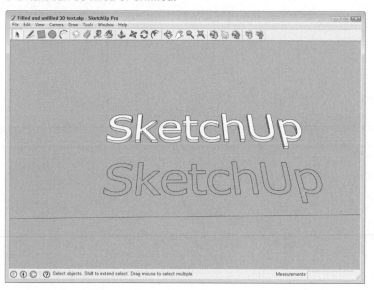

FIGURE 11.11

The Extrusion value sets how tall the 3-D text is.

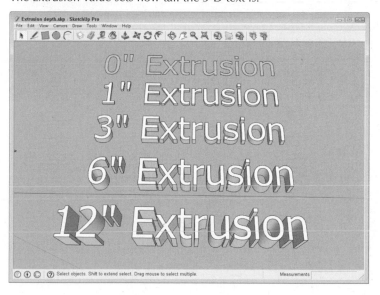

Summary

With the Text tool and the 3D Text tool, you can quickly add the needed information to your drawings. One of the nice features of the Text tool is that SketchUp automatically identifies the dimension for the object, making it easy to document your drawings.

This chapter covered the following topics:

- Creating Leader text and adding dimensions and callouts
- Adding titles with the Text tool
- Editing text
- Adding 3D Text objects

There are only a few more tools to cover before you've got them all. One of the last groups of tools is the Construction tools, which I cover in the next chapter. These tools help to measure lengths and angles.

Chapter 12

Using the Construction Tools

Measurements are among the key components of drawings. This is especially important if you are creating design plans or schematics. Within the Tools menu are several tools that help to measure specific lengths and angles. These tools can also be used to create guide lines used to aid you in your drawing tasks. There is also a Dimension tool that is used to add dimensions to objects. Because SketchUp knows the exact position of all points in the current model, it can automatically compute the distance between two points.

IN THIS CHAPTER

Measuring lengths

Creating guide lines

Measuring angles

Adding dimensions

Moving and orienting axes

Measuring Distance with the Tape Measure Tool

The Tape Measure tool is used to measure distances within the scene. It is found in the Construction Toolbar or by choosing Tools ⇨ Tape Measure. You can also access this tool by pressing T. When you select this tool, the cursor changes to a small tape measure icon, and the tip of the icon is the point from where the measurements are taken.

The Tape Measure tool, like the Line tool, also works by inference. This helps get accurate measurements from endpoints and corners of objects. To use the Tape Measure tool, simply click on a starting point and drag to the ending point. As you stop over the top of an object, its length is measured and displayed in a tooltip, as shown in Figure 12.1. When you release the mouse button, the measurement appears in the Measurements Toolbar.

NOTE If the measurement value has a small tilde (~) sign in front of it, the measurement is an approximation. The tilde mark stands for "about."

205

FIGURE 12.1

The Tape Measure tool is used to measure distance.

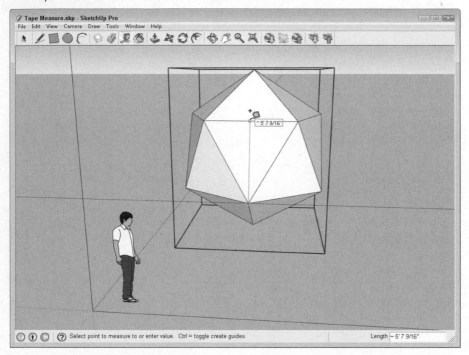

Using guide lines

The Tape Measure tool can also be used to create guide lines. Guide lines are dashed lines that extend through the entire scene. They are helpful when lining up objects.

To create a guide line, simply click and drag from a point on an edge or from the midpoint that runs parallel to the guide line you want to create. The dragged distance is displayed in the Measurements Toolbar. You can type a new distance value in the Measurements Toolbar by typing a new value. When you release the mouse, a guide line runs through the scene, as shown in Figure 12.2.

FIGURE 12.2

Guide lines are helpful for lining up objects.

Guide Lines

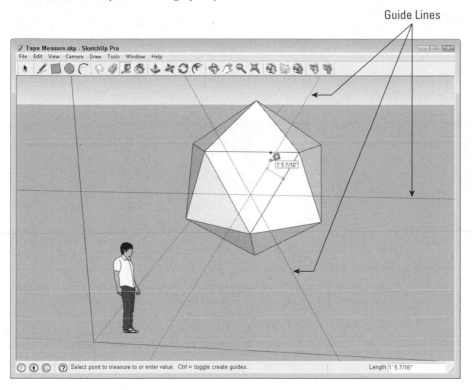

Using guide points

If you click and drag from an endpoint while holding down the Ctrl key, you create a guide point. Guide points extend from where you drag to where you stop and mark a specific point. Figure 12.3 shows a guide point.

FIGURE 12.3

Guide points mark specific points.

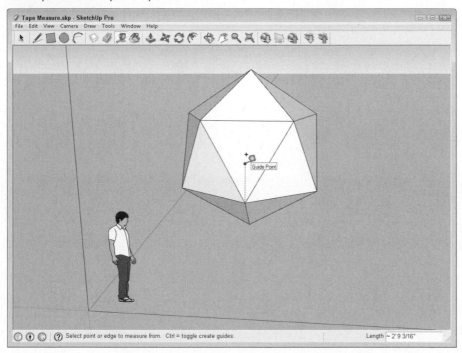

Editing and removing guide lines

Guide lines can be selected and transformed just like regular lines. When selected with the Select tool, guide lines turn blue. Guide lines can also be hidden or erased using the right-click pop-up menu. Selected guide lines can also be deleted by simply pressing the Delete key.

Guide lines are not intended to be part of the end drawing. You can remove all guide lines at once by choosing Edit ⇨ Delete Guides.

Tutorial: Creating guide lines for a keypad

Positioning guide lines can really help a drawing go easier. For example, imagine creating a ten-digit keypad. If the numbers aren't lined up just right, the drawing will look off. Guide lines can help with this.

To create a series of guide lines for a keypad, follow these steps:

1. **Choose View ⇨ Standard Views ⇨ Top to switch to the top view.**

2. **Click and drag with the Rectangle tool until the dashed line appears to create a Golden Section.** This rectangle will be one of the digit's areas.

3. **Select the Tape Measure tool.** Click and drag from the midpoint of the right edge out to the right a distance of 2', and release the mouse button to create a guide line. Then drag from the midpoint on the bottom edge down a distance of 1' to create another guide line. Then create two more guide lines on the left and top sides.

4. **Create a guide line that is 2' from the rightmost guide line and another guide line that is 1' from the top guide line.** These new guide lines define the upper-left corner for the second digit.

5. **Select the first rectangle.** Choose Edit ⇨ Copy to copy the rectangle. Choose Edit ⇨ Paste and click and drag the pasted rectangle to the second position.

6. **Drag with the Tape Measure tool from the right edge of the second rectangle to create two more guide lines that are spaced exactly 2' apart.** Copy and paste to position the third rectangle.

7. **Drag with the Tape Measure tool to create two more guide lines that are 1' apart from the lower edge of the rectangles.**

8. **With the Select tool, hold down the Ctrl key and click on all three rectangles and the two lower horizontal guide lines.** Copy and paste these objects to the bottom of the lowest guide line.

9. **Repeat Step 8 to create two more rows of rectangles.**

Figure 12.4 shows the resulting array of rectangles. These rectangles are equally spaced.

Using the Tape Measure tool to rescale the scene

If you use the Tape Measure tool to measure the length between two endpoints in the current scene, the distance is displayed in the Measurements Toolbar. If you type a new value for this measured distance, the entire scene is rescaled to this new entered value relative to the measured value. For example, if you have a model that has 1-foot sides and you measure the side and then type a value of 6 inches, the entire model is rescaled to half its size.

A warning dialog box appears before the rescaling is done.

 **Rescaling only impacts new items drawn into the scene. Any external components or loaded objects are not affected.**

FIGURE 12.4

Guide lines help maintain the spacing of regularly spaced objects.

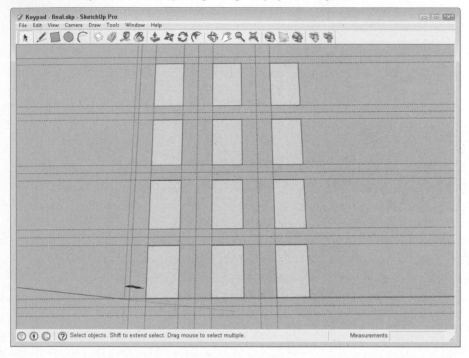

Measuring Angles with the Protractor Tool

The Protractor tool works just like the Tape Measure tool, except you can use it to measure angles instead of distances. The Protractor tool can also create guide lines. The Protractor tool is found on the Construction toolbar or by choosing Tools ⇨ Protractor.

When you select the Protractor tool, the cursor changes to a protractor icon that is the same as the Rotate tool. To measure an angle, place the center of the protractor at the point where the two lines intersect and click. This places the protractor and lets you click to specify the first line; click again to select the second line. The angle measurement appears in the Measurements Toolbar, as shown in Figure 12.5.

When measuring an angle, a guide line is created automatically or you can force a guide by pressing the Ctrl key. If the measured angle doesn't place the guide line where you want, you can type a new value in the Measurements Toolbar to correct the guide line.

 SketchUp values for rotational angles in the Measurements Toolbar can be expressed as degrees, such as 120, or they can be a rise over run slope ratio, such as 1:4.

When dragging the protractor around the scene before placing the center point, the protractor automatically aligns to the face that it is over. If you hold down the Shift key while dragging the protractor, the protractor stays aligned to the current face even when it moves over another face.

FIGURE 12.5

The Protractor tool measures angles and creates radial guide lines.

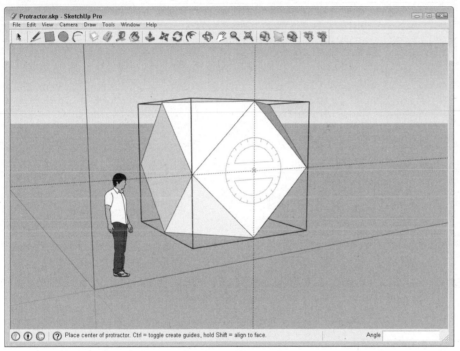

Adding Dimensions with the Dimension Tool

Although the Text tool can be used to label and highlight dimensions, it is really meant to add call-outs to the scene and to point out specific objects. The Dimension tool, however, is intended to create dimensions for the scene objects. The Dimension tool is found in the Construction Toolbar or by choosing Tools ⇨ Dimensions.

To use the Dimension tool, simply click on two points in order and the dimension between the two points is listed. You can then drag to position the dimension text and the dimension lines are automatically positioned to match the text. Figure 12.6 shows a simple object with a dimension added using the Dimension tool.

FIGURE 12.6

The Dimension tool measures and labels selected dimensions.

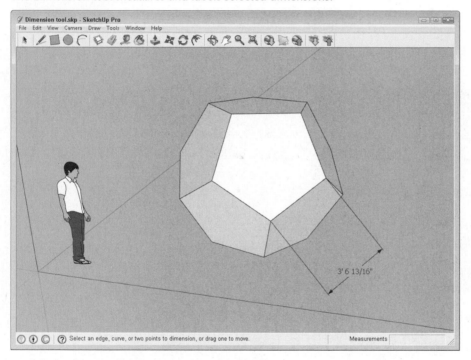

Configuring dimensions

The way the dimensions look, including their font, size, and positioning, is configured using the Dimensions panel in the Model Info dialog box, as shown in Figure 12.7. You can open this dialog box by choosing Window ➪ Model Info.

NOTE Most of the same dimension settings found in the Dimensions panel of the Model Info dialog box are also found in the Entity Info dialog box, which is opened by choosing Window ➪ Entity Info or by right-clicking on a dimension object and selecting Entity Info from the pop-up menu.

At the top of the Dimensions panel, the current font and font size is listed. To change the font, click Fonts. This opens the Font dialog box, as shown in Figure 12.8. The Font dialog box lists all the current system fonts in a list and provides a sample of the selected font. The Font dialog box also lets you change the font style and size. Font size can be set using a Point value or a Height value with units.

FIGURE 12.7

The Dimensions panel of the Model Info dialog box lets you configure the look of dimensions.

Text color swatch

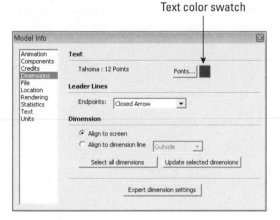

FIGURE 12.8

The Font dialog box lets you change the font, style, and text size.

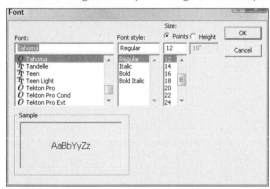

Next to the Fonts button on the Model Info dialog box is a text color swatch that shows the current text color. Clicking this color swatch opens the Choose Color dialog box, as shown in Figure 12.9, where you can specify a different color and the brightness of the selected color. The Picker drop-down list lets you change the Color Picker between the Color Wheel, HLS, HSB, or RGB options.

CROSS-REF You can learn about the various color pickers in Chapter 18.

On the Model Info dialog box in the Dimensions panel under Leader Lines is a drop-down list for configuring the look of the endpoints of the leader lines. The options include the following:

- **None:** This option displays only a line with no arrow at its end.
- **Slash:** This option places a slash at the end of the leader.
- **Dot:** This option places a dot at the end of the leader.
- **Closed Arrow:** This option displays a single solid arrow at the end of the leader.
- **Open Arrow:** This option displays an arrow as two angle lines receding back from the end of the leader.

FIGURE 12.9

The Choose Color dialog box lets you change the text color.

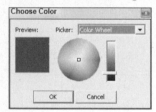

In the Dimension section, you can set the dimension to align to the screen, which causes the dimension text to be horizontally aligned to the view. This horizontal orientation stays horizontal as the scene is rotated. If you select the Align to dimension line option, the dimension text is aligned to the dimension line, as shown in Figure 12.10. You can also choose to have the text posi-tioned above, centered, or below the dimension line.

CAUTION If the Align to dimension line option is selected, the dimension text remains aligned to the dimension lines when the scene is rotated. This could result in a dimension that is illegible if viewed on edge or obscured by other objects.

FIGURE 12.10

Dimension text can also be aligned to the dimension lines.

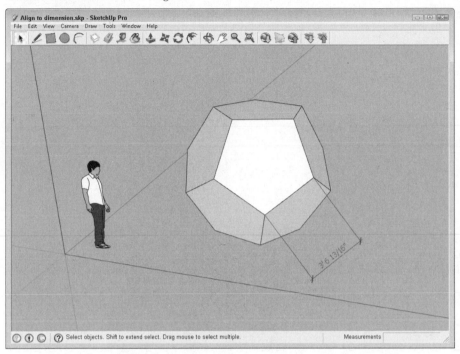

If you make any configuration changes in the Dimensions panel of the Model Info dialog box, you can instantly apply them to all dimensions in the current scene by first clicking Select all dimensions and clicking Update selected dimensions.

Using the Expert Dimension Settings

For even finer configuration settings, click Expert dimension settings. This opens the Expert Dimension Settings dialog box, as shown in Figure 12.11.

The first option, Show radius/diam prefix, lets you enable SketchUp to identify radius and diameter measurements with a prefix, as shown for a diameter measurement in Figure 12.12.

 **If you right-click on a diameter measurement, you can change it to a radius dimension, or vice versa using the Type menu in the pop-up menu.**

FIGURE 12.11

The Expert Dimension Settings dialog box provides finer control over dimensions.

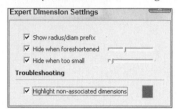

FIGURE 12.12

Diameter measurements are identified by a prefix.

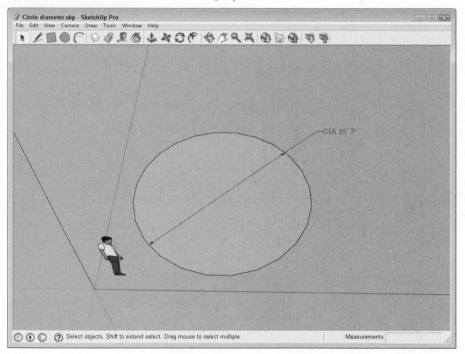

If you rotate a scene, the dimension lines could become foreshortened, which leaves the dimension text floating without clearly being able to tell what the dimension represents. To prevent this problem, you can select the Hide when foreshortened option in the Expert Dimension Settings dialog box. Next to the option is a slider that you can adjust to change the foreshadowing threshold.

A similar problem can happen when you zoom out of the current scene. If a dimension is so small that it cannot be distinguished, then selecting the Hide when too small option causes the dimension to be hidden. This option also has a slider that you can adjust.

When the Highlight non-associated dimensions option is selected, a color swatch appears to its right. When enabled, all dimensions that aren't associated with the current model are highlighted using the color swatch's color. This helps to remove any dimensions that don't really apply to the current model. This often happens when deleting a face but forgetting to delete the edge entities.

Using the Axes Tool

The Axes tool allows you to reset the coordinate system for the current scene. The Axes tool is found in the Construction Toolbar or by choosing Tools ➪ Axes. To use the Axes tool, click on a point to be the new scene origin, then drag to specify the direction of the red X-axis. Click and drag again to specify the direction of the green Y-axis. Figure 12.13 shows the scene after the axes have been moved and reoriented. The new shape is created by rotating about a different set of axes.

FIGURE 12.13

The Axes tool is used to reposition and reorient the coordinate axes.

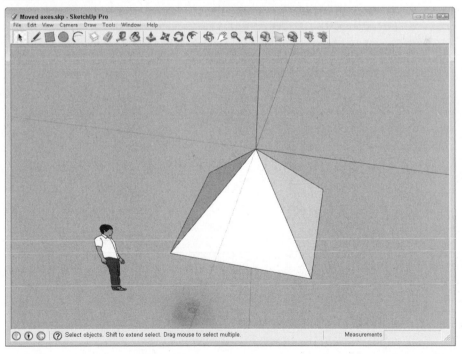

If you want to move the axes back to their original positions, right-click on the axes and select Reset from the pop-up menu. If you select Move from the right-click pop-up menu, the Move Sketching Context dialog box, as shown in Figure 12.14, appears where you can type precise dimensions to move and rotate the axes.

The right-click pop-up menu also includes an option to Align View, which changes the current view orientation so it is looking straight down on the newly aligned axes.

FIGURE 12.14

The Move Sketching Context dialog box lets you precisely move and orient the axes.

Summary

Drawing objects with precision yields a dividend when you need to add dimensions to the drawing. To help with the task, the Tape Measure and Protractor tools are helpful. They can also be used to add guide lines to the scene to help keep objects aligned. The Dimension tool automatically measures and labels dimensions.

This chapter covered the following topics:

- Measuring lengths with the Tape Measure tool
- Creating and using guide lines
- Measuring angles with the Protractor tool
- Adding dimensions with the Dimensions tool
- Moving and orienting axes

Another helpful technique is to load a background reference photo that can guide you as you draw. Matching a background photo is covered in the next chapter.

Chapter 13

Matching a Background Photo

A common trick for presenting architectural designs is to match the SketchUp models to a background photo. This helps others to visualize how the finished structure will look in its new environment.

The scale used to build models in SketchUp is based on a real-world 1:1 ratio. This ratio works great when models are combined, but when a background photo is added to the drawing, the scale needs to be altered to match the photo's scale. This is accomplished by choosing Camera ⇨ Match New Photo.

The Match New Photo feature lets you orient the view to be aligned to the location where the digital camera was when the building location was shot. After you define this location, you can build a model that fits with the background image.

Another way to use this features is to start with a background image or a series of background images that are used to align the axes in the current document, allowing you to build the model based on the background image.

Aligning the Current Model to a Background Image

If you have a scene that you've built in SketchUp and you want to see how it looks at a given location, you can use the Match Photo feature to position the background image and use the alignment tools to match the model's axes to the perspective in the background image.

The first step in this process is to start with the model loaded, like the model displayed in Figure 13.1.

The scene model needs to be loaded first before the background.

Choose Camera ➪ Match New Photo from the menu. The Match Photo dialog box appears (which is a file dialog box) where you can locate and load the background photo. After you load the background photo, it appears behind the model along with several alignment controls, as shown in Figure 13.2. After the photo is loaded, SketchUp switches to Match Photo mode, as indicated by the label in the margin to the left.

FIGURE 13.2

The model with the background image loaded

Match Photo Label   Red axis grip   Green axis grip

Origin

The Match Photo command also creates a separate scene for the background photo that is selected using the Scene tab at the top of the interface. When the background photo is loaded, use the Match Photo dialog box controls, shown in Figure 13.3, to configure the photo.

The square markers in the drawing area can be clicked and dragged to align the model to the background photo. The origin grip is the point where the three axes meet. It is easiest if you place this origin at the corner of the building in the background photo.

Once the origin is set, you can move the red and green grips to align the red and green axes. There are four grips, two for each axis. These should be moved to be aligned with the horizontal plane and the receding plane, as shown in Figure 13.4.

FIGURE 13.3

The Match Photo dialog box holds the controls for matching the photo.

New Matched Photo

    Edit Matched Photo

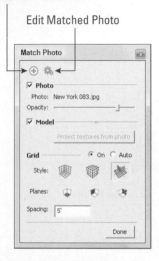

FIGURE 13.4

The Match Photo feature aligns the model to the background photo.

After aligning the model to the photo, you can scale the model by clicking and dragging the solid red, green, or blue axis lines. Figure 13.5 shows the scene after it is correctly scaled.

To exit Match Photo mode, click Done in the Match Photo dialog box or click in the margin to the left of the drawing area.

FIGURE 13.5

After being scaled, the model objects fit with the scale of the photo.

Modeling to a Background Image

If you want to start with the background image, the process is a little different. For this case, simply align the SketchUp axes to the background image, and then you can model using the aligned scene using a sketching mode.

The first step here is to choose Camera ⇨ Match New Photo and select the photo you want to match. The photo is added to the background and SketchUp is placed in Match Photo mode, as shown in Figure 13.6.

FIGURE 13.6

To begin with a photo, the first step is to load the background photo.

Next, locate and drag the Origin grip to a corner in the photo to establish the origin location. Then select the various red and green grips and align them to the background photo, as shown in Figure 13.7.

FIGURE 13.7

Align the red and green grips to the background photo to match the axes.

Click Done in the Match Photo dialog box to access an overlay 2-D drawing mode. This is identified with the Sketch Over label in the upper left of the drawing area, as shown in Figure 13.8. While in Sketch Over mode, you can draw, and the lines are aligned to the background image.

NOTE If you navigate the current scene with the Orbit tool, you'll automatically exit Sketch Over mode.

FIGURE 13.8

Sketch Over mode lets you draw objects that are aligned with the photo.

Editing Matched Photos

After you match the model with a background photo, if you need to revisit the matching parameters you can choose Camera ➪ Edit Matched Photo. This option adds the alignment grips to the scene again.

You can also revisit these controls by clicking on the Edit Matched Photo button at the top of the Match Photo dialog box, as shown in Figure 13.3. This same command is also available in the right-click pop-up menu.

Working with multiple photos

If you have multiple photos of the location, you can use the New Matched Photo button in the top of the Match Photo dialog box, as shown in Figure 13.3, or you can choose Camera ➪ Match New Photo again to add another background image to the scene. This new photo will get its own scene tab and further define the building location.

Hiding the background photo and model

Within the Match Photo and the Sketch Over dialog boxes are options that you can use to hide and show the loaded photo or the current model. The Opacity slider affects how opaque and transparent the background photo is.

 Making the background photo semiopaque makes it easier for the viewers to focus on the new drawing.

Projecting textures

If you are re-creating a building or structure from an existing photo, then the Project textures from photo button in the Match Photo dialog box is an easy way to have a portion of the background photo applied to the sketched face as a texture. Figure 13.9 shows a face with a projected texture. The photo has been hidden.

FIGURE 13.9

The Project textures from photo command causes the background photo to be applied to the drawing faces.

Working with grids

It is often helpful to have a grid added to the drawing area so you can see the axes planes. Within the Sketch Over dialog box, you can set grids to be On, which shows the grids at all times; or you can set grids to Auto, which displays the grid only when selecting the respective axes.

Also in the Sketch Over dialog box, you have three Grid Style options that let you choose the grids that best match the background photo. The left choice is good for interior photos where you can choose the corner of a wall where it meets the floor. The middle choice is good for outdoor buildings when the photo is taken from above where you can see the upper corner of a building. The right choice is good for photos taken outdoors at street level where the corner of the building meets the road.

The Planes options let you toggle on and off the various planes of grid lines that are aligned by color: red, green, and blue. These planes are helpful when you are trying to line things up. There are separate buttons for each of the base planes indicated by Red/Green, Red/Blue, and Blue/Green. Once a plane is displayed you can alter the distance between adjacent grid lines using the Spacing value. The default Spacing value is set to 1".

Summary

Background photos, like materials and textures, can add a lot to the realism of the current scene, but if the photo isn't aligned correctly, the background photo can actually detract from the scene. The Match New Photo feature includes the controls and settings that make it easy to align the model to the background photo.

This chapter covered the following topics:

- Aligning the current model to a background photo
- Modeling a design based on a background photo
- Working with the background photo options

The next chapter shows how TIN surfaces can be used to create organic surfaces like terrains.

Chapter 14

Working with TIN Surfaces

Almost all models created with the conventional SketchUp tools consist of straight-lined objects. This is great for buildings, machines, and mechanical-type objects, but if you want to create objects that are more organic, you can use the Sandbox tools. The Sandbox tools are used to create organic shapes like terrains, plants, and animals.

The organic surfaces are called Triangulated Irregular Network surfaces or TIN surfaces. These surfaces break down into triangular faces and are most often used to create terrain objects. These terrains are irregular in that they have a randomness to them.

Creating TIN Surfaces

Before you can use the Sandbox tools, you need to enable them using the Extensions panel in the System Preferences dialog box, as shown in Figure 14.1. After the extensions are enabled, the Sandbox submenu appears in the Draw menu. SketchUp does not need to be restarted once the extensions are enabled.

Enabling the Sandbox tools also adds a toolbar to the interface. The Sandbox toolbar, shown in Figure 14.2, includes buttons for each of the available Sandbox tools.

The Sandbox Toolbar includes two tools for creating TIN surfaces. These tools are the From Contours tool, which creates surfaces using a set of selected contour lines, and the From Scratch tool, which creates a rectangular surface that can be sculpted into an organic surface like a terrain.

FIGURE 14.1

The Extensions panel in the System Preferences dialog box lets you add features to SketchUp.

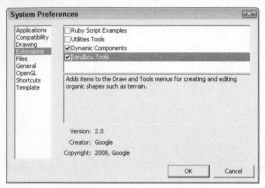

FIGURE 14.2

The Sandbox Toolbar includes buttons for each of the Sandbox tools.

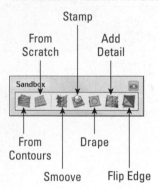

Creating objects from contour lines

The first Sandbox tool, From Contours, lets you create terrain objects based on curves and lines that represent the contours of the land. The contours are drawn using any of the basic line tools such as the Line, Arc, or Freehand tools. Each of these lines needs to be offset from the others to describe the height of the terrain at each section. Figure 14.3 shows a set of contour lines created with the Freehand tool with lines at different heights.

FIGURE 14.3

Contour lines define the height of the object at different intervals.

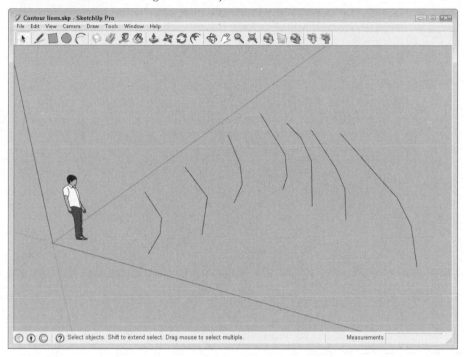

After you draw the contour lines, simply select them all and choose Tools ➪ Sandbox ➪ From Contours. This menu command creates a surface based on the contour lines called a TIN surface. TIN surfaces are comprised of triangulated polygons, which give them the ability to be deformed into unique shapes. Figure 14.4 shows the resulting surface created from the contour lines.

FIGURE 14.4

Contour lines are made into a surface using the From Contours tool.

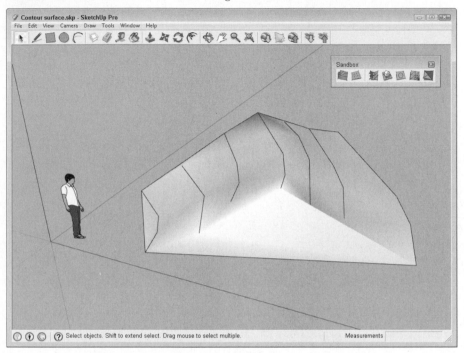

Creating TIN surfaces from scratch

If you don't have contour lines to start from, the From Scratch tool can be used to create a simple rectangular TIN plane that can then be sculpted as needed to form an object.

To use the From Scratch tool, click to specify a starting point, then drag to specify the plane's length. Then drag perpendicular to the length to establish the width of the TIN plane. Figure 14.5 shows a sample TIN surface created with the From Scratch tool.

When dragging to specify the width and length, the width and length are displayed in the Measurements Toolbar. If you type a custom value in the Measurements Toolbar, the TIN surface is updated to the custom value.

FIGURE 14.5

Contour lines are made into a surface using the From Scratch tool.

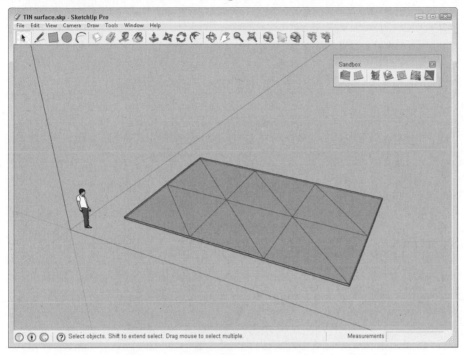

Modifying TIN Surfaces

The remaining Sandbox tools let you modify an existing TIN surface. These tools include the Smoove tool for creating smooth hills and valleys; the Stamp tool for pushing an object into a surface to make an impression; the Drape tool for projecting edges onto a surface; the Add Details tool for increasing the surface resolution; and the Flip Edge tool for changing the direction of the crossing face edges.

All of the surface-editing tools are located in the Tools⇨Sandbox menu.

Using the Smoove tool

What do you get when you combine a tool that moves the surface points smoothly? The answer is the Smoove tool. To sculpt an existing TIN surface (either a rectangular TIN surface created with the From Scratch tool or a terrain created with the From Contour tool), select and use the Smoove tool.

When the Smoove tool is selected, its radius is listed in the Measurements Toolbar. You can change its radius by typing a new value. Larger radius values have a larger impact on the surface. The next step is to click on the base point where the greatest movement will be. When the cursor is over a point or edge that you want to move, the tool's radius is displayed, as shown in Figure 14.6.

CAUTION   The surface needs to have sufficient density before it can be altered. The Add Details tool can add density to a surface.

If you click on a TIN surface with the Smoove tool, the entities within the radius area are shaded, as shown in Figure 14.7. The entities closest to the center of the radius area are shaded more than those near the edge. The amount of shading indicates how much the selected entities will move with the tool.

FIGURE 14.6

The Smoove tool's radius is displayed as it moves edges and points.

Smoove Tool radius

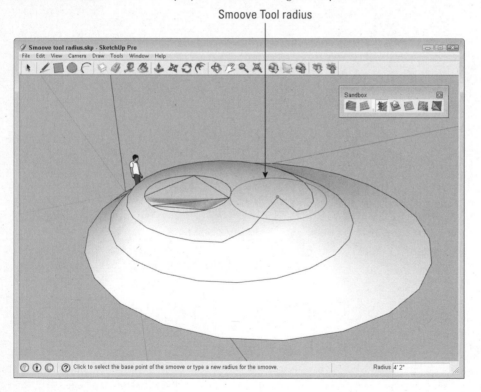

FIGURE 14.7

The Smoove tool highlights all those entities that will move with the Smoove tool.

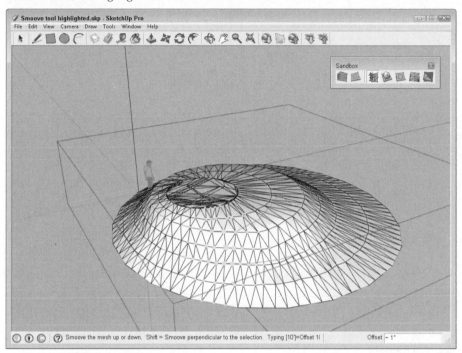

Dragging the selected entities moves them up or pushes them down into the surface causing a smooth peak, as shown in Figure 14.8, or an indentation, as shown in Figure 14.9. You can also type the move distance in the Measurements Toolbar for more accurate results. Because the influence of the Smoove tool decreases for those entities near the edge of the radius area, the resulting deformation is smooth and gradual.

FIGURE 14.8

The Smoove tool creates smooth peaks in the surface.

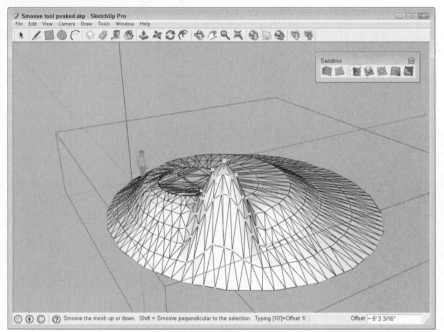

Holding down the Shift key while dragging with the Smoove tool causes the selected entities to move in a horizontal direction, as shown in Figure 14.10.

FIGURE 14.9

The Smoove tool can also create smooth valleys in the surface.

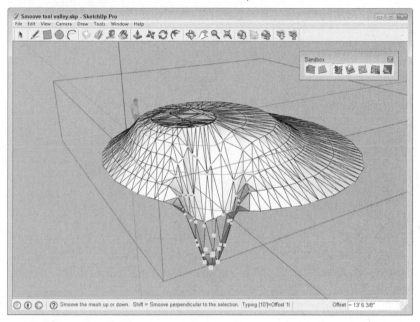

FIGURE 14.10

Holding down the Shift key moves the points horizontally.

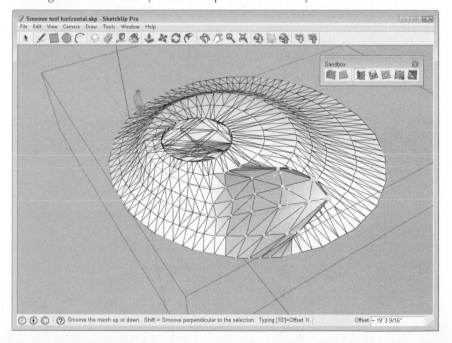

Stamping objects into surfaces

The Stamp tool allows you to create an indentation in a TIN surface by pushing another object into the surface. To use the Stamp tool, you need to create a separate stamp object in addition to the TIN surface. Position the stamp object above the TIN surface where you want the stamp to be located, as shown in Figure 14.11.

FIGURE 14.11

The Stamp tool requires a stamping object above the surface.

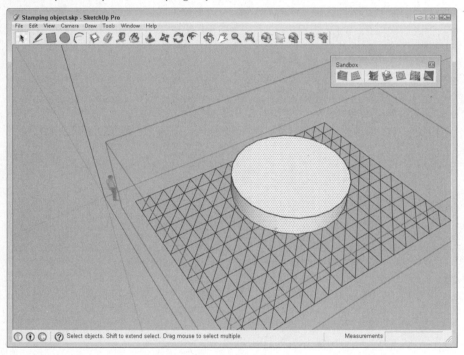

 **TIP** The Stamp tool is useful for creating building excavations. It can also be used to create a simple lake in a terrain.

Select the Stamp tool and then select the stamp object. You can then adjust the offset around the stamp object to determine how wide the stamp is. Then click on the TIN surface and drag the mouse up and down to set the depth of the indentation and click to apply the stamp. Figure 14.12 shows a circular disc being stamped into a TIN surface.

FIGURE 14.12

The Stamp tool lets you indent into a surface using another object's shape.

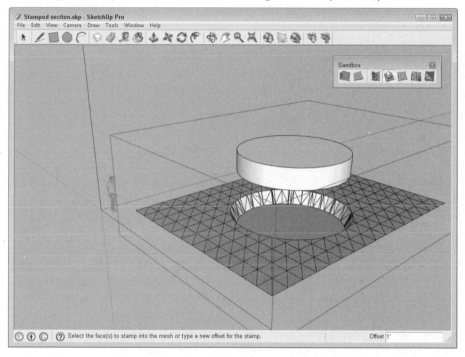

Using the Drape tool

The Drape tool is similar to the Stamp tool, but instead of indenting the stamp shape, it simply projects the separate object on top of the TIN surface. This is useful for adding details like a road to the surface of a terrain.

Like the Stamp tool, you need to create a drape object and position it above the TIN surface where you want it to be projected, as shown in Figure 14.13. Only the edges of the drape object are projected onto the TIN surface.

Select the Drape edges and then choose the Drape tool. Click on the TIN surface, and the edges are projected onto the surface. Even though the edges are projected, the original edges still remain. Figure 14.14 shows the edges projected onto the underlying surface.

FIGURE 14.13

The Drape tool requires a set of edges above the surface.

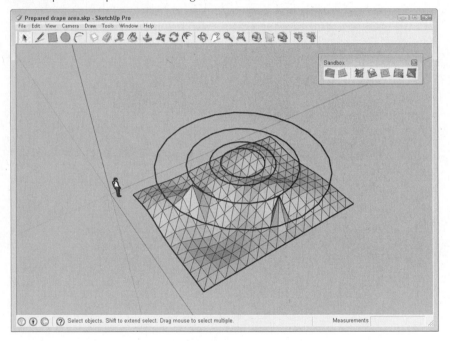

FIGURE 14.14

The Drape tool projects edges onto a surface.

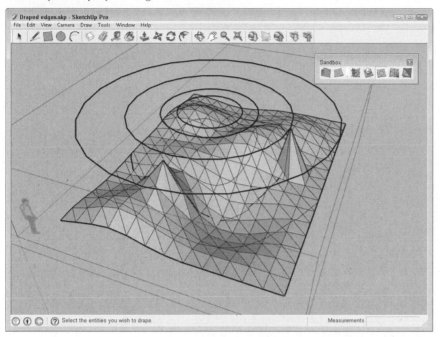

Increasing surface resolution

When a TIN surface is created, the surface is divided into triangles that are regularly spaced. Each square is composed of two triangles. Using the Add Detail tool, you can further divide specific areas of the surface into triangles with denser triangles.

If, for example, you have a terrain that is mostly flat, then the default triangulation will work just fine, but if you want to add a river cutting through the terrain, the Add Detail tool can be used to increase the resolution where the river is located so it is smoothly created.

Using the Add Detail tool becomes an important step before using the Smoove and/or Stamp tools. Using these tools without sufficient resolution prevents the changes caused by these tools to be easy to see.

The easiest way to use the Add Detail tool is to select the entire surface that you want to increase and click the Add Detail tool. Figure 14.15 shows a simple surface created with the From Scratch tool.

FIGURE 14.15

The From Scratch tool creates a surface with a coarse resolution.

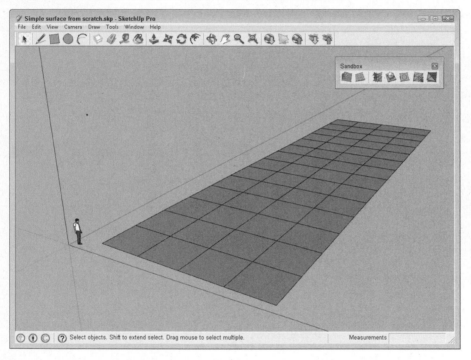

To increase the resolution on this surface, select the faces that you want to increase in resolution. Select the entire surface with the Select tool and select the Add Detail tool. The resolution of the selected faces is automatically increased, as shown in Figure 14.16. If you repeat this step, the resolution increases even more, as shown in Figure 14.17.

CAUTION Remember that TIN surfaces are grouped and need to be double-clicked to expose the group before you can select the individual surfaces.

FIGURE 14.16

The Add Detail tool can increase the resolution of all the faces of a surface.

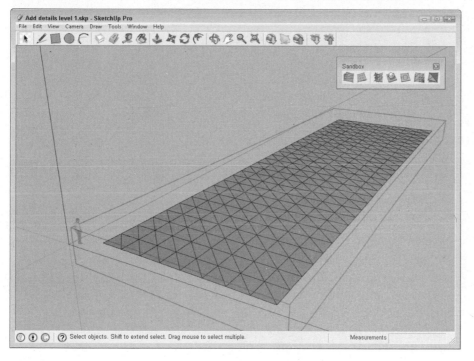

FIGURE 14.17

The Add Detail tool can be used multiple times on a surface.

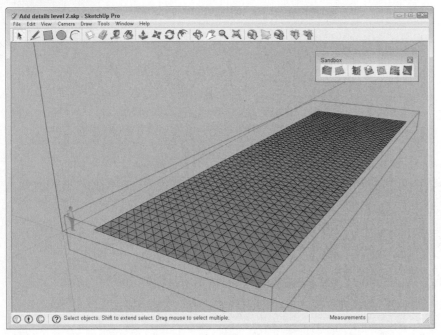

If you want to localize the resolution to a specific area, you can select just certain faces before selecting the Add Detail tool, as shown in Figure 14.18.

If there isn't a selection when the Add Detail tool is clicked, click on individual faces, edges, and vertices to subdivide them with the Add Detail tool. Once selected, you can drag the mouse up or down to lift or drop the selected entity, as shown in Figure 14.19. Holding down the Ctrl key increases the resolution without moving the selected entity.

FIGURE 14.18

The resolution can be localized by selecting specific entities before selecting the Add Detail tool.

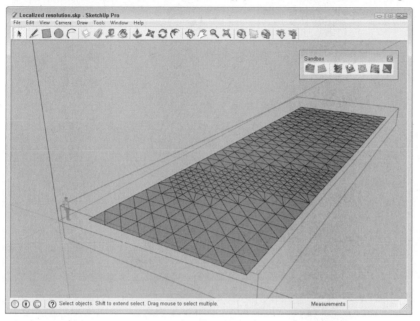

FIGURE 14.19

The resolution can be localized by selecting specific entities with the Add Detail tool.

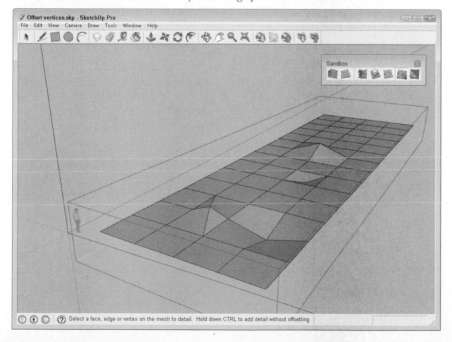

Flipping edges

When a TIN surface is triangulated, each polygon is automatically split into two triangles by adding a crossing edge. These crossing edges always run the same direction, which is against the flow of the terrain at times.

To fix the crossing triangulation lines, select the Flip Edge tool, click on the line that you want to flip, and it will automatically run between the opposite corners, as shown in Figure 14.20.

The Flip Edges tool reverses the direction of the crossing edge.

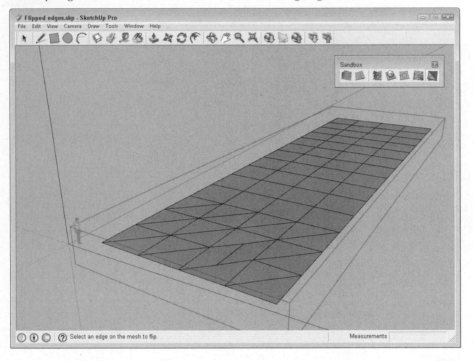

Tutorial: Creating a terrain object

Simple terrain objects are useful for certain architectural projects and are fairly easy to create with the Sandbox tools.

To create a simple terrain, follow these steps:

1. **Choose Window ⇨ Preferences and select the Extensions panel.** Make sure the Sandbox Tools option is enabled and close the System Preferences dialog box.

2. **Zoom out of the current scene so you can see a large portion of the drawing area.** This gives you the room to create a large terrain object.

3. **Choose Draw ⇨ Sandbox ⇨ From Scratch.** Click and drag a line parallel to the X-axis that fills the drawing area and click to set the length. Then click and drag along the Y-axis and click to set the width. This creates a large surface with a grid on it, as shown in Figure 14.21.

FIGURE 14.21

The From Scratch tool is used to create an initial surface.

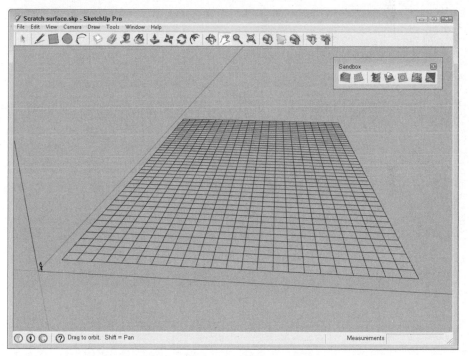

4. **Double-click on the surface with the Select tool to open the group.** Click and drag over all the faces to select them all.

5. **Choose Tools ⇨ Sandbox ⇨ Add Detail to subdivide all the selected faces.** This increases the resolution of the surface by triangulating every face.

6. **Choose Tools ⇨ Sandbox ⇨ Smoove, and move the Smoove tool over the surface.** A red ring shows the radius size. Type a new radius value in the Measurements Toolbar that is large enough to cover about a quarter of the surface. Then click and drag at random places in the surface to add some slight elevation.

7. **Reduce the radius value from Step 6 to half its current value and continue to push and pull the surface.**

Figure 14.22 shows the completed terrain.

FIGURE 14.22

Terrains are quickly created using the various Sandbox tools.

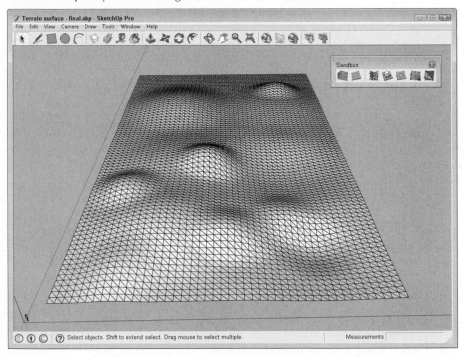

Summary

The Sandbox tools are great for creating flowing organic surfaces. They allow you to create surfaces from a set of contour lines or from scratch as a rectangular surface. Once created, you can use the other Sandbox tools to modify the surface. The Smoove tool is used to create rolling hills, valleys, and peaks; the Stamp and Drape tools indent or project objects and edges onto the surface; the Add Detail tool increases the resolution of the surface; and the Flip Edges tool changes the direction of the crossing edge.

This chapter covered the following topics:

- Creating TIN surfaces from contours or from scratch
- Modifying surfaces with the Smoove tool
- Stamping objects into the surface
- Projecting edges onto the surface with the Drape tool
- Using the Add Details tool to increase surface resolution
- Flipping edges to make the surface flow better

The next chapter begins a part on organizing scenes and objects, starting with the Component Browser.

Part IV

Organizing Scenes

Chapter 15

Using Component Libraries

After working with SketchUp for a while, you'll find some drawing parts that you want to reuse in other drawings. SketchUp provides a way to organize and make these reusable parts accessible. Reusable parts are called components, and they are saved in the Components Browser.

As the Components Browser becomes populated with reusable parts, the time needed to create complex scenes is significantly reduced. The key to making components useful is to save them at the right scale that is consistent for all available components.

If you want to look beyond your own set of components, you can access a huge variety of models using the 3D Warehouse. The 3D Warehouse is an external resource of objects made of uploaded models from users around the world.

IN THIS CHAPTER

Using the Components Browser

Creating new components and libraries

Accessing 3D Warehouse

Using the Components Browser

The Components Browser holds all the preloaded objects that are available for use in your current scene. Choose Window ⇨ Components to open the browser, which is displayed in Figure 15.1.

All components within the Component Browser are divided into categories or collections. The components in the current category are displayed as thumbnails in the browser panel. The default category is the Components Sampler category that is installed with SketchUp, but you can switch between different collections marked as favorites or recently opened collections using the drop-down arrow icon to the right of the Home icon.

FIGURE 15.1

The Component Browser includes prebuilt models.

Component Thumbnail

Component Name   Component Description

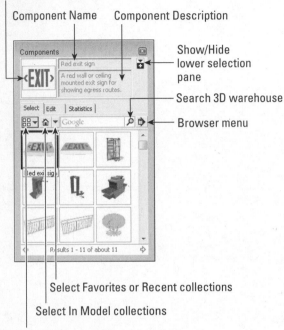

Show/Hide
lower selection
pane

Search 3D warehouse

Browser menu

Select Favorites or Recent collections

Select In Model collections

Browser Preview mode

After you select a component thumbnail, its preview is displayed at the top of the browser along with its name and a description if it has one. The selected components can then be placed into the current scene by dragging and dropping it into the scene. Figure 15.2 shows a component added to the current scene.

NOTE   **The Components Browser only allows a single object to be dropped onto the drawing area at a time.**

At the top of the thumbnails is a Search field that you can use to enter a keyword. This keyword is used to search the 3D Warehouse repository for models that match the keyword. All applicable models are displayed as thumbnails in the browser. Figure 15.3 shows the Component Browser after searching for the keyword, "torpedo."

FIGURE 15.2

Components can be dragged and dropped from the Components Browser.

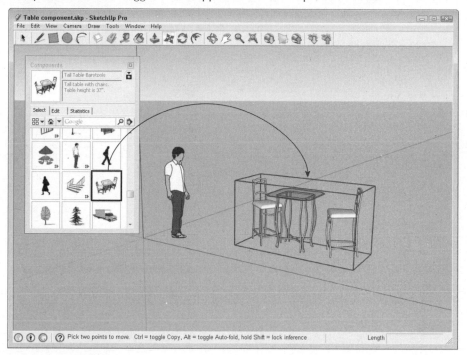

FIGURE 15.3

Models can be searched and loaded directly into the browser from 3D Warehouse.

All the recent searched collections are saved at the bottom of the Selection list. At the top of the Selection list are a list of Favorite collections. These are always available in the Selection menu. You can add or remove collections from the Favorites list using the Browser menu. The Home button lets you see the In Model category, which shows all the components in the current scene.

Using the Browser Preview Menu, you can switch between Small and Large Thumbnails or views with Details. Figure 15.4 shows the browser with the Details option enabled.

FIGURE 15.4

The Browser Menu includes options for changing the thumbnail size and for viewing component details.

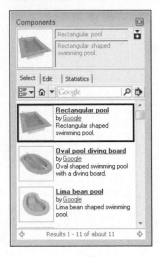

The Browser Preview Menu also includes an option to display the components as a list. Figure 15.5 shows the browser in List View.

Working with collections

Any open collection can be added to your list of Favorites using the Add to Favorites menu option in the Browser menu. If a favorite collection is viewed within the browser, then you also have the option to Remove from Favorites.

Favorite collections can be accessed from 3D Warehouse or from your local drive. If you want to save a collection to your local drive, then the Open or Create a Local Collection menu option can be used. This menu lets you select a folder where the local collection is saved. This same menu can then be used to access any models within the collection.

FIGURE 15.5

Components can also be displayed as a list.

Selecting the Save as a local collection menu saves all the components in the current In Model set to the local collection folder.

You can also view the selected component within 3D Warehouse using a menu option.

Moving components between libraries

The Components Browser can open two selection panels at once using the Show/Hide Lower Selection panel button at the top right of the browser. Both selection panels, as shown in Figure 15.6, include the same buttons for selecting the viewed components. They also both include a search field and browser menu button.

One way to use both selection panels is to keep the various libraries open in one panel and thumbnails of the components in the other. Another way is to move components between the various libraries by dragging a thumbnail from one panel to the other. If a dragged thumbnail is dropped on another library thumbnail, the dropped thumbnail is added to the library.

FIGURE 15.6

Using the lower selection pane, you can move components between collections.

Using the Edit tab

In the top selection panel are two additional tabs for accessing the Edit and Statistic panels. The Edit panel, shown in Figure 15.7, presents several options for controlling the alignment of the dropped component. These options are only available when you select a component from the In Model library.

When a component is selected from the In Model library, you can edit its name and description fields by typing a new name or a description.

The Glue to option lets you constrain the alignment of the selected component. The options include None, Any, Horizontal, Vertical, and Sloped. This setting defines how the component is oriented when dropped in the scene. For example, if you specify the Vertical option for a door, then the door is automatically aligned to be vertically upright when placed, as shown in Figure 15.8.

FIGURE 15.7

The Edit panel includes options for setting the component alignment.

FIGURE 15.8

Glued components are forced to be Vertical, Horizontal, or Sloped.

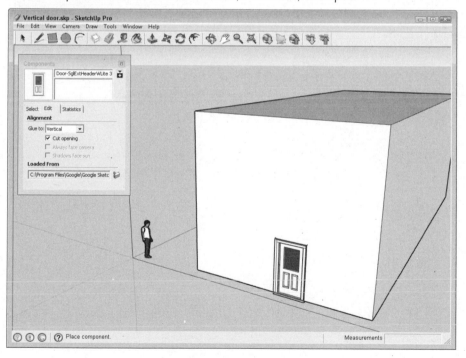

The Vertical option is useful for gluing doors and windows to the side of a building; items such as air conditioners would be glued to the top of a building using the Horizontal option. For any of the gluing options besides the None option, you can select the Cut opening option to cause a hole to be cut into the surface of the gluing object when dropped.

If the None option is selected, you can specify that the object Always face camera. This creates a billboard object that is rendered as a 2-D object that is always facing the camera. Figure 15.9 shows a person added to the top of the building. This person, like the default character standing near the origin, is set to always face the camera.

The Shadows face sun option is only available when the Always face camera option is selected. It causes the component's shadow to be cast as if it were turned to face the sun providing the widest possible shadow. This works well for components like trees and poles, but if the shadow is unique, like a chair, then this option creates an unrealistic shadow.

FIGURE 15.9

Components that are set to always face the camera are rendered as 2-D objects.

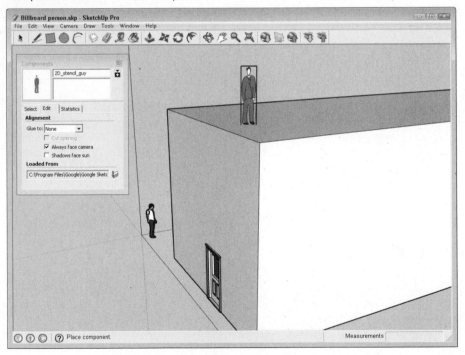

CROSS-REF You can learn more about using shadows in Chapter 21.

At the bottom of the Edit panel is the path to the selected component's location on the hard drive.

Using the Statistics tab

The Statistics panel, shown in Figure 15.10, lists all the various entities contained in the current component. From the drop-down list, you can choose to view all of the geometry entities or just the components that make up the selection. Selecting the Expand option shows the entities for each component. At the bottom of the panel, the number of instances of the selected component are listed.

FIGURE 15.10

The Statistics panel lists the number of different entities that make up the current component.

Creating Components

After you go through the available prebuilt components, you'll want to start creating your own components. You can also create your own libraries to store the components in.

There are several ways to create a component. One way is to choose Edit ⇨ Make Component (or you can press G). The Make Component button is only available when a set of objects that can be made into a component is selected.

All of these options cause the Create Component dialog box to appear, as shown in Figure 15.11. With this dialog box, you can type a name and description. You can also set the same options that are available in the Edit tab of the Components Browser. There is also a Replace selection with component option that causes the selected objects to be considered a component instead of just objects.

Once you have a newly defined component, it is automatically added to the In Model library, but you can move it to another library by simply clicking and dragging the component thumbnail to the library that you want to add it to that is opened in the lower selection panel.

TIP Components can also be added to library folders by clicking and dragging them directly from Windows Explorer or the Finder.

When you create a new component, it is not initially saved to the hard drive and is identified in the Loaded From field as an Internal Component. Although the Component is saved with the current scene, you need to save the file if you want to reuse it in other scenes. You can save a new component by right-clicking on its thumbnail and selecting the Save As menu command.

FIGURE 15.11

The Create Component dialog box lets you set the options of new components.

Accessing the 3D Warehouse

If you need more components, there are a couple of places that you can visit. The Google SketchUp Web site includes a page of component collections that you can download and use. 3D Warehouse is a repository of SketchUp models uploaded by users.

Getting more components

Although SketchUp gives you the ability to create and save new components and libraries, to really jump-start your components collection, you can use the Get More menu command found at the bottom of the Components Browser menu. This command opens a Web page, as shown in Figure 15.12, on the Google SketchUp Web site that features more than 2000 pre-built components that you can add to your component set.

Getting 3D Warehouse models

3D Warehouse is a sharing repository available online for SketchUp users. On this site, you can find a vast assortment of models and collections. To access 3D Warehouse, simply choose File ⇨ 3D Warehouse ⇨ Get Models, or you can click the 3D Warehouse button in the Components Browser. Both of these options open a Web page, as shown in Figure 15.13.

On the 3D Warehouse home page are several featured collections. There is also a search feature that you can use to locate specific items. If you browse or search for uploaded items, the items are presented as thumbnails. If you click on a model thumbnail, a larger picture of the model is displayed, as shown in Figure 15.14, along with thumbnails of related items. Beneath the image is a link to download the model.

FIGURE 15.12

The Google SketchUp Web site features expanded collections of components that you can download.

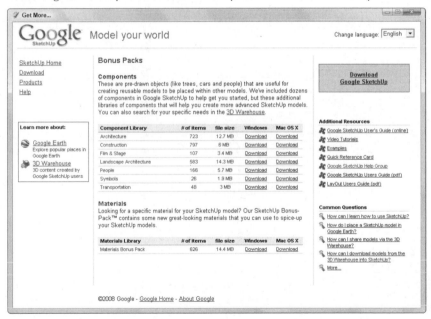

FIGURE 15.13

3D Warehouse is an online repository of SketchUp models and collections.

FIGURE 15.14

Items can be downloaded by clicking the Download Model link.

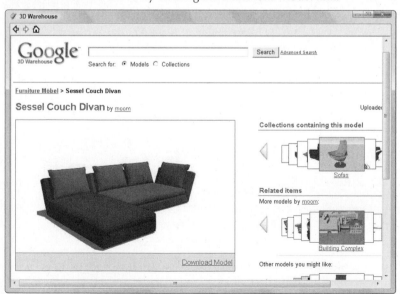

CAUTION Before downloading and using models found on 3D Warehouse, be aware of any copyright restrictions that are attached to the model. Using models without the permission of the creator is not permitted.

Sharing models

3D Warehouse also makes it easy to upload your own models. Simply choose File ➪ 3D Warehouse ➪ Share Model. You need a Google account before you can share SketchUp models, and you must accept a Terms of Service agreement. You can then access a page where you can give your model a title and description. You can also add a logo, Web site address, and any identifying tags to the model before uploading it.

Summary

Grouping provides a way to quickly combine several objects so they move together, but to create a grouping that can be reused in other scenes you'll want to use components. All components are organized and displayed in the Components Browser, and from the browser you can drop components into the current scene. Models can also be downloaded and used in the current scene from 3D Warehouse, an online repository of models.

This chapter covered the following topics:

- Using the Components Browser
- Adding components to the current scene
- Setting component properties
- Creating new components and libraries
- Downloading models from 3D Warehouse
- Uploading models to 3D Warehouse

In the next chapter, you look at layers as another way to organize the scene.

Chapter 16

Working with Dynamic Components

Y ou can use the Components Browser to add new objects to the current model, but for most standard components, you only get what is available. Dynamic Components, on the other hand, allow you to change many aspects of the component using preset parameters.

SketchUp 7 includes a number of default Dynamic Components that you can use, and if you own the Pro version you can even create you own custom Dynamic Components.

Using Default Dynamic Components

Within the Components Browser is a category called Dynamic Components Training. This set of Dynamic Components can be selected using the Selection drop-down list. The set of Dynamic Components shown in Figure 16.1 includes shelves, a table, fences, frames, blinds, and grids.

CROSS-REF You can learn more about using the Components Browser in Chapter 15.

IN THIS CHAPTER

Using the default Dynamic Components

Creating custom Dynamic Components

Using the Component Attributes dialog box

The Components Browser includes several preset Dynamic Components.

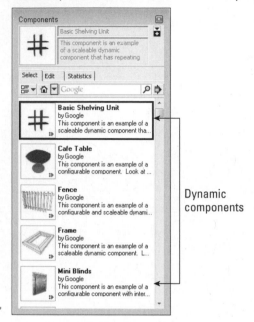

Dynamic
components

Enabling Dynamic Components

Dynamic Components are a set of plug-ins that must be enabled before you can access them. To enable Dynamic Components, choose Window ➪ Preferences to open the System Preferences dialog box. Click the Extensions panel and then select Dynamic Components, as shown in Figure 16.2, then click OK.

Manipulating Dynamic Components

Dynamic Components are placed in the current scene just like any other component; however, after you place them, you can change how they look using the various dynamic parameters. To access the dynamic parameters, use the Dynamic Component tools found on the Dynamic Components Toolbar, as shown in Figure 16.3. You can access this toolbar by selecting the View ➪ Toolbars ➪ Dynamic Components menu.

FIGURE 16.2

Dynamic Components are enabled using the Extensions panel of the System Preferences dialog box.

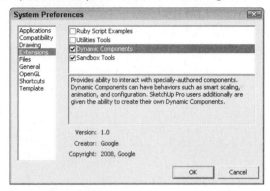

FIGURE 16.3

The tools for working with Dynamic Components are found in the Dynamic Components Toolbar.

Interacts with Dynamic Components

Component Attributes

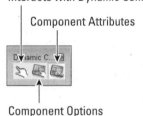

Component Options

The Interaction tool allows you to work directly with certain components such as doors and windows. You can use this tool to open a door interactively by clicking and dragging with the tool. This tool highlights any objects in the scene when it is positioned over the top of an object that uses it.

Not all Dynamic Components have interactive parameters, but all have parameters that you can access in the Component Options dialog box, as shown in Figure 16.4. This dialog box is opened by clicking on the Component Options tool in the Dynamic Components toolbar. The exact parameters will change for each component.

After a parameter value is changed, the Apply button at the bottom of the Component Options dialog box is enabled. Clicking this button makes the change to the dynamic component.

Figure 16.5 shows three sets of shelves that have been manipulated by changing their dynamic parameters. For this shelf component, you can alter the shelf depth and thickness, and also the number of rows and columns, their spacing, and even the material colors.

FIGURE 16.4

The Component Options dialog box lists the various parameters that you can alter.

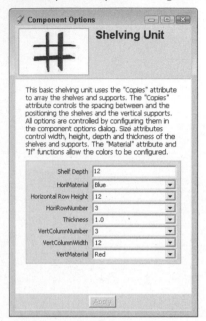

FIGURE 16.5

Multiple variations can quickly be made by altering the parameters of a Dynamic Component.

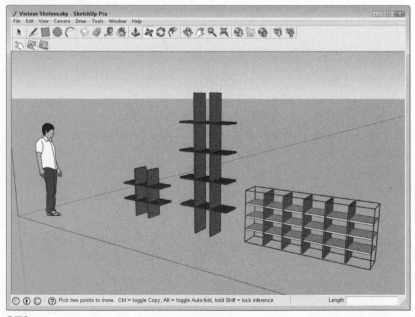

Creating Dynamic Components

Although the standard version of SketchUp 7 can use and manipulate Dynamic Components, the Pro version includes the ability to create your own Dynamic Components. The dynamic parameters are defined using the Component Attributes dialog box, as shown in Figure 16.6. This dialog box is opened by clicking the Component Attributes button on the Dynamic Components Toolbar.

Using the Component Attributes dialog box

The Component Attributes dialog box holds all the defined parameters along with the formulas used to compute those values. Some of the values are dependent on other values such as the item cost, which is determined by the size of the object.

FIGURE 16.6

The Component Attributes dialog box lets you define the parameters of the Dynamic Components.

Delete Attribute   Refresh   Toggle Formula View

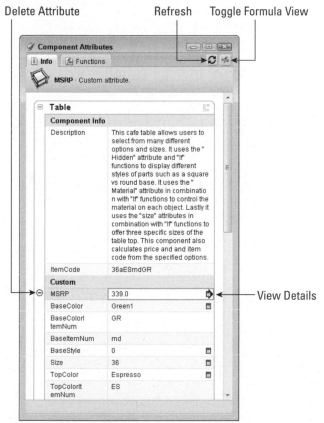

View Details

All parameters are divided into a hierarchy of subparts. For example, for the Table Dynamic Component, as shown in Figure 16.7, there are parameters for the whole table and parameters for the different parts that make up the table. Each of these parts is at a level beneath the main table object. Using the Expand/Contract button to the left of each part's name, you can expand each part to view its parameters.

To rename an attribute, simply double-click the attributes name and a simple dialog box appears where you can rename the attribute. Some attributes are reserved and cannot be renamed.

For each defined parameter, a value is displayed. This value is the default value that is used when the dynamic component is dropped into the scene. This value can also be changed as the user changes the values in the Component Options dialog box. The resulting value is determined by the formula that is attached to each parameter. To see the formula, click the Toggle Formula View button at the top of the Component Attributes dialog box. Figure 16.8 shows the formulas for the various table parameters.

FIGURE 16.7

The Component Attributes dialog box parameters are divided into subparts.

Expand button

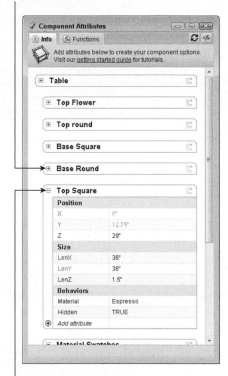

Contract button

The keywords used to create the formulas are standardized for SketchUp, and you can find a detailed listing of these keywords in the SketchUp help files.

Click the Refresh button to update the parameter values to reflect any changes to the current formula.

Not all parameters appear in the Component Options dialog box. Some parameters are only used to compute other values. For example, you could define a square box's length, width, and height values, and use these values to compute a volume parameter that appears on the Component Options dialog box. That way the user only needs to change one parameter to get a larger or smaller box.

FIGURE 16.8

Click the Toggle Formula View button to see all the parameter's formulas.

Clicking the Details button to the right of the parameter value allows you to access options for the units and displays the parameter in the Component Options dialog box. Figure 16.9 shows the details options for the MSRP parameter. Using these details, you can set the default units, whether the parameter is visible in the Component Options dialog box, and whether the user can change the value or select a value from a drop-down list. There are also options to set the display label and the display units.

Click the Details button to set which parameters are visible in the Component Options dialog box.

Adding new attributes

To add a new attribute to the subpart of a dynamic component, simply click the Add Attribute link at the bottom of each subpart. This opens a pop-up menu of available attributes, as shown in Figure 16.10. Within the list of available attributes are categories for Position, Size, Rotation, and Behaviors. You can also define a custom attribute by typing a new name.

Creating formulas

When a new attribute is added to the Component Attributes dialog box, you can set its value using a formula. To create a formula, click in the value field and type an equals (=) sign. This identifies the variables and values used to calculate the result. Formulas can use the common mathematical functions to add, multiply, and subtract values from one another. To use another attribute as a variable for the current formula, simply click the attribute's name and its name is added as a formula variable.

FIGURE 16.10

Clicking the Add Attribute link opens a pop-up menu of available attributes.

Add attribute link

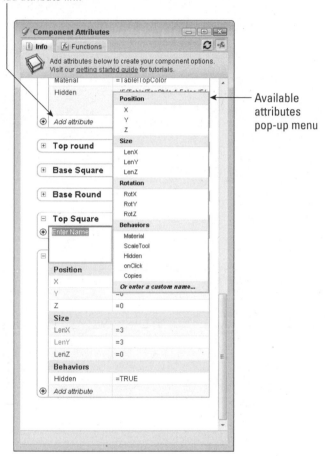

Available attributes pop-up menu

You can also access formula functions to perform a wide variety of mathematical operations. You can find all these functions by clicking the Functions tab at the top of the dialog box. The functions are in a drop-down list, as shown in Figure 16.11. Selecting a function and clicking the insert button adds the function to the current selected formula. Beneath the drop-down list is a description of the selected function.

FIGURE 16.11

The Functions tab holds the available functions that you can use.

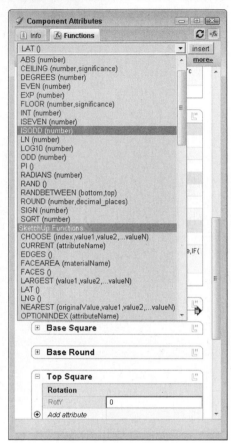

 A complete listing of the available functions can be found in the help files.

Summary

Dynamic Components offer a way to create multiple new objects by simply changing the attributes of the defined component. Changes to the Dynamic Component are made using the Component Options dialog box. If you have a Pro version, you can create custom Dynamic Components.

This chapter covered the following topics:

- Accessing Dynamic Components in the Components Browser
- Enabling Dynamic Components
- Changing Dynamic Component attributes
- Creating new Dynamic Components

The next chapter looks at layers as another way to organize the scene.

Chapter 17

Using Layers

A s your scenes get more and more complex, you'll need a way to organize the various objects that makes sense. Groups and components
are helpful ways to organize sets of parts, but to organize an entire
scene that includes many different objects, the Layer Manager is a good way
to go.

The Layer Manager lets you divide your scene into logical sets. For example, a
scene can have a background layer that holds all the distance objects, a street
layer for the objects surrounding the buildings, a plants and trees layer, a
layer for the buildings, another for the interior objects, and a final layer for
the people. When divided in this manner, it becomes easy to quickly hide all
the plants and trees or to remove all the people from the scene.

Another common way to use layers is to divide a model by its material
assignments. For example, if you have a model of a car, you can set one layer
to hold all the parts that get the body color, another layer for the glass
objects, a third for the tires, and a fourth for the rims.

Accessing the Layer Manager

All layers are listed in the Layers Manager, as shown in Figure 17.1. You can
access the Layers Manager from the Windows menu. All projects include a
Layer0 by default. Even if you choose not to use layers, all objects are automatically placed on Layer0. Layer0 cannot be deleted or renamed.

FIGURE 17.1

The Layers dialog box lists all layers for the current model.

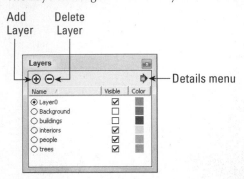

Add Layer

Delete Layer

Details menu

Creating new layers

To create a new layer, simply click the Add Layer button in the Layers dialog box. This adds a new layer to the list that is initially named Layer and a sequential number. When created, the new layer's name is automatically selected and can be renamed by typing a new name. Other layers can be renamed at any time (except for Layer0) by double-clicking the layer's name and typing a new one. New layers are also assigned a random color.

Deleting layers

You can select a layer by clicking on it. The selected layer is highlighted. Multiple layers can be selected at once. Highlighted layers can be deleted by clicking the Delete Layer button.

If the selected layer is empty, then clicking the Delete Layer button simply removes the layer from the Layers dialog box. If the layer is not empty, the warning dialog box shown in Figure 17.2 appears giving you the following options:

- **Move contents to Default layer:** Select this option to move all the layer objects to Layer0.

- **Move contents to Current layer:** Select this option to move all layer objects to the current active layer.

- **Delete contents:** Select this option to delete all the objects on the layer.

To quickly remove all empty layers in the Layers dialog box, select the Purge option from the Details pop-up menu.

FIGURE 17.2

If you try to delete a layer that contains objects, this warning dialog box appears.

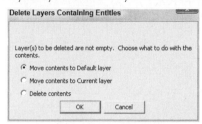

Working with Layers

There are several ways to work with layers using the Layers dialog box. The key to working with layers is to identify the current active layer and the various layer properties.

Setting an active layer

The column of radio buttons to the left of the layer names is used to identify the active layer. Only one layer can be active at a time. All new objects are automatically added to the current active layer. By default, Layer0 is the active layer when you first start SketchUp, so all new objects are automatically added to this layer. The active layer can be different from the selected layer, as shown in Figure 17.3.

FIGURE 17.3

The active layer is indicated by the filled radio button to the left of the name.

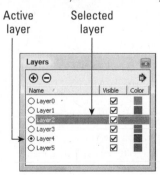

All new objects drawn into the current project are automatically added to the current active layer, but you can move objects between layers using the Entity Info dialog box, which can be accessed from the right-click pop-up menu.

Learning the layer properties

All layers have the following properties, and each of these properties is listed in a column:

- **Active:** Indicated by the radio button to the left of the name. Only one layer is active at a time.
- **Name:** Each layer has a distinct name. If you try to change a name to be the same as another name, an error dialog box appears.
- **Visible:** This check box determines whether the objects contained on a given layer are visible or hidden.
- **Color:** Each layer can be assigned a color that provides a way to view all objects that are on a layer and it also lets you know what layer an object is on.

You can sort all layers by property by clicking on the column heading. For example, clicking once on the Name column sorts all layers in ascending alphabetical order; clicking a second time reverses the order. Sorting by Visibility causes all visible layers to be grouped together and all hidden layers to be grouped together. Sorting by color groups all colors with the same hue.

Hiding layers

After you separate the model into layers, you can quickly hide a specific layer using the Visible check box. When enabled, all objects on that layer are hidden. These objects remain hidden even when you choose View ➪ Hidden Geometry. Figure 17.4 shows a car with the windows layer hidden.

CAUTION   The active layer cannot be hidden. If you make an invisible layer active, the Visible check box is automatically selected, and if you try to deselect the Visible check box on the active layer, a warning dialog box appears.

Identifying objects on layers

The color swatch is used to identify which objects are contained on which layer. By choosing Color by Layer in the Details pop-up menu, every object is colored based on its layer color. Figure 17.5 shows a car that uses this option.

FIGURE 17.4

Deselecting the Visible check box causes all objects on a layer to be hidden.

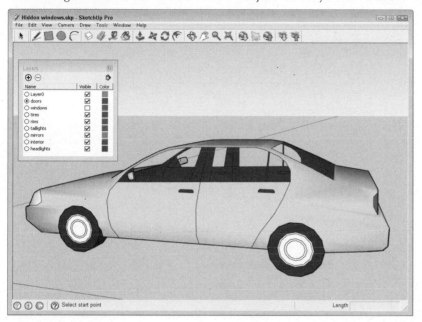

FIGURE 17.5

The Color by Layer option shows each object using its layer color.

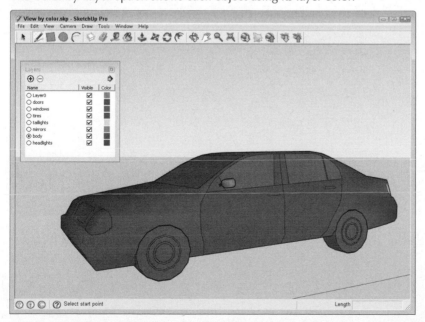

Moving objects between layers

The layer for each object is listed in the Entity Info dialog box. If you open this dialog box by choosing Window ⇨ Entity Info, you can use the Layer drop-down list to change the layer assignment for the selected entity, as shown for the door in Figure 17.6.

Objects can be switched to a different layer using the Entity Info dialog box.

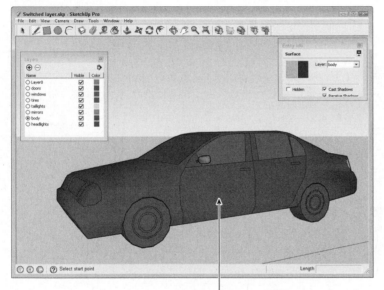

Layer assignment changed

Tutorial: Separating into layers

The best time to use layers is as you are creating a project, but if you create an entire scene and need to separate it into layers after it is built, you can do that, also.

To separate an existing scene into layers, follow these steps:

1. **Open the** Street scene.skp **file from the Chapter 17 folder on the CD-ROM.** This file includes a basic scene created using default components.

2. **Choose Window ⇨ Layers to open the Layers dialog box.** Some of the components are on different layers, but most are on Layer0.

3. **Click the Add Layer button in the Layers dialog box to create five new layers.** Name those new layers People, Buildings, Vehicles, Trees, and Ground.

4. **With the Select tool, Shift+click on both tree objects to select them.** Then choose Window⇨Entity Info to open the Entity Info dialog box. Select the Trees layer from the drop-down list.

5. **Continue to use the Entity Info dialog box and the Select tool to assign the people, ground, and vehicle objects to their appropriate layers.**

6. **Select all remaining layers in the Layers dialog box and click the Delete Layer button.** Select the option to move all the objects on those layers to the default layer.

7. **Select the building objects and move them to the Buildings layer.**

8. **Change the Layer color swatches to be unique and enable the Color by Layer pop-up menu command from the Layers dialog box.** Figure 17.7 shows the resulting objects by layer color.

 **If you leave the color swatch for Layer0 to red, the objects not assigned to a layer are easy to spot.**

FIGURE 17.7

Viewing layers by color helps you quickly identify which objects are on which layers.

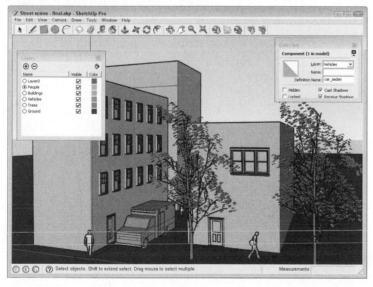

Summary

Using layers effectively provides another helpful way to organize a scene. It also makes a quick way to hide a certain group of layers. Although the Layers dialog box is simple, it is quite powerful for organizing the scene.

This chapter covered the following topics:

- Accessing the Layer Manager
- Creating and deleting layers
- Hiding layer objects
- Viewing layer objects by color
- Moving objects between layers

The next chapter covers splitting the current project into multiple scenes and animating between scenes.

Chapter 18

Using the Scenes Manager

I f you're making a presentation of your drawing, you often don't want to have to deal with the various configuration settings during your presentation. SketchUp includes a way to save the current project with one set of settings for instant recall and another set of settings for a different look using the Scenes dialog box.

After you define two or more scenes, you can use the Animation features to create an animation between the adjacent scenes. Scene animations can be exported if you're using the SketchUp Pro version.

IN THIS CHAPTER

Opening the Scenes Manager

Creating new scenes

Learning the scene properties

Animating scene transitions

Exporting scene animations

Accessing the Scenes Manager

If you like a specific view of the current drawing with all its settings, you can save the scene using the Scenes Manager. The Scenes Manager, shown in Figure 18.1, allows you to create and manage all the defined scenes. Choose Window ⇨ Scenes to open the Scenes Manager.

All new scenes are listed in the Scenes dialog box. You can select a scene from the Scenes dialog box, and all of the properties for the selected scene, including its name and description, are displayed.

The Scenes dialog box lets you create and manage defined scenes.

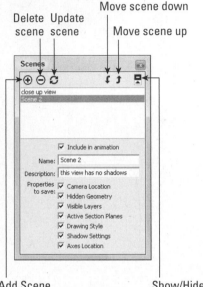

Delete scene
Update scene
Move scene down
Move scene up
Add Scene
Show/Hide details

Working with Scenes

Using the Scenes dialog box, you can create new scenes and change their properties. These properties determine what is saved with the scene.

Adding new scenes

To create a new scene, click the Add Scene button at the top of the Scenes dialog box. This adds a new scene to the list named Scene followed by a sequential number. You can change the scene's name by typing a new name in the Name field. You can type a description in the Description field.

When a new scene is added to the Scenes dialog box, a tab for the named scene is placed at the top of the drawing area, as shown in Figure 18.2. Using the Scenes dialog box, you can alter a scene's name, description, or properties, but you use the drawing area tabs to switch to the defined scene. The current scene is highlighted.

The scenes in the Scenes dialog box are listed in the order they are created, but you can alter this order using the Move Scene Down and Move Scene Up buttons at the top of the Scenes dialog box.

You can also delete the selected scene in the Scenes dialog box using the Delete Scene button. Deleting a scene also deletes its tab.

FIGURE 18.2

The drawing area tabs let you switch between the different scenes.

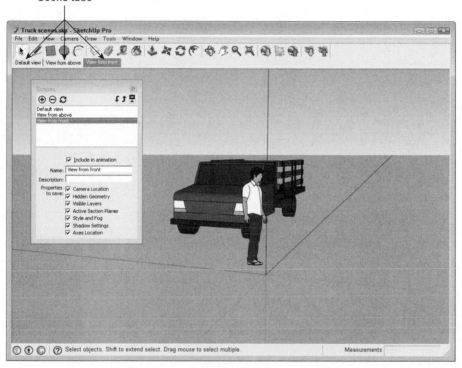

Learning the scene properties

Each scene can have several properties saved with it using the properties check boxes. The available scene properties include the following:

- **Camera Location**: Records the position in the camera in the scene including all camera properties such as zoom distance and location
- **Hidden Geometry**: Stores any hidden geometry with the scene
- **Visible Layers**: Causes all visible layers to be saved with the scene
- **Active Section Planes**: Saves any specified section planes with the scene
- **Drawing Styles**: Displays the scene using the selected style
- **Shadow Settings**: Saves all the shadow settings with the scene
- **Axes Location**: Saves and displays the drawing axes for the scene

If you make any changes to the scene, you can update its display using the Update Scene button at the top of the Scenes dialog box.

Animating Scenes

Another benefit of working with scenes is that you can use the animation feature to animate between the saved scenes. You can see a sample of this when you switch between the saved scenes using the scene tabs at the top of the drawing area. When switching between scenes, the camera is animated moving between the current scene to the selected scene.

Scenes can be animated moving from one scene to the next. This is useful for creating a simple animation of a camera moving through the scene or to see the shadows changing as the time of day changes. To create a scene animation, select the Include in Animation option for all scenes that you want to include. The animation will move from the first scene in the list through to the last included scene.

If the Include in Animation option is disabled for a scene, then the scene's name is enclosed within parentheses in both the Scenes dialog box and in the scene tab, as shown in Figure 18.3.

FIGURE 18.3

Scenes that are surrounded with parentheses are not included in the animation.

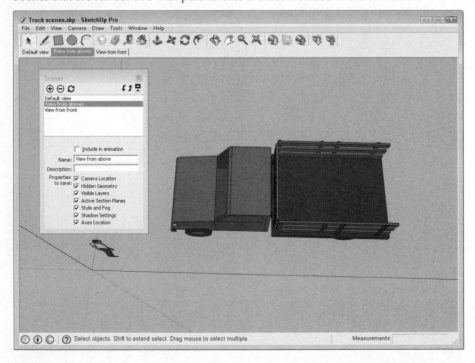

Because the order of the list directly affects the animation, you can alter a scene's position in the list using the Move Scene Up and Move Scene Down arrows.

Exporting animations

Abrupt view changes can make it hard for viewers to understand your drawing, but using the animation features for scenes lets you animate the transition between two scenes. When two or more scenes are created, you have the option to export the scene animation to an external file by choosing File ⇨ Export ⇨ Animation. This opens the Export Animation dialog box, as shown in Figure 18.4.

 **The ability to export scene animations is only available in SketchUp Pro.**

FIGURE 18.4

Scene animations can be exported using the options in the Export Animation dialog box.

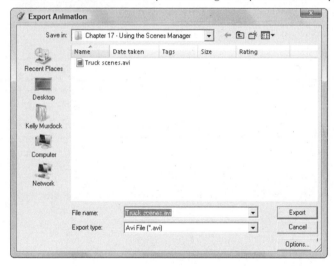

Using the Export Animation dialog box, you can export scene animations to the following formats:

- **AVI**: The default Windows video format
- **JPEG**: A compressible image format common on the Web
- **PNG**: A newer image format that supports transparent backgrounds
- **TIF**: A common image format
- **BMP**: A common image format for Windows

Exporting to video

If the AVI export format is selected, the scene animation can be exported as a single video file. Clicking Options from the Export Animation dialog box opens the Animation Export Options dialog box, as shown in Figure 18.5.

FIGURE 18.5
_____

The Animation Export Options dialog box lets you set the animation's size.

Link Aspect Ratio

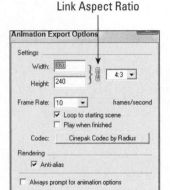

Within the Animation Export Options dialog box are settings for the video's Width and Height. Clicking on the chain icon (Link Aspect Ratio) to the right of the dimension values locks the Width and Height values to the selected aspect ratio. This causes the Width to change automatically when the Height value is changed, and vice versa. The available aspect ratios are 4:3 (standard) and 16:9 (widescreen).

The Animation Export Options dialog box also lets you set the Frame Rate, which is the number of images (or frames) displayed each second. Other common frame rates include 30 frames per second for television, 24 frames per second for movies, and 12 frames per second for Web video. Higher frame rates result in smoother videos, but result in larger file sizes.

Selecting the Loop to starting scene option causes the animation sequence to start over at the first scene when finished. Selecting the Play when finished option opens the system's default video player and automatically plays the video after it is saved.

The Codec button opens the Video Compression dialog box, as shown in Figure 18.6. Video files are comprised of a single image for each frame, so if you have a video with a 640-x-480-pixel image running for 3 seconds at 30 frames per second, then a total of 90 images are required. This can result in a huge file. To keep the file size of videos smaller, video formats like AVI use a codec to compress the video images. A codec is a file utility that compresses video images as they are being saved. It also uncompresses the images when they are being played.

There are a large number of available codecs, each with advantages and disadvantages, but the Video Compression dialog box lets you choose which codec to use. The available codecs depend on your system. Most codecs have an option to set the amount of compression applied to the video images: the greater the compression setting, the smaller the resulting file size and the lower the quality of the images.

FIGURE 18.6

The Video Compression dialog box lets you choose a video codec.

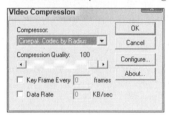

The Compressor drop-down list in the Video Compression dialog box also includes an option to save the video file using Full Frames (uncompressed), which doesn't compress the video images at all.

The Animation Export Options dialog box includes an option to enable anti-aliasing for the drawing. This reduces any jagged edges for lines by softening the transition between black and white pixels. Selecting the Anti-alias option adds to the time to render and save the image, but it improves the image quality dramatically.

The final option, Always prompt for animation options, causes the Animation Export Options dialog box to appear every time an animation file is exported.

Exporting to sequenced images

If any of the other image formats are selected in the Export Animation dialog box, the scene animation is exported as a series of sequential image files with the filename followed by four digits. The digits represent the frame number. Clicking Options opens the Animation Export Options dialog box, as shown in Figure 18.7.

FIGURE 18.7

The Animation Export Options dialog box for images has fewer settings.

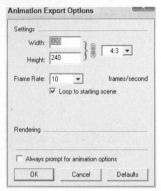

When saving a scene animation as a set of sequential images, the Animation Export Options dialog box has only settings for the dimensions, the frame rate, and whether the image loops or not.

A series of sequential images can then be loaded into video editing packages, like Adobe Premiere, where you can add effects like transitions and titles before saving the file to a video format.

Tutorial: Animating a view change

Abrupt view changes can make it hard for viewers to understand your drawing, but using the animation features for scenes lets you animate the transition between two scenes.

To animate a view change, follow these steps:

1. **Open the** `Sidewalk.skp` **file from the Chapter 18 folder on the CD.** This file includes a simple project created using default components.

2. **Choose Window ⇨ Scenes to open the Scenes Manager.**

3. **Click the New Scene button in the Scenes dialog box.** Name the new scene Front camera.

4. **Use the Orbit tool to rotate the view to the front of the object.** Click the Update Scene button in the Scenes dialog box.

5. **Click the New Scene button to create a second scene.** Name this scene Rear camera.

6. **Rotate the camera around to the back of the object, and click the Update Scene button.**

7. **Click the Front camera scene tab at the top of the drawing area and then the Rear camera scene tab to see the transition between each.**

8. **Choose File ⇨ Export ⇨ Animation, and choose the AVI animation file type.** Type a name and click Export.

Figure 18.8 shows one frame of the transition between scenes.

FIGURE 18.8

Scene animation provides an easy way to show transitions between cameras.

Summary

Using the Scenes Manager, you can create snapshots of the current project that can be recalled with a single click. This is helpful for presentations. Scenes are automatically animated between scenes in the drawing area when you click on the Scene tabs, and these scene animations can be exported to an external file.

This chapter covered the following topics:

- Opening the Scenes Manager
- Creating new scenes
- Specifying scene properties
- Animating scene transitions
- Exporting scene animations to video and image formats

This chapter concludes the part on organizing scenes. The next part deals with applying materials, styles, and effects beginning with materials.

Part V
Working with Materials, Styles, and Effects

Chapter 19

Creating and Applying Materials

There is only so far you can go with geometry, but you can get an even greater level of detail from the materials and textures that are applied to your objects. Think of a billboard. Without an ad plastered to the front of it, it would be fairly boring, but the level of detail you get from the textured images adds a lot to the end result.

Materials in SketchUp are applied using the Material Browser. The Material Browser also includes settings for defining how the materials look. SketchUp includes several default materials that you can apply, but to really get the power of the Material Browser, you'll want to create your own custom materials.

Using the Material Browser

The Material Browser is opened by choosing Window ⇨ Materials. You can also open the Material Browser by selecting the Paint Brush tool by choosing Tools ⇨ Paint Brush. The Material Browser, shown in Figure 19.1, divides the available materials into folders.

The top left of the Material Browser shows a preview of the currently selected material. This is the material that is applied to any faces that are clicked on with the Paint Brush tool. Beneath the material preview are two tabbed panels — Select and Edit. These panels are used to select materials from the current library of predefined materials and edit the current material.

FIGURE 19.1

The Material Browser includes several folders of predefined materials.

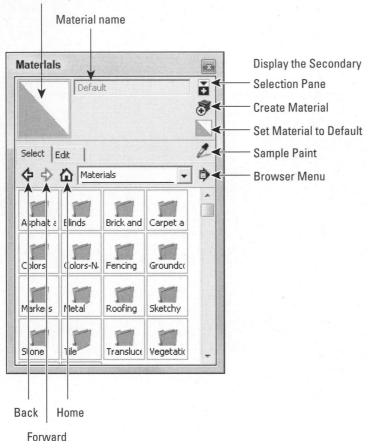

Selected material preview

Material name

Display the Secondary
Selection Pane

Create Material

Set Material to Default

Sample Paint

Browser Menu

Back | Home

Forward

Selecting a predefined material

All default materials are located in folders within the Materials folder where SketchUp is installed. You can navigate these folders of materials within the Material Browser by clicking on the various folders or by selecting the folder name from the drop-down list. When a material folder is open, thumbnails of the materials are displayed in the Material Browser, as shown in Figure 19.2. Click on a thumbnail to make it the current selection.

FIGURE 19.2

When a material folder is open, its material thumbnails are displayed.

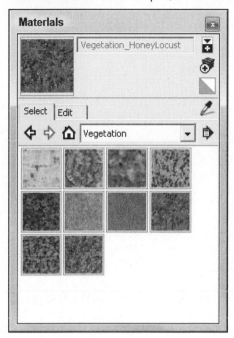

After navigating through the various material folders, the Back and Forward buttons become enabled allowing you to move through the visited folders. There is also a Home button that opens the In Model folder. The In Model folder holds all the materials that exist in the current scene.

Exploring the default materials

The default installation of SketchUp includes several libraries of predefined materials, and even more materials can be downloaded from the SketchUp Web site at http://sketchup.google.com. The default material categories include the following:

- **Asphalt and Concrete:** This material library includes textures for different roads and sidewalks.

- **Blinds:** This library includes several different styles of window coverings including cloth, Roman, vertical, and bamboo.

- **Brick and Cladding:** This library includes several brick patterns and siding materials.

- **Carpet and Textiles:** This material library includes several different styles of carpet and rugs including Berber and plush.

- **Colors:** This library includes a large assortment (310) of colors indexed by number.

- **Colors-Named:** This library includes a library of 137 colors listed by name.

- **Fencing:** This material library includes several styles of fencing including chain link, lattice, picket, and railing.

- **Groundcover:** This library includes several groundcover materials such as bark chips, gravel, and sand.

- **Markers:** This library includes several marker colors.

- **Metal:** This material library includes several types of metals including aluminum, brass, and rusted.

- **Roofing:** This library includes several types of roofing such as shingles, slate, and tile.

- **Sketchy:** This library includes several sketched patterns including crosshatching and stone.

- **Stone:** This material library includes a variety of stone textures including granite, marble, and sandstone.

- **Tile:** This library includes several styles of tiles including ceramic, hexagon, and limestone.

- **Translucent:** This library includes several types and colors of glass.

- **Vegetation:** This material library includes several plant textures including bark, grass, and ivy.

- **Water:** This library includes several water textures.

- **Wood:** This library includes several styles of wood floors including cherry, parquet, and plywood.

If you select the Get More option from the pop-up menu, the SketchUp Web site loads where you can download a Bonus Pack of materials, as shown in Figure 19.3.

CROSS-REF User-created materials can be downloaded from 3D Warehouse. Chapter 15 covers accessing 3D Warehouse.

Changing the browser display

Using the browser menu, you can switch between Small, Medium, Large, and Extra Large Thumbnails. Figure 19.4 shows the browser with Extra Large thumbnails.

The browser menu also includes an option to display the components as a list. Figure 19.5 shows the browser in List view.

FIGURE 19.3

The SketchUp Web site offers a Bonus Pack of materials that you can download.

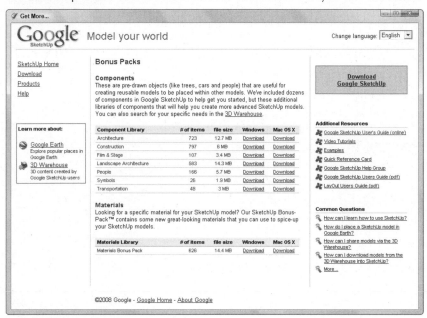

FIGURE 19.4

The browser menu includes options for changing the thumbnail size.

FIGURE 19.5

Components can also be displayed as a list.

Moving materials between libraries

The Materials Browser can open two selection panels at once by clicking the Display Secondary Selection Pane button at the top right of the browser. Both selection panels include the same Forward, Back, and Home buttons for navigating through the viewed components. They also include a library drop-down list and browser menu.

One way to use both selection panels is to keep the various libraries open in one panel and thumbnails of the components in the other, as shown in Figure 19.6. You can move components between the various libraries by clicking and dragging a thumbnail from one panel to the other. Dragging and dropping a thumbnail on another library thumbnail adds the dropped thumbnail to the library.

You can also move the current material to the In Model folder by right-clicking on the material thumbnail and select the Add to Model menu.

Creating a new material library

If you plan on creating your own new materials, you'll want to save them in a new library where you can easily find them. To create a new material library, simply select the Open or create a library option from the browser menu. This opens a Browse For Folder dialog box, as shown in Figure 19.7.

FIGURE 19.6

Using two panels, you can move materials between the different folders.

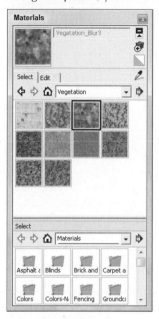

FIGURE 19.7

The Browse For Folder dialog box lets you select and/or create a new material folder.

All default material folders are located in the Materials folder where SketchUp is installed. You can place the new material library folder anywhere you want. Once created, the new folder is opened within the Material Browser and you can move materials into it using the two-panel method explained earlier or by using Windows Explorer or Mac Finder.

At the bottom of the library folder drop-down list is a separator line that divides all categories from a list of favorites, as shown in Figure 19.8. To add a material folder to these favorites, simply select the Add library to Favorites option in the browser menu. To remove a material folder from the Favorites section, use the Remove Library from Favorites menu command.

If the In Model folder is selected, the browser menu includes a Save Library As option that lets you save the current set of materials to a named library folder. There is also a Purge Unused option that you can select to remove all materials from the In Model folder that aren't applied to an object.

FIGURE 19.8

At the bottom of the Favorites list is a section of favorites.

Applying Materials to Objects

After a material is selected in the Material Browser, its thumbnail is displayed in the material preview at the top of the Material Browser. This material can be applied to object faces using the Paint Bucket tool.

Using the Paint Bucket tool

The Paint Bucket tool lets you apply material that you select in the Material Browser to object faces in the current scene. To select the Paint Bucket tool, choose Tools ➪ Paint Bucket, click the Paint Bucket icon in the Principal toolbar, or press B.

 **Applied materials and colors are only visible if the Shaded or Shaded with Textures display option is selected in the View ➪ Face Style menu.**

Selecting the Paint Bucket tool automatically opens the Material Browser and changes the cursor to a paint bucket. Clicking on a single face with the Paint Bucket tool applies that material to that face only, as shown in Figure 19.9. If you select multiple faces with the Select tool and click on one of the selected faces, the current material is applied to all selected faces.

If you hold down the Ctrl key when clicking on a face with the Paint Bucket tool, all adjacent faces to the selected face are also painted with the current material, as shown in Figure 19.10. If some faces have a different material applied, the original material remains and only those faces that have the same material as the face that is clicked on are changed. Also, if a set of faces is selected before applying materials, only those faces within the selection have materials applied.

Holding down the Shift key when applying materials with the Paint Bucket tool causes all faces with the material on the face you click on to be replaced. This provides a way to quickly change all instances of a certain material in the scene with a single click. You can limit the faces that get replaced by selecting them before using the Paint Bucket tool.

If the Shift and Ctrl keys are held down together when using the Paint Bucket tool, only the faces on the current object that have the same material as the clicked-on face get replaced.

To apply materials to groups and components, first double-click on the group or component to get access to the individual faces before you can paint on them. If you apply a material before opening the group or component, the material is applied to the entire group or component.

FIGURE 19.9

The Paint Bucket tool applies the selected material to the face you click.

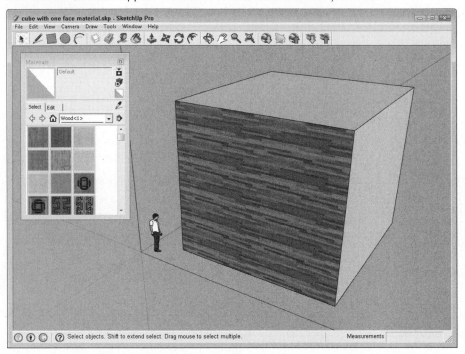

Sampling existing materials

Sometimes, when applying materials, it can be tough to remember from which exact library a material came. If the material is already applied to the scene, then you can recall and load any scene material into the Material Browser using the Sample Paint button in the Material Browser. Clicking this button changes the cursor to an eyedropper and loads any applied material into the material preview when clicked.

You can also access the Sample Paint tool by holding down the Alt key and clicking on a face with an applied material. After you sample a material, you can reapply it to other faces using the Paint Bucket tool.

FIGURE 19.10

Holding down the Ctrl key when using the Paint Bucket tool applies the material to all object faces.

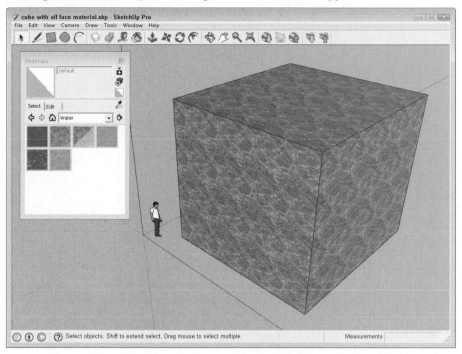

Tutorial: Applying materials to a truck

Virtually painting a truck in SketchUp is a snap and certainly a lot easier than messing with a body shop. In this tutorial, you get the chance to apply materials using the Paint Bucket tool.

To apply materials to a truck, follow these steps:

1. **Open the** `Truck with materials.skp` **file from the Chapter 18 folder on the CD.** This file includes a truck component from the Component library, which is all white by default.

2. **Because the truck is a component, you need to double-click on it with the Select tool to get access to the faces before you can apply materials.**

3. **Choose Tools ⇨ Paint Bucket, or press B to access the Paint Bucket tool.** This opens the Material Browser.

4. **In the Material Browser, select the Colors category from the drop-down list.** Click the Red color swatch to load this material into the material preview, then Ctrl+click with the Paint Bucket tool on the sides of the truck. This covers the truck body with the red color. Also click on the truck's front.

5. **Click on the gray material in the Material Browser.** Click on the panel on the side and the back of the truck.

6. **In the Material Browser, select the Translucent category from the drop-down list.** Click on the Translucent_Glass_Blue thumbnail to load this material into the material preview. Then click with the Paint Bucket tool on the windows.

Figure 19.11 shows the truck with materials applied.

FIGURE 19.11

Even simple colors help to distinguish objects.

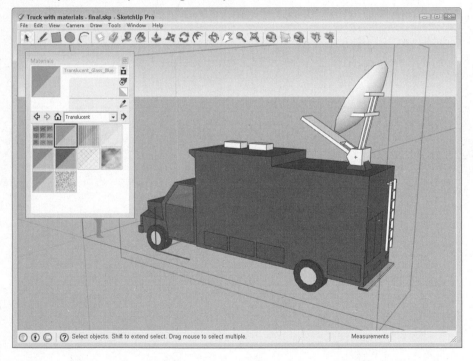

Editing Materials

The Edit panel in the Material Browser includes controls and settings for altering the material's color, texture, and opacity. By learning how to use these settings you can create an infinite number of materials. If you want to reset the material to its default settings, click the Set Material to Default button at the top of the browser.

Creating new materials

Clicking the Create Material button in the Material Browser opens the Create Material dialog box, as shown in Figure 19.12. The new material is named Material1 by default, but you can type a new material name in the Name field. The Material preview shows what the current material settings look like.

FIGURE 19.12

The Create Material dialog box includes all the settings for defining a new material.

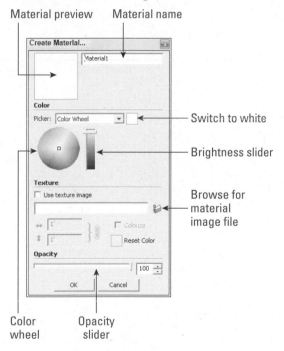

Material preview   Material name

Switch to white

Brightness slider

Browse for material image file

Color wheel   Opacity slider

Changing colors

The color is set using the color wheel. Simply click or drag within the color wheel to select the color you want and then drag the Brightness slider to adjust the color's brightness. Clicking on the Default white color swatch resets the color to pure white.

Using the Picker drop-down list you can change the default color picker. The options include Color Wheel, HLS, HSB, and RGB. The HLS picker, shown in Figure 19.13, sets values for the Hue, the Saturation, and the Light values. The Hue value sets the color, the Saturation value sets the amount of color where 0 is gray and 100 is a pure color, and the Light value adjusts how light or dark the color is.

The HSB color picker, shown in Figure 19.14, is similar to the HLS system with Hue and Saturation values, except it deals with a Brightness value instead of a Light value. The Brightness value ranges from pure black to a light version of the current hue.

FIGURE 19.13

The HLS color picker defines colors by hue, saturation, and light.

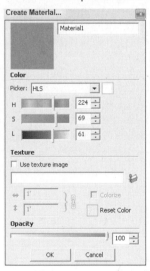

The RGB color picker, shown in Figure 19.15, is a common color picker for many programs including Web colors and Photoshop. It deals with three values for the amount of Red, Green, and Blue added to the current color. By mixing different amounts of each of these component colors, you can create different resulting colors. The RGB values range from 0 (no color) to 255 (pure color).

FIGURE 19.14

The HSB color picker defines colors by hue, saturation, and brightness.

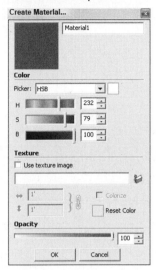

FIGURE 19.15

The RGB color picker defines colors by red, green, and blue components.

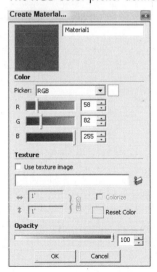

Loading textures

To have a loaded texture appear as part of the current material, select the Use texture image option from the Create Material dialog box. The image texture file can be loaded using the Browse for Material Image File button, and the filename, once loaded, is displayed to the left of the browse button, as shown in Figure 19.16. The image formats that SketchUp recognizes include JPEG, PNG, TIF, TGA, and BMP.

CROSS-REF You can learn more about these various image formats in Chapter 4.

The width and height values below the image name define the size of the repeating texture on the face. For example, if these values are set to 1 inch by 1 inch, then the material is applied to the face as a series of 1-inch-by-1-inch repeating tiles. If the dimensions are set to a larger value, the texture appears larger across the face. Figure 19.17 shows two box objects. The one on the left has a small tiling value resulting in a pattern that repeats more often and smaller. The box object on the right has a larger tiling value resulting in a larger texture that repeats less often.

FIGURE 19.16

Loaded textures are displayed in the material preview at the top of the browser.

Reset to original image width

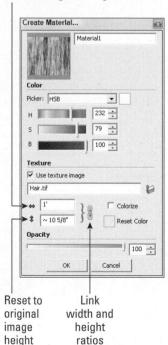

Reset to original image height

Link width and height ratios

To the right of the Width and Height values is a Link button. When this button is enabled, then the aspect ratio of the width and height values are maintained, so that changing one value automatically changes the other to keep the current aspect ratio. This is helpful to prevent any image distortion to the texture image.

TIP When working with repeating texture patterns, it is helpful to make the image files into a seamless image by matching the patterns to its opposite side. Seamless images are images where the seam between the repeating sides isn't visible.

The Colorize option causes all colors within the image to have the same hue. You can also set the image color back to its original color by selecting the Reset Color option.

If you want to save the current material as an image file, right-click on the material thumbnail and select the Export Texture Image menu. This opens a file dialog box where you can save the material's image.

FIGURE 19.17

The texture dimensions set the size of the texture repeating on the object face.

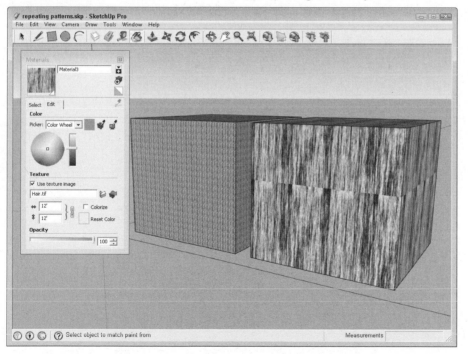

Adding transparency

The Opacity slider is used to set the material's opacity or transparency. Semitransparent materials allow objects on the opposite side of the face to be visible, such as glass and water. Figure 19.18 shows two objects with materials applied. The object on the right has a semitransparent material, and the left object is opaque.

FIGURE 19.18

Semitransparent materials are partially see-through.

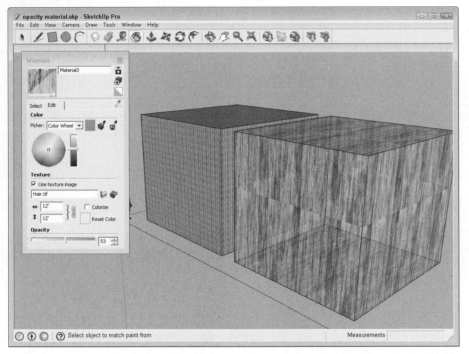

Editing current materials

Selected materials can be edited with the same settings found in the Create New Materials dialog box by opening the Edit panel, as shown in Figure 19.19. The Edit panel is identical to the Create New Materials dialog box, except it includes two additional buttons for matching colors — Match Color of Object in Model and Match Color on Screen.

The Match Color of Object in Model button causes the material color to be set to match the color of an object that you click on. The Match Color on Screen changes the material color to match the color of the color that is selected anywhere in the screen.

FIGURE 19.19

The Edit panel includes buttons for matching colors.

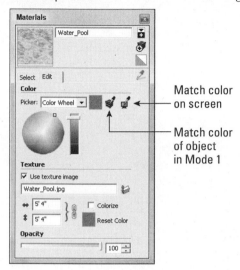

Match color
on screen

Match color
of object
in Mode 1

Using the Position Texture Tool

Placing random seamless texture to represent grass or tile on the surface of objects works well without having to align the image, but if the texture image file is a photo or an image with text such as a soup can label, then having it aligned incorrectly will not give you the effect you want. SketchUp includes a tool that lets you interactively set the alignment of a texture image on the surface of an object. This tool is called the Position Texture tool and it is accessed by right-clicking on the face that has a textured material applied to it and choosing Texture ➪ Position.

 **The Texture pop-up menu only appears when you right-click on a selected face.**

This command displays four pin controls, as shown in Figure 19.20. You can click and drag the controls to change the placement of the texture image. These pins include the following, and each pin is color-coded:

- **Move (red):** This pin allows you to move the texture.
- **Scale/Rotate (green):** This pin lets you uniformly scale the size of the texture by dragging left and right or to rotate the texture about the Move pin by dragging up and down.

317

- **Scale/Shear (blue):** This pin lets you vertically scale the texture by dragging up and down, or you can shear the texture by dragging to the side.
- **Distort (yellow):** This pin lets you change the perspective of the texture.

When the Position Texture tool is active, you can select from some useful menu options using the right-click pop-up menu. These options include Reset, to undo any changes made with the tool; Flip, either Left/Right or Up/Down; Rotate, 90, 180, or 270 degrees; and Undo and Redo.

After clicking the Done option, the manipulated texture is frozen to the selected face. Figure 19.21 shows a texture that has been enlarged and rotated.

FIGURE 19.20

The texture pins control the image placement.

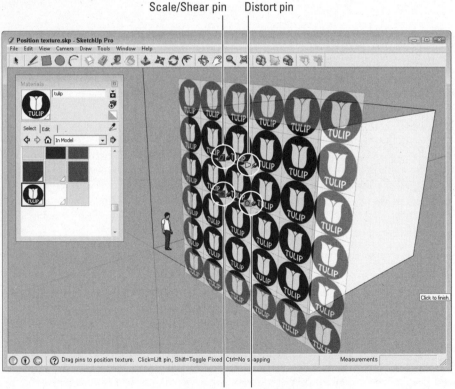

FIGURE 19.21

Once placed, the texture is frozen to the selected face.

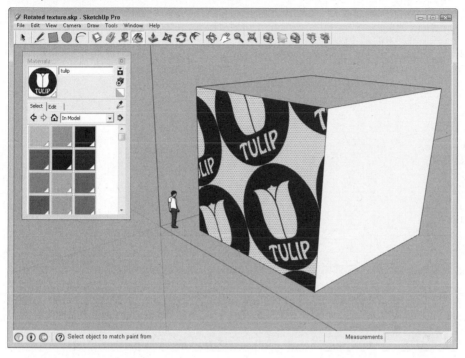

Summary

The ability to add materials and textures to objects helps a great deal in improving the visual look of the scene objects. Materials are selected using the Material Browser and applied using the Paint Bucket tool. The Paint Bucket tool includes some keyboard help for applying materials to many faces at once. The Material Browser can also be used to create new materials and to edit existing materials. Finally, the Position Texture tool is used to move, scale, shear, and rotate applied textures.

This chapter covered the following topics:

- Using the Material Browser to select and organize materials
- Applying materials with the Paint Bucket tool
- Creating new materials with color, texture, and opacity
- Controlling texture placement with the Position Texture tool.

Another way to change the look of models is with Styles using the Styles Browser, which is covered in the next chapter.

Chapter 20

Using Styles

When I sketch, I like to use a wet, black ink pen. In fact, I'm so particular about the pen I use that I keep it close by my sketching book at all times. I used to like a pencil with a gummy eraser that enabled me to erase lines and to draw lightly at first, but now I find that the pen gets me to results quicker.

The drawing tool that I use to sketch on paper gives my sketches a specific look that I like with clean, crisp lines. However, if I happen to drag my hand over the wet ink, it smears, which often ruins the drawing.

SketchUp has a way to apply specific styles to the current model that simulate drawing with different types of pens and pencils. These styles are selected and applied from the Styles browser, and happily, they don't ever smear the ink.

IN THIS CHAPTER

Using the Styles browser

Applying styles

Editing style edges, faces, and backgrounds

Adding watermarks

Using the Styles Browser

The Styles browser holds all the preloaded styles that are available for use in your current scene. You can open this browser by choosing Window ➪ Styles. The browser is displayed in Figure 20.1.

CROSS-REF You can also create your own custom styles using Style Builder, which is covered in Chapter 21.

All styles within the Styles browser are divided into categories separated into folders. The styles in the current category are displayed as thumbnails. The available categories are displayed when you select the Styles category from the drop-down list. You can change the displayed category by selecting a new category from the selection drop-down list or by clicking on the folder thumbnail. The default style categories include the following:

FIGURE 20.1

The Styles browser includes several predefined styles.

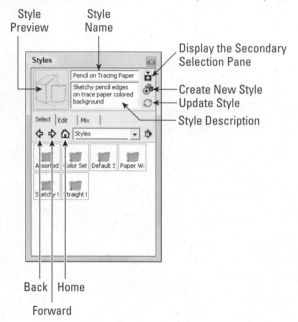

- **Assorted Styles:** This style folder includes many common drawing styles such as blueprint, Google Earth, monochrome, pencil on tracing paper, spray paint on brick, standard CAD, watercolor, and white board.

- **Color Sets:** This style folder holds a number of key color-coordinated drawing styles including blues, greens, red brick, and so on.

- **Default Styles:** This style folder includes the default drawing methods that are available in the View menu.

- **Paper Watermarks:** This style folder holds several watermark methods including Canvas, Chipboard, Masonite, and Watercolor Paper.

- **Sketchy Edges:** This style folder includes a large assortment of different drawing utensils such as airbrush, brush, charcoal, conte, crayon, marker, pen, pencil, and so on.

- **Straight Lines:** This style folder contains a series of straight lines ranging in thickness from 1 pixel to 10 pixels.

Applying a style

When a style thumbnail is selected, its preview is displayed at the top of the browser along with its name and a description, if it has one. The selected styles can then be applied into the current scene by simply clicking on the style thumbnail. Figure 20.2 shows a scene with the blueprint style applied.

Styles are applied by simply clicking on the style thumbnail in the Styles browser.

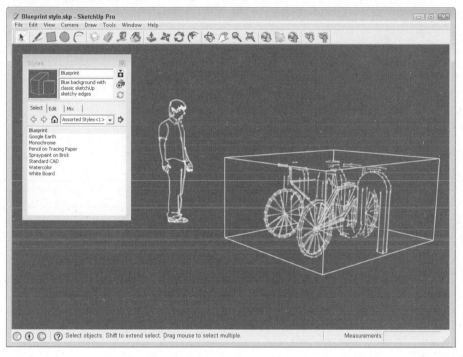

As you move back and forth through the various categories, SketchUp keeps track of your navigation and lets you move forward and back through your selections using the Forward and Back buttons. The Home button lets you see the In Model category, which shows the styles available in the current scene.

Changing the browser display

Using the browser menu, you can switch between Small, Medium, Large, and Extra Large Thumbnails. Figure 20.3 shows the browser with Extra Large thumbnails.

The browser menu also includes an option to display the styles as a list. Figure 20.4 shows the browser in List view.

FIGURE 20.3

The browser menu includes options for changing the thumbnail size.

FIGURE 20.4

Styles can also be displayed as a list.

Moving styles between libraries

The Styles browser can open two selection panes at once using the Display Secondary Selection Pane button at the top right of the browser. Both selection panes include the same Forward, Back, and Home buttons for navigating through the viewed styles. They also both include a library drop-down list and browser menu button.

One way to use both selection panes is to keep the various libraries open in one pane and thumb-nails of the styles in the other. You can move styles between the various libraries by clicking and dragging a thumbnail from one pane to the other. If a dragged thumbnail is dropped on another library thumbnail, the dropped thumbnail is added to the library. Figure 20.5 shows the Styles browser with both panes open.

FIGURE 20.5

When both selection panes are open, you can easily move styles to different folders.

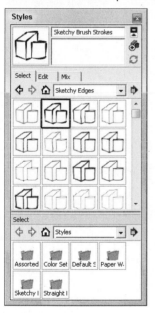

Editing Existing Styles

In the top selection pane are two additional tabs for accessing the Edit and Mix panes. The Edit pane, shown in Figure 20.6, presents several options for controlling the various style settings. The Edit pane consists of five panes that are located right under the Edit tab. Each of these panes lets you access a different set of style settings including Edge, Face, Background, Watermark, and Modeling. The name of the current pane is displayed to the right of the pane icons.

FIGURE 20.6

The Edit pane includes options for changing the style settings.

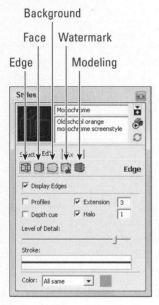

If any of the settings found in the Edit pane are changed, the changes are immediately shown in the style preview and a small overlay is placed on top of the thumbnail to indicate that a change has been made to the style, as shown in Figure 20.7. To make these changes permanent, click the thumbnail or click the Update Style button. If you select a different style before making the changes permanent, the setting changes are lost.

FIGURE 20.7

The update style symbols are shown on the style thumbnail when a setting has been changed.

Changing edge style

The Edge settings allow you to turn on or off the various types of edge highlighting. If the Display Edges option is deselected, the edges are only visible by shading or by a change in material, as shown in Figure 20.8.

FIGURE 20.8

If the Display Edges option is deselected, the edges aren't marked.

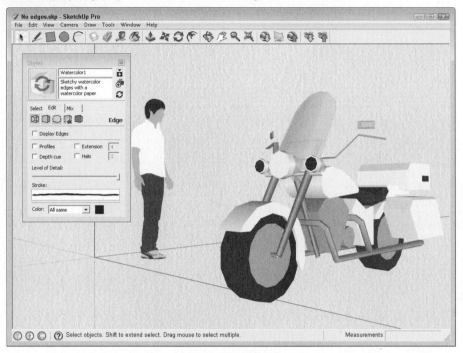

By selecting the Display Edges option, all model edges are displayed, as shown in Figure 20.9. The thickness, style, and color of the lines can be altered.

FIGURE 20.9

If the Display Edges option is selected, the edges are visible.

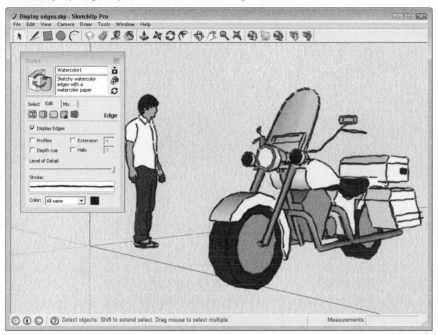

The Profiles option causes lines that make up the model's profile to be emphasized. This is most apparent when the Display Edges option is deselected, as shown in Figure 20.10, but it can be used in conjunction with the Display Edges option, also.

FIGURE 20.10

The Profiles option causes the outer lines of each object to be highlighted.

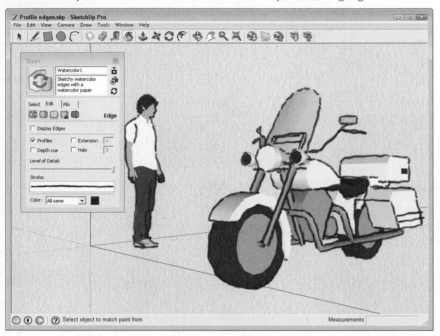

The Depth Cue option causes edges that are closer to the camera to be thicker, and the edge thickness gradually decreases for objects farther from the camera causing a depth cue effect. This option is only available when the Display Edges option is selected. Figure 20.11 shows this effect in the road that recedes to the back.

FIGURE 20.11

The Depth Cue option causes lines farther from the camera to be thinner.

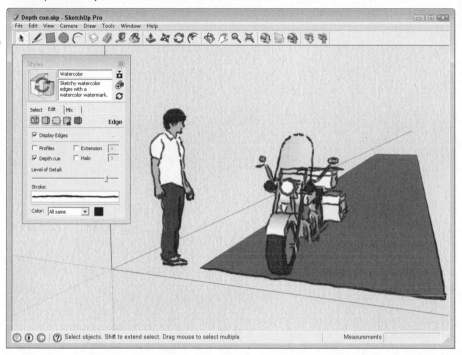

The Extension option gives the model a hand-drawn look by extending the line a given distance beyond where it would normally end, as shown in Figure 20.12. The value to the right of the Extension option is the length in pixels to extend the line. This option is only available if the Display Edges or the Profiles option is selected.

FIGURE 20.12

Selecting the Extension option causes the lines to extend beyond where they should end.

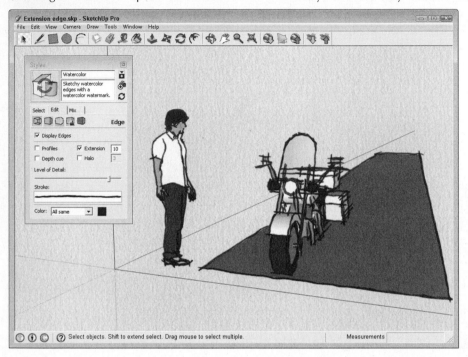

The Halo option simplifies the interior lines by causing the line to end before it intersects with another line. This clears a lot of the lines that complicate the drawing, and you can set the distance away from the intersection where the line should stop. Figure 20.13 shows this effect. This option is only available when the Display Edges or the Profiles option is selected. It is also only available for Sketchy Edge styles.

FIGURE 20.13

The Halo option stops drawing a line before it intersects with another.

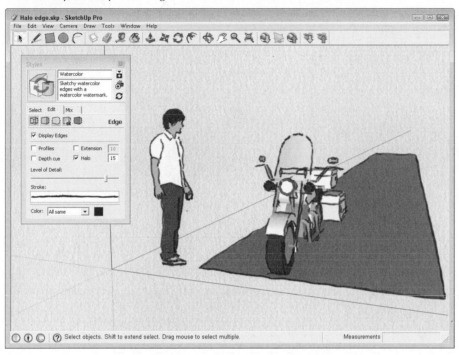

The Level of Detail slider provides another way to simplify the number of lines. For example, items that are located farther from the camera shouldn't be drawn with the same number of lines as those items that are close to the camera. By lowering the Level of Detail slider, you can reduce the total number of lines that are drawn, as shown in Figure 20.14.

By lowering the Level of Detail slider, you can simplify the number of lines.

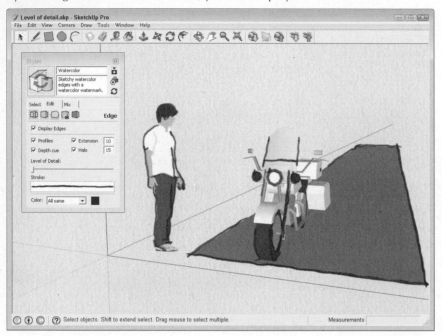

The Color drop-down list has three options:

- **All same:** Selecting this option causes all lines to be drawn using the same color. The color is set using the color swatch to the right of the color drop-down list.

- **By material:** This option colors the edges using the assigned material color.

- **By axis:** This color option causes all edges to be displayed using the color that corresponds to the axis that the line is parallel to, so all lines that are parallel to the X-axis are colored red and so on, as shown in Figure 20.15. Any lines that aren't exactly parallel to an axis are colored using the designated color swatch.

FIGURE 20.15

The Color By axis option causes all lines that are parallel to an axis to match the axis color.

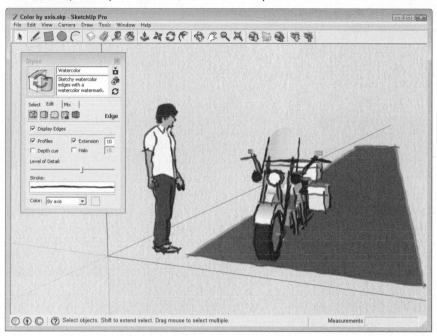

The Edge pane, shown previously, applies for Sketchy Edge styles, but for other style types, the Edge pane includes some other settings including Endpoints and Jitter, as shown in Figure 20.16. Notice also that for this pane, the Profiles and Depth Cue settings have a value where you can change the line thickness.

FIGURE 20.16

For nonsketchy styles, the Edge pane has some additional options.

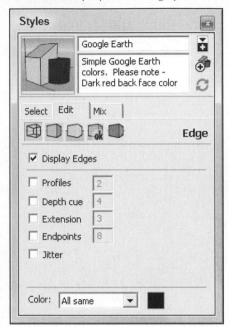

The Endpoints option highlights the end of each line with a thicker line, as shown in Figure 20.17. The value next to the Endpoints option defines the distance in pixels from the end of the line that is highlighted. This option is only available when the Display Edges or the Profiles option is selected.

FIGURE 20.17

The Endpoints option highlights the end of each line.

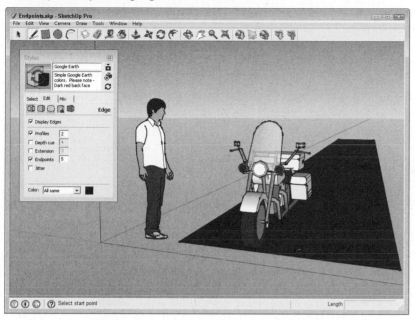

The Jitter option causes the lines to be drawn multiple times at random offsets, which gives the resulting drawing a hand-drawn look, as shown in Figure 20.18.

FIGURE 20.18

The Jitter option gives the drawing a hand-drawn look.

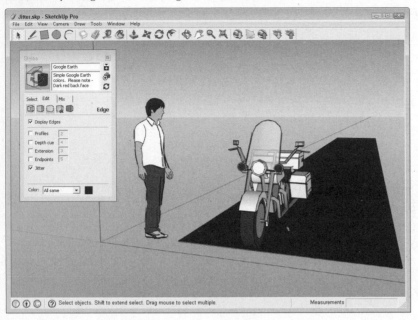

Changing face style

The Face pane in the Styles browser, shown in Figure 20.19, offers settings for controlling the look, style, and color of the face entities. The Front and Back color swatches are used to set the colors for all front and back faces. These colors provide a way to identify the direction that the model faces are pointing. If a material is applied to a face, then the material takes precedence over the front and back colors.

> **TIP** If you are unsure of the direction a face entity is pointing, try setting the Front and Back colors to a bright, easy-to-spot color like green or red. This will immediately highlight any problem faces.

FIGURE 20.19

The Face pane includes settings for selecting the various default display options.

Wireframe   Shaded using all same

Shaded

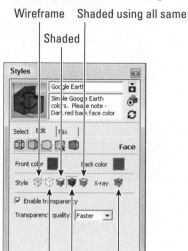

Hidden Line   X-Ray

Shaded with Textures

The Style icons in the Face pane let you switch among the various display settings. The Wireframe setting displays all lines without any face shading or textures. The lines are subject to the settings in the Edge pane. Figure 20.20 shows the Wireframe option.

 **Face entities cannot be selected when the Wireframe display is selected.**

FIGURE 20.20

The Wireframe display option shows all model lines.

Wireframe display option

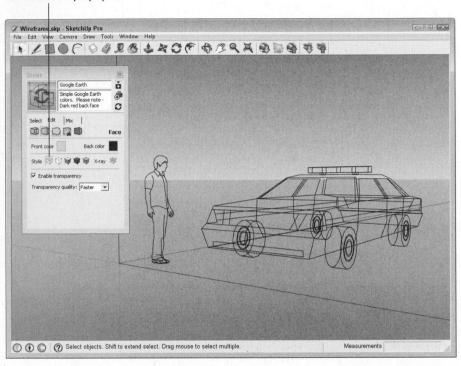

The Hidden Line display option displays all faces using the same flat color along with the lines that are facing the camera, as shown in Figure 20.21. All lines that are obscured by a face entity are hidden from view.

 **The Hidden Line display option is a good choice if you are printing the drawing on a black-and-white printer.**

FIGURE 20.21

The Hidden Line display option shows all faces using the same flat color.

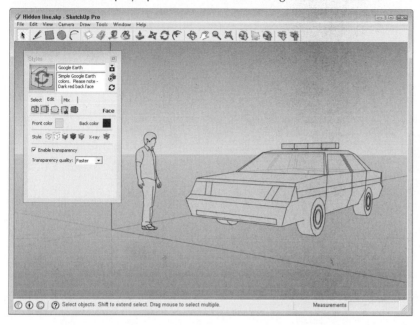

The Shaded display option displays all faces using any applied material colors. It also shades faces based on their orientation to the light source, but each face is shaded equally across its entire face with the same color, as shown in Figure 20.22.

FIGURE 20.22

The Shaded display option displays faces using any applied material colors.

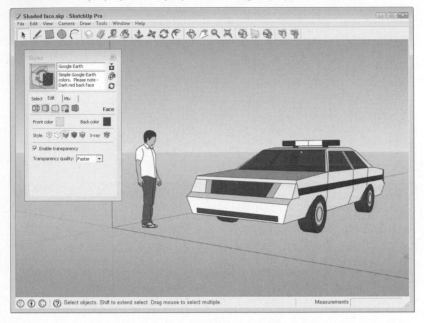

The Shaded with Texture display option works just like the Shaded option, but it also displays any material textures that are applied to face objects, as shown in Figure 20.23.

FIGURE 20.23

The Shaded with Textures display option also displays any applied material textures.

Shaded with textures display option

The Shaded Using All Same display option is also referred to as the Monochrome option. It displays entire objects using either the Front or Back color, depending on which side is facing the camera, as shown in Figure 20.24.

FIGURE 20.24

The Shaded Using All Same, also called the Monochrome, display option colors all objects using the front or back color.

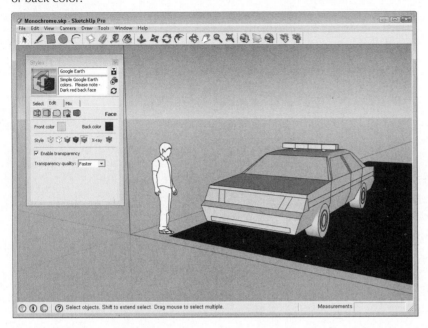

The X-ray option can be selected simultaneously with any of the other display styles. It causes all faces to be semitransparent, making it possible to see the edges on the back side of the object, as shown in Figure 20.25.

FIGURE 20.25

The X-ray display option can be selected along with any of the other display styles.

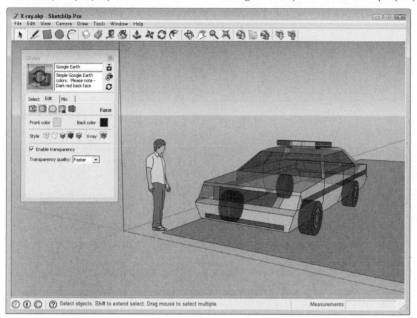

The Enable transparency option lets you turn all semitransparent materials within the entire model on or off. Figure 20.26 shows the model with the Enable Transparency option deselected. Because drawing transparent faces can take some time, you may experience a slowdown in your refresh rate as you navigate the model with the Enable Transparency option selected, so SketchUp offers three Transparency Quality options. The Faster option is the quickest, but results in the poorest results. The Medium option is faster; the Nicer option has the best quality.

FIGURE 20.26

By deselecting the Enable Transparency option, you can turn off all semitransparent materials.

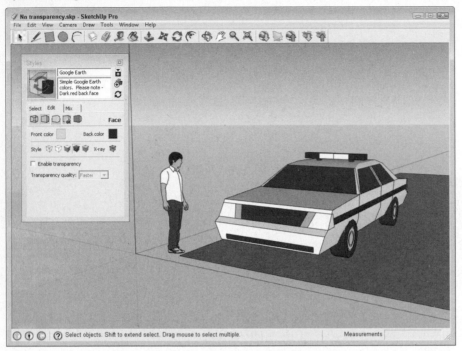

Changing the background style

The Background pane in the Styles browser, shown in Figure 20.27, offers settings for controlling the color and transparency of the background, sky, and ground.

The Background color swatch lets you change the background color that is applied to the entire background, as shown in Figure 20.28.

FIGURE 20.27

The Background pane includes an option to change the background color.

FIGURE 20.28

The Background color swatch controls the background color.

Background color swatch

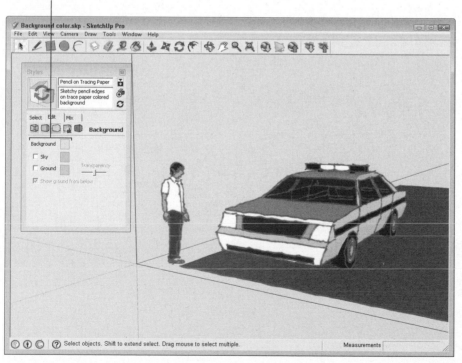

If the Sky and Ground options are selected, they are displayed over the top of the background color. The Sky color gradually lowers to meet the horizon as a gradient, but the ground color is constant, as shown in Figure 20.29.

The Transparency slider to the right of the Ground color lets you control the transparency of the ground plane. If you rotate the model so the view is underneath the ground plane, you can cause the ground plane to be visible with the Show ground from below option. If the ground plane is semitransparent, then you can see the model through the ground plane, as shown in Figure 20.30. If the Show ground from below option is not selected, the ground plane isn't visible when viewed from beneath.

FIGURE 20.29

The Sky and Ground options and color swatches let you add a recessed horizon to the scene.

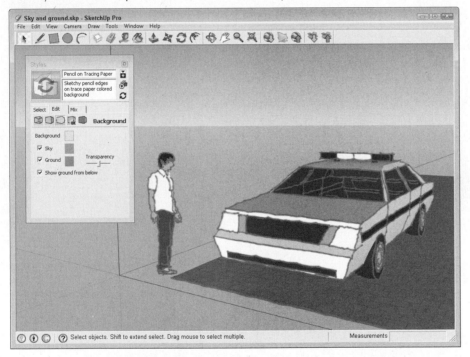

FIGURE 20.30

You can make the ground plane visible from beneath the model.

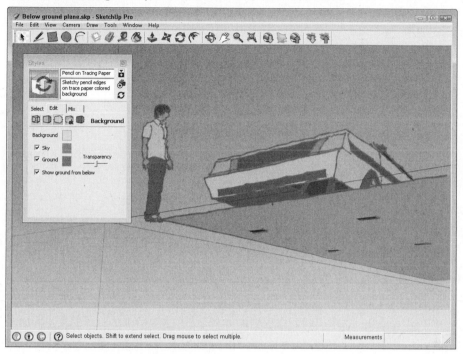

Adding a watermark

Watermarks are any image that is added to a drawing as an overlay. They are usually used to identify a company logo or specific copyright information. You can add watermarks to the current model using the Watermark pane in the Styles browser. The Watermark pane, shown in Figure 20.31, lets you open several watermark images and organize them within the drawing.

To add a new watermark image to the drawing, click the Add Watermark button in the Watermark pane. This opens a file dialog box where you can browse for an image to open. The available image formats include JPEG, PNG, TIF, TGA, and BMP. After selecting an image file, the Create Watermark dialog box, shown in Figure 20.32, appears. This dialog box is the first of a three-step wizard that lets you specify the settings for the watermark. The Next and Previous buttons let you move forward and back through the wizard pages.

CROSS-REF   You can learn more about these different image formats in Chapter 4.

FIGURE 20.31

The Watermark pane lets you open and add watermark images to the drawing.

Add Watermark

Delete Watermark

Edit Watermark Settings

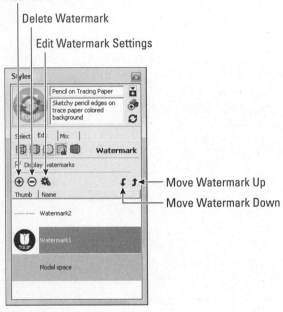

Move Watermark Up

Move Watermark Down

FIGURE 20.32

The Create Watermark dialog box lets you name the watermark file.

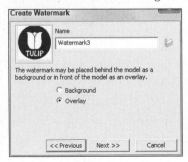

The first page of the Create Watermark Wizard lets you type a name for the watermark file. This name is displayed in the Watermark pane of the Styles browser. This first page also lets you choose to place the watermark as a Background image or as an overlaid image. The Create Watermark dialog box also shows a preview of the watermark file in the upper-left corner.

The second page of the Create Watermark Wizard, shown in Figure 20.33, lets you specify to use the brightness of the watermark image as a mask and to change the watermark's transparency to blend with the model or to be opaque.

FIGURE 20.33

The second page of the Create Watermark Wizard also lets you blend the image with the model.

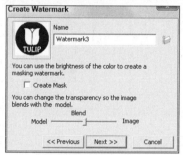

The third and final page of the Create Watermark Wizard, shown in Figure 20.34, lets you select how the watermark is fitted to the drawing.

FIGURE 20.34

The final page of the Create Watermark Wizard sets how the watermark is positioned.

When two or more watermark images are added to the Watermark pane, the Move Watermark Up and Down buttons become active, allowing you to change the order of the watermarks.

After you add a watermark image to the list of watermarks, you can revisit any of the settings made in the Create Watermark Wizard by selecting the watermark and clicking the Edit Watermark Settings button. This opens the Edit Watermark dialog box, as shown in Figure 20.35.

FIGURE 20.35

The Edit Watermark dialog box lets you change any of the watermark settings.

Watermark   Browse
preview   for Image

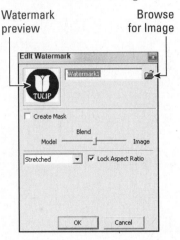

In the first page of the Create Watermark Wizard, you can specify whether the watermark image is posted as a background, as shown in Figure 20.36, or as an Overlay, as shown in Figure 20.37. For each type of watermark, you can set the Blend amount using the slider, which ranges between fully transparent at the Model end of the slider to fully opaque at the Image end of the slider.

The Create Mask option causes the dark areas of the watermark image to be colored using the background color, which is set in the Background pane of the Styles browser, and all white areas in the watermark image are made transparent, as shown in Figure 20.38.

The Background option causes the watermark image to appear in the background behind the model.

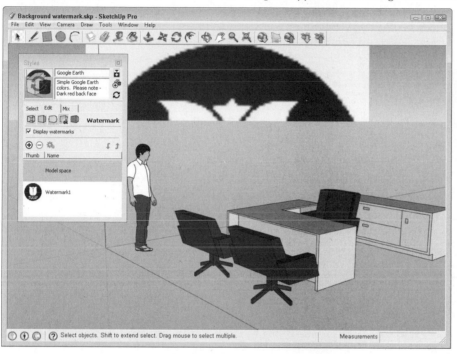

FIGURE 20.37

The Overlay option causes the watermark image to appear on top of the current model.

FIGURE 20.38

The Create Mask option colors the black areas of the watermark mask to the background color.

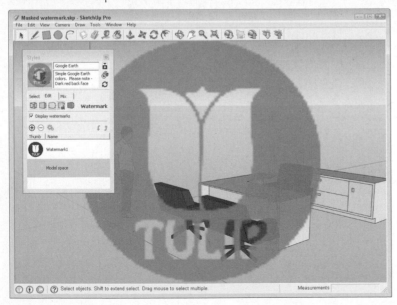

The watermark display drop-down list under the Blend slider includes three options. These same options can be set in the third page of the Create Watermark Wizard. These options include the following:

- **Stretched:** This option sizes the watermark image to fill the entire drawing area. If the Lock Aspect Ratio option is selected, the image keeps its width-to-height ratio. Figure 20.39 shows a watermark with the Stretched option when the Lock Aspect Ratio option is deselected.

FIGURE 20.39

The Stretched display option causes the watermark to fill the drawing area.

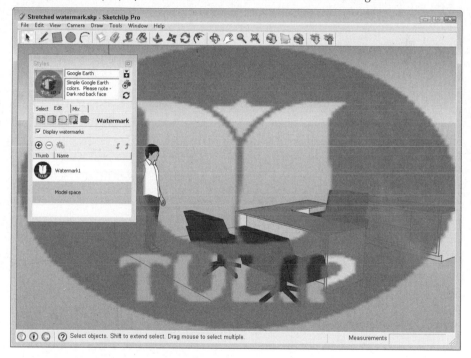

- **Tiled:** This option tiles the watermark end to end to fill the entire drawing area. When this option is selected, a Scale slider appears under the display drop-down list that you can use to set the size of the individual tiles. Figure 20.40 shows this display option.
- **Positioned:** This option lets you scale and position the watermark image in the center or in the corners or edges of the drawing area using the controls that appear in the Edit Watermark dialog box, as shown in Figure 20.41. Figure 20.42 shows an example of this option.

FIGURE 20.40

The Tiled display option causes the watermark to fill the entire drawing area.

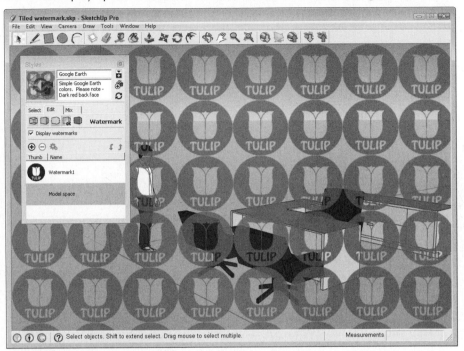

FIGURE 20.41

The Edit Watermark dialog box lets you specify where the watermark is located.

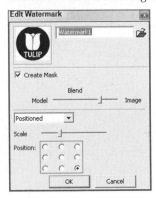

FIGURE 20.42

Using the Watermark Settings panel, you can place a nice watermark logo in the lower-right corner of the scene.

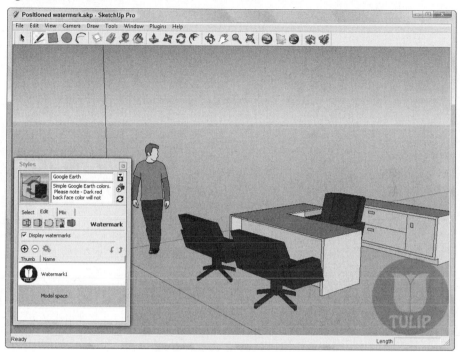

One unique way to use watermarks is to add a textured image as an overlay watermark to give the drawing area the look as if it were drawn on a textured paper. The Paper Watermark folder in the Styles browser offers some examples of this. Figure 20.43 shows a canvas texture applied as a watermark.

FIGURE 20.43

Texture images can be overlaid as a watermark to give the drawing area a texture.

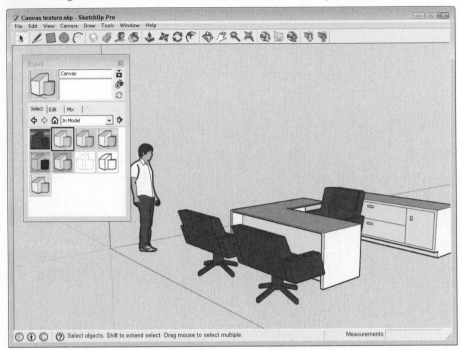

Changing modeling colors

The Modeling pane, shown in Figure 20.44, includes settings for the various colors for different modeling objects. This pane also includes options for hiding or displaying specific object types.

The available colors that you can set in the Modeling pane include the following:

- **Selected:** This color marks the highlighted color for the selected objects.
- **Locked:** This color marks the highlighted color for any locked objects.
- **Guides:** This color marks the color used for any guides.
- **Inactive Section:** This color marks the color for any inactive section objects.
- **Active Section:** This color marks the color for any active section objects.
- **Section Cuts:** This color marks the color used to show any section cuts. There is also a Section Cut Width value measured in pixels that you can set.

FIGURE 20.44

The Modeling pane in the Style browser lets you change the color of different objects.

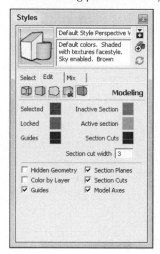

Below the modeling colors are several display options, including the following:

- **Hidden Geometry:** This option makes any hidden geometry visible in the current style.
- **Color by Layer:** This option makes any hidden geometry visible in the current style.
- **Guides:** This option displays any guides when enabled.
- **Section Planes:** This option makes any section planes visible in the current style.
- **Section Cuts:** This option makes any section cuts visible in the current style.
- **Model Axes:** This option makes the model axes visible in the current style.

Most of these display options are also available in the View menu, but the Modeling pane defines their visibility for the current style.

Mixing styles

If you have a style edge setting that you like that you want to add to a new style that you're creating, you can use the Mix pane to combine different style definitions. When the Mix pane is selected, two panes are displayed, as shown in Figure 20.45. To add a set of definitions from the style displayed in the lower pane, simply click and drag the desired style onto the type of settings that you want to mix into the current style.

For example, if you have a base style in the top preview, but you want to mix in the edge settings from another thumbnail, then find the thumbnail of the style that has the edge settings that you want to borrow and click and drag from that thumbnail to the Edge Settings row in the Mix pane. The edge settings are then copied into the current style.

FIGURE 20.45

The Mix pane lets you combine specific settings to the current style.

Summary

The Styles browser lets you define the look and settings for several key entities including the edges and faces. By defining unique styles that can be saved into libraries, you can give your drawing a custom look that makes it unique. There are several style aspects that you can change including the edge, face, and background settings. You can also use the Styles Brower to add watermarks to your model.

This chapter covered the following topics:

- Using the Styles browser
- Adding styles to the current scene
- Setting style edge and face properties
- Changing the background colors
- Adding and configuring watermark images
- Mixing different styles together

The next chapter presents adding certain effects to the model, including fog, and sectioning a model.

Chapter 21

Using Style Builder

Although the Styles palette has a large number of available presets, it might not have the exact look that you want for your model. To help define your own custom look, you can use the Style Builder program.

The tool, which is actually a separate application, ships with SketchUp and lets you create your own custom styles.

CROSS-REF You can learn more about styles and the Styles Browser in Chapter 20.

Learning the Style Builder Interface

The Style Builder interface is similar to the other SketchUp applications that use various menus, panels, and windows. The main interface, shown in Figure 21.1, is divided into three panels. The left panel holds the Sample Strokes, the top panel holds the current selection set of sketched strokes, and the bottom panel displays a preview model.

FIGURE 21.1

The Style Builder interface is divided into three panels.

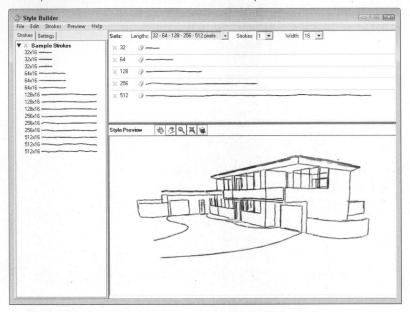

Loading Sample Strokes

In the left window, you can switch between two panels using the tabs at the top. The Strokes panel shows a collection of sample strokes loaded from a template. These template files are image files that hold the various strokes. These files can be PNG, BMP, or TIFF files. Each stroke is 8, 16, 32, or 64 pixels high, and 16, 32, 64, 128, 256, or 512 pixels wide depending on the size of the stroke.

You can quickly create each of the needed template sizes by choosing File ⇨ Generate Templates to open the Style Template Generator dialog box, as shown in Figure 21.2. After selecting the specific Stroke lengths, the Stroke per set, and the Stroke width values that you need, click Save As to create the template files.

The drawing style for each stroke is made by combining strokes of several different lengths together. By matching the length of the actual line to a stroke that is similar in length, the style ends up being unique. For each stroke set, you can choose the stroke lengths, but you should use a style that includes a variety of stroke lengths. You can also set the number of strokes per set. If only one stroke is defined for each length, then the style looks redundant. Using several different strokes per set gives the style a great variation, which helps if you are going for a hand-drawn sketch look. Finally, you can set the Stroke width value. This determines the vertical size of each stroke. With a larger vertical space, the stroke can deviate a greater distance from the midline.

FIGURE 21.2

The Style Template Generator creates a document with all the specified strokes.

The Style Template file includes spaces for all the necessary strokes. It also includes a UPC code at the top of the template. This code is used by the Style Builder program to automatically load the new strokes into the interface. Figure 21.3 shows a sample template file saved as a PNG file. The template includes marks on either side of the space to show the midline for each line.

FIGURE 21.3

The Style Template file includes a space for each unique stroke.

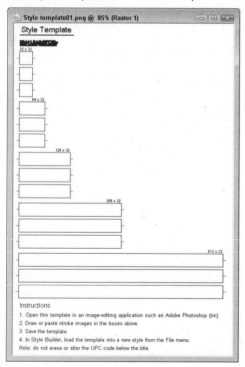

 As long as the midlines are consistent at each end, the lines will connect seamlessly.

New strokes can be loaded into the Sample Strokes panel by choosing File ⇨ Load Template. Figure 21.4 shows a figure with a new set of strokes loaded.

FIGURE 21.4

Loading a new set of strokes into the Sample Strokes panel gives you more samples to choose from.

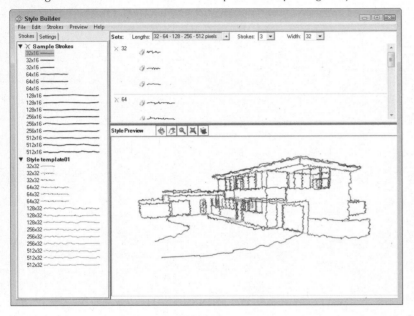

Defining a New Style

Clicking the Settings tab opens several settings that help to define the new style, as shown in Figure 21.5. Using these fields, you can give the style a name. This name is the name that is used within SketchUp's Style palette. You can also specify a Dropout length, which is the length at which the line fades out. High Dropout length values cause only the longest lines to remain. The Fade factor value sets the length over which the line fades out. There is also a color swatch for changing the line color.

The Edge effects section lets you include several edge effects. These are the same effects that are available within the Styles palette in SketchUp.

CROSS-REF You can learn more about the various edge effects in Chapter 20.

After defining a style and setting its attributes, you can save the style by choosing File ➪ Save As. Styles are saved as STYLE files, and these files can then be opened and used within SketchUp's Styles palette. To add a new style to SketchUp's Styles palette, just place the saved STYLE file within the Styles folder where SketchUp is installed and restart SketchUp. Figure 21.6 shows the default SketchUp interface with the Squiggle lines style applied.

FIGURE 21.5

The Settings panel lets you name and specify the line characteristics.

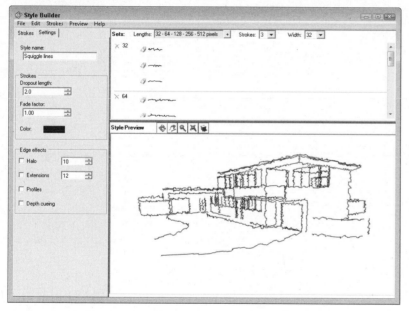

New defined styles can be used within SketchUp.

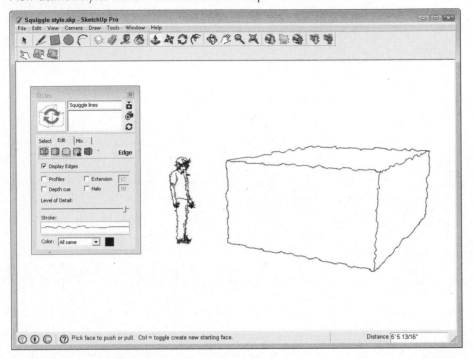

Selecting a stroke set

When a new set of stroke samples is loaded into the Stroke Sample panel, the new strokes are automatically applied to the current style, but you can selectively choose which strokes are used by clicking and dragging strokes from the left panel to the top panel.

If you drop a stroke of one size into a space with a different size, then a Resizing Strokes dialog box appears, as shown in Figure 21.7. You can use this dialog box to either Scale the stroke image or Crop or pad the stroke image.

Using the settings at the top of the Sets panel, you can add or remove stroke lengths, increase or decrease the number of strokes in the set, or change the width of the stroke. When adjusting the Width setting, a Change Stroke Width dialog box, as shown in Figure 21.8, appears. This dialog box lets you change the stroke width by either scaling the stroke vertically or by cropping or padding the vertical space. This dialog box can be eliminated using the Preferences dialog box.

FIGURE 21.7

If different-sized strokes are dropped, then you can scale or crop or pad the stroke.

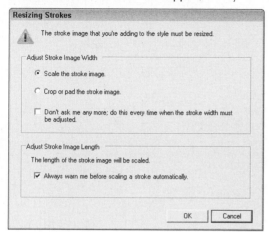

> **CAUTION** Be aware that if you select the Crop or padding option, then any portions of the stroke that are above that specified width are removed, which could result in some open gaps.

FIGURE 21.8

The Change Stroke Width dialog box lets you alter the stroke width by scaling or cropping or padding.

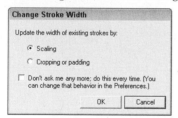

Controlling the preview

The Style Preview pane provides a quick look at the current style. The default house model can be switched out for a different model by choosing Preview ⇨ Change Model. Figure 21.9 shows Style Builder with a different loaded model.

FIGURE 21.9

Style Builder lets you load a different model.

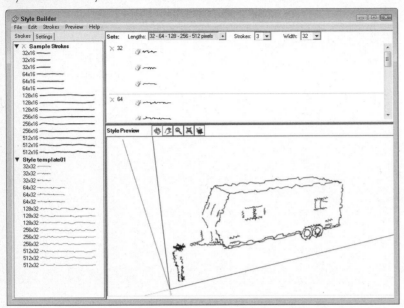

At the top of the Style Preview pane are several navigation tools for controlling the position and orientation of the preview model. These tools include the Orbit, Pan, Zoom, Zoom Extents, and Toggle Shadows tools, as shown in Figure 21.10.

NOTE You can also press Alt+middle scroll mouse wheel and Shift+middle scroll mouse wheel to rotate and pan the preview pane.

FIGURE 21.10

The Style Preview pane includes tools for navigation of the Style Preview pane.

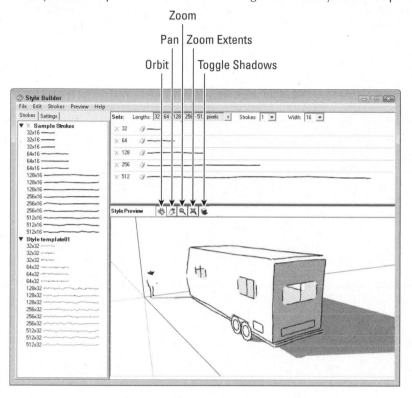

Setting preferences

The Preferences dialog box, as shown in Figure 21.11, offers several ways to have the program warn you with a dialog box when the style has a blank stroke, has no name, or when the stroke needs to be adjusted. Choose Edit ➪ Preferences to display this dialog box.

FIGURE 21.11

The Preferences dialog box lets you turn warning dialog boxes on or off.

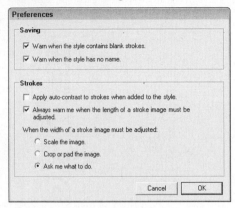

Summary

The Style Builder program provides a unique way to create and implement your own custom styles. Styles created with this program can be added to the Styles folder, which loads them directly to the Styles palette in SketchUp.

Using the templates that Style Builder can create, you can quickly create your own custom strokes.

This chapter covered the following topics:

- Learning the Style Builder interface
- Loading sample strokes
- Defining style settings
- Selecting a stroke set
- Using the Style Preview window
- Setting preferences

The next chapter presents adding certain effects to the model, including fog, and sectioning a model.

Chapter 22

Adding Effects

Before continuing on, there are a couple of additional features that are considered miscellaneous. These features are being called effects because they are unique from the other tools.

The Fog effect adds a layer of fog over the top of the drawing, causing all objects to become brighter. The Section Plane effect lets you cut and display the interior of a model.

IN THIS CHAPTER

Adding and configuring fog

Sectioning an object

Extracting a cross section

Exporting section slices

Adding Fog to the Scene

The Fog effect is useful for casting a light or heavy fog over the entire drawing. One of the benefits of this effect is that you can set a scene with fog and another without fog and animate between them. Using fog in this manner can be used to slowly fade out a current drawing.

CROSS-REF You can learn more about creating and animating scenes in Chapter 17.

Fog is applied to the current drawing using the Fog panel, shown in Figure 22.1. Choose Window ⇨ Fog to open this panel.

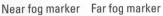

FIGURE 22.1

The Fog panel is used to apply fog to the drawing.

Near fog marker   Far fog marker

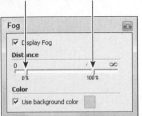

Enabling fog

Fog can be turned on and off using the Display Fog option in the Fog panel. You can also choose View ⇨ Fog. For most scenes, the fog effect appears as a brightening in the scene. Figure 22.2 shows a scene without fog, and Figure 22.3 shows the same scene with fog.

FIGURE 22.2

This scene has no fog.

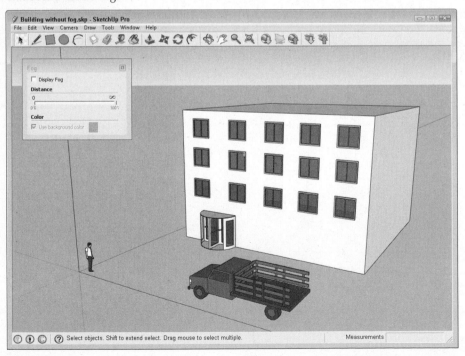

FIGURE 22.3

Adding fog hides some of the details.

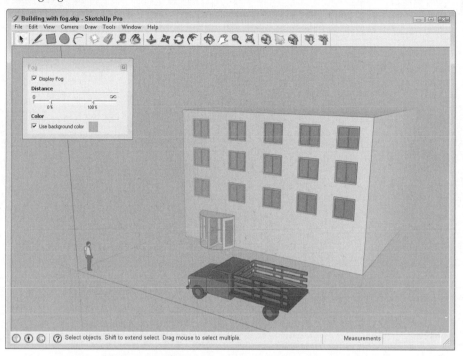

Setting fog distance

On the Distance slider in the Fog panel, you find two markers. The left marker is the Near fog marker. It marks where the fog starts and is measured relative to the camera. Setting the Near fog marker to 0 starts the fog right in front of the camera. The Near fog marker can be moved to the right to make the fog appear behind the foreground objects. This is a good effect if you have a background that you want to partially obscure with fog.

The right marker on the Distance slider is the Far fog marker. It marks the location where the fog is at a maximum value. The fog gradually thickens as the distance approaches the Far fog marker. If the two markers are close together, then the fog changes abruptly, as shown in Figure 22.4.

Notice also in Figure 22.4 how the fog is always parallel to the camera plane. The fog remains parallel as you rotate the camera. Figure 22.5 shows the fog from a different angle.

FIGURE 22.4

A small distance between the fog markers results in thick fog.

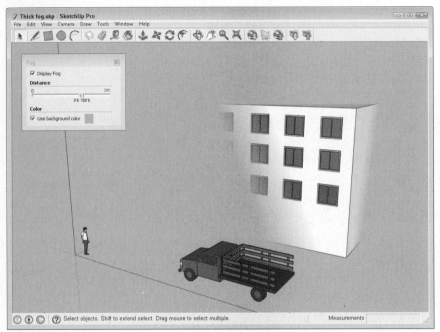

FIGURE 22.5

The fog changes as the camera rotates about the scene.

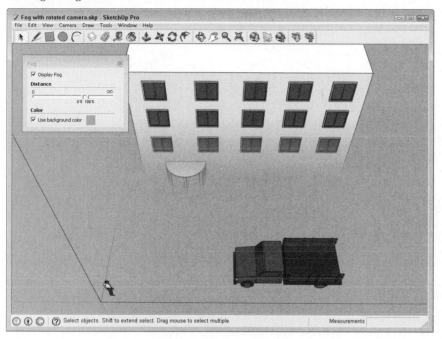

Changing fog color

By default, the fog color is set as the background color. This causes the fog to blend into the background, but you can change the fog color by deselecting the Use Background Color option and clicking on the color swatch. Figure 22.6 shows the scene with a black fog.

FIGURE 22.6

You can change the fog color using the color swatch.

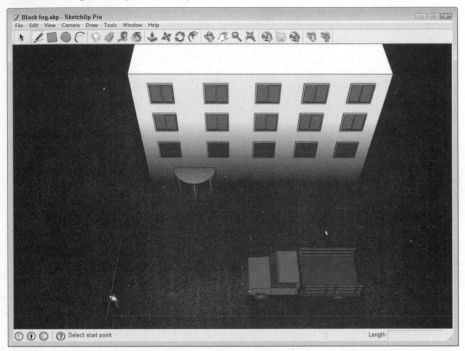

Sectioning an Object

The other key effect covered in this chapter is the Section Plane tool that lets you cut and display the interior of the model. This tool places a plane in the scene that can be moved to precisely where you want the section to appear.

Defining a section plane

To make the section plane appear, choose Tools ⇨ Section Plane. This causes a section plane object, as shown in Figure 22.7, to appear.

A section plane defines where to cut the model.

Section Plane

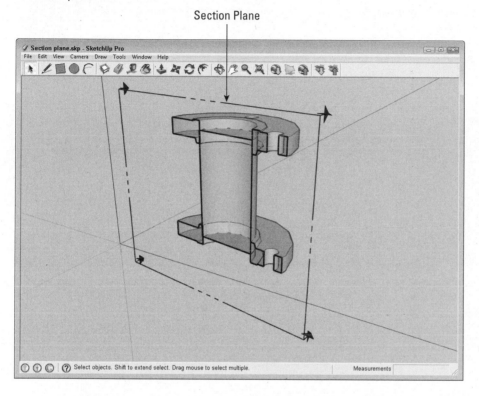

Manipulating the section plane

After you add a section plane to the scene, it can be selected and manipulated just like other objects. Section plane objects are orange by default, but they turn blue when selected just like other objects. When selected, the transform tools can be used to move the section plane, as shown in Figure 22.8. You can also see a different section of an object by moving the object through the section plane.

 **NOTE**   Only the Move and Rotate transform tools can be used on section planes.

FIGURE 22.8

Section planes can be moved to show a different section.

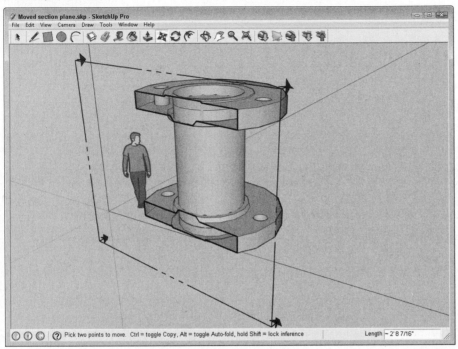

Reversing the section cut

At each corner of the section plane is an arrow that points toward the area of the object that is visible. To reverse these arrows and change the side of the section that is visible, simply right-click on the section plane border and select the Reverse option from the pop-up menu. Figure 22.9 is a reversed view of the object in Figure 22.8.

FIGURE 22.9

The visible section of the sectioned object can be reversed.

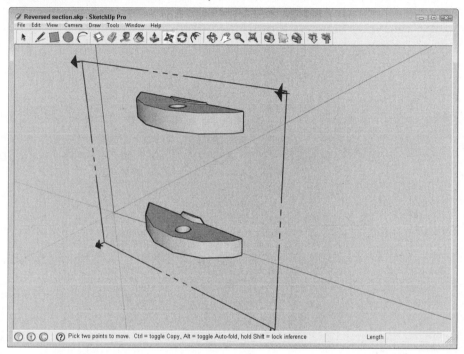

Extracting a cross section

The Create Group from Slice menu command from the right click pop-up menu causes a cross section of the current section to be separated from the section. This slice can be moved and viewed independent of the section. Figure 22.10 shows a cross section created in this manner.

You can also align the view to be perpendicular to the current section using the right-click Align View menu command.

FIGURE 22.10

Cross sections can be separated from the section and moved within the scene.

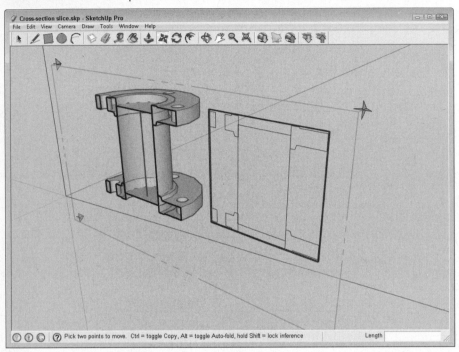

Hiding the section plane

When you finish a drawing that includes a section plane, you can hide the section plane using the Hide command on the right-click pop-up menu. Choosing View ⇨ Hidden Objects makes the hidden object visible so you can work with it again if you need to.

Exporting Section Slices

Cross-section slices that have been created can also be exported for use in CAD packages. Slices show accurate dimensions that aren't impacted by perspective.

 The ability to export section slices is only available in Google SketchUp Pro.

To export a section slice, first select the section slice object and choose File ⇨ Export ⇨ Section Slice. This opens a file dialog box where you can specify a location and name for the image file. Section slices can be saved in either the DWG or DXF file formats. Both of these are vector-based formats.

In the Export 2D Section Slice dialog box, you can access a dialog box of options by clicking Options. The 2D Section Slice Options dialog box, shown in Figure 22.11, includes settings for controlling the scale and line width.

FIGURE 22.11

The 2D Section Slice Options dialog box includes settings for saving section slices.

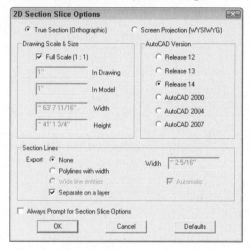

The Projection option lets you export the section slice as a True Section (Orthographic). Orthographic sections are created by looking straight down an axis. It measures the dimensions of objects without any distortion and is useful for CAD drawings. The Screen Projection (WYSIWYG) option shows the section as it is displayed on the screen. The WYSIWYG acronym stands for "What you see is what you get." This option often has perspective and doesn't represent the actual dimensions of the object.

The Drawing Scale & Size options define how the section slice is sized during the export. The Full Scale option exports the slice at a 1-to-1 ratio. The In Drawing and In Model values let you set a unique ratio for the exported drawing where the In Drawing value is the ratio of the exported dimensions and the In Model value is the ratio of the current SketchUp drawing. For example, to export a section slice at 1/4 size, set the In Drawing value to 1 inch and the In Model value to 4 inches.

The AutoCAD Version section lets you choose the AutoCAD version to support. The options include Release 12, 13, 14, AutoCAD 2000, AutoCAD 2004, and AutoCAD 2007. The image formats are typically not backwards compatible, so make sure you save the file in a version that is older or equal to your current version. For example, if you use AutoCAD 2000, then you can open files saved for AutoCAD 2000 or any earlier version, but you won't be able to open the file saved for any later versions.

The Section Lines section lets you set the line thickness. The None option outputs the lines at their normal width. The Polylines with width option lets you specify the width of the lines. The Wide line entities option is only available in AutoCAD 2000 or later and exports lines as a wide-line type. The Separate on a layer option causes the lines to appear on their own layer.

If the Always Prompt for Section Slice Options option is selected, the Options dialog box automatically appears every time a section slice is exported. Clicking Defaults resets all settings to their default values.

Summary

To add to the current drawing, you can use fog and section planes. The fog feature adds a layer of fog, but also lets you configure the fog by changing where it starts and where it reaches a maximum value. You can also change the fog's color. The Section Plane feature lets you cut through an object to show its interior. Section slices can be separated from the sliced object and exported to a CAD package.

This chapter covered the following topics:

- Adding fog to the scene
- Changing the fog distance and color
- Adding and manipulating a section plane
- Reversing the section
- Extracting a section slice
- Exporting a section slice

Another effective drawing technique that is especially good at showing depth is to add shadows to the drawing. This is covered in the next chapter.

Chapter 23

Using Lights and Shadows

IN THIS CHAPTER

Learning the Shadow Settings

Enabling and disabling shadows

Changing shadow time and date

Setting which objects cast and receive shadows

Mother nature provides an excellent way to give 3D objects a sense of depth with shadows. Effective shadows help define the 3D look of an object. Shadows in SketchUp provide support for changing the shadow to a different time and date.

Accessing the Shadow Settings

Lights are enabled by default, but you have complete control over the shadows cast by an object. To access the shadow settings, choose Window ⇨ Shadows to open the Shadow Settings dialog box, as shown in Figure 23.1.

Click the Show/Hide Details button in the top-right corner to show or hide all of the settings beneath the Date setting.

You can also access many of these same shadow settings using the Shadows toolbar, as shown in Figure 23.2. Choose View ⇨ Toolbars ⇨ Shadows to open the Shadows toolbar.

FIGURE 23.1

The Shadow Settings dialog box includes settings for the time and date of the shadows.

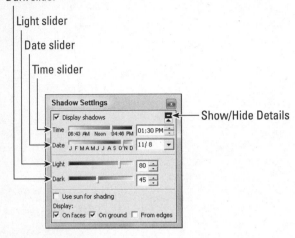

FIGURE 23.2

The Shadows toolbar includes many of the same settings as the Shadow Settings panel.

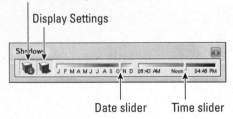

Turning shadows on and off

The first option to learn is the Display Shadows option. This simple check box is used to turn the shadows on and off. Figure 23.3 shows the model without any shadows and Figure 23.4 shows the same model with shadows turned on. Notice how the shadows are cast onto the ground plane and also onto the model objects.

 Shadows can also be turned on and off by choosing View ➪ Shadows.

FIGURE 23.3

The model without any shadows enabled

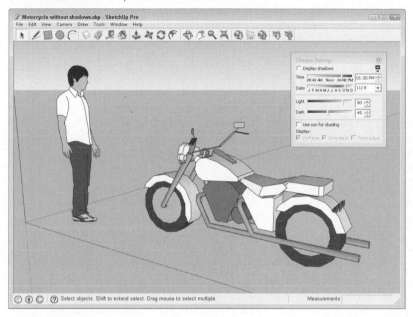

FIGURE 23.4

The same model with shadows enabled

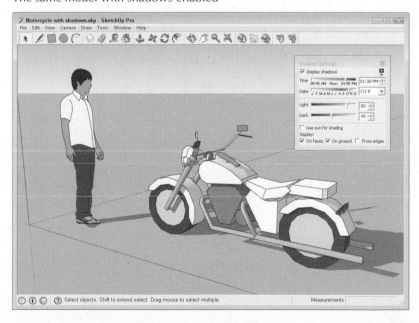

Setting shadow time and date

We all know from experience that shadows at high noon are short and close to the object, but as the day progresses and the sun begins to head toward the horizon shadows get longer and more pronounced. Using the Time slider, you can change the time for the shadow. The center of the slider represents noon and either end is sunrise and sunset.

Figure 23.5 shows the model during the sunrise hours. Notice how the shadow is cast toward the left. Figure 23.6 shows the same scene as the shadows approach noon. During the bright hours of the day, the colors on the model also get brighter.

FIGURE 23.5

During the morning hours the shadows extend to the left.

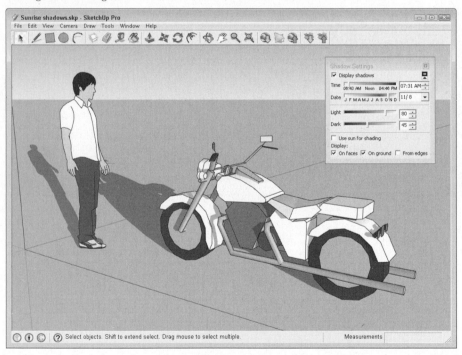

FIGURE 23.6

At noon the shadows are small and the model colors are brighter.

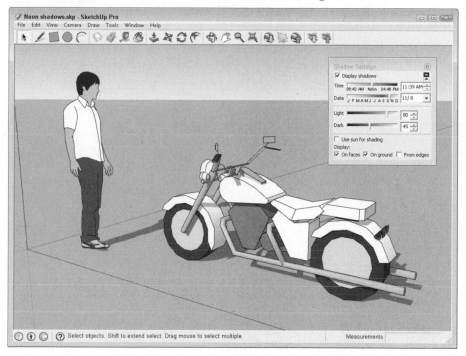

Figure 23.7 shows the model in the evening hours. The shadow is now being cast in the opposite direction and the model colors are much darker. Figure 23.8 shows the model at night when no shadows are cast and the model colors are all dark.

In addition to the slider, you can also set the time by typing a value in the time field to the right of the slider.

Beneath the Time slider in the Shadow Settings panel is the Date slider. The Date slider is identified by the letters, J, F, M, A, M, J, J, A, S, O, N, and D. These letters stand for the first letter of each month and represent a full year.

FIGURE 23.7

During the evening hours the shadows extend to the right.

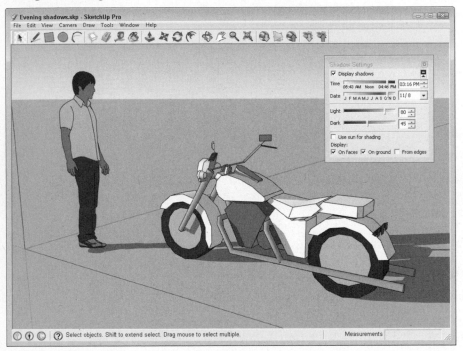

> **TIP**   You can do a daily or yearly shadow study by saving two scenes at different times and using the scene animation feature animating between the two different times or dates.

It isn't as obvious, but the sun moves farther south and north in the sky during different months of the year. For the Northern hemisphere, the sun takes a path that is closer to the south end of the sky during the summer months and then moves north to be more directly overhead during the summer months. This impacts the direction that the shadow is cast.

If you drag the Date slider back and forth, you'll notice that the shadows are close to the object during the summer months and they extend outward away from the object during the winter months. Figure 23.9 shows the shadows in January, and Figure 23.10 shows the shadows after the Date slider has moved to July.

In addition to dragging the Date slider, you can type a date into the Date field or click the drop-down list to access a pop-up calendar of dates, as shown in Figure 23.11.

FIGURE 23.8

At night there are no shadows and the model colors are dark.

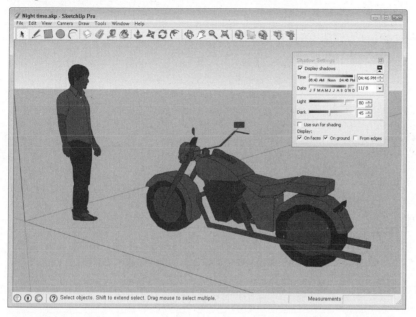

FIGURE 23.9

During the winter months, the shadow extends farther from the object.

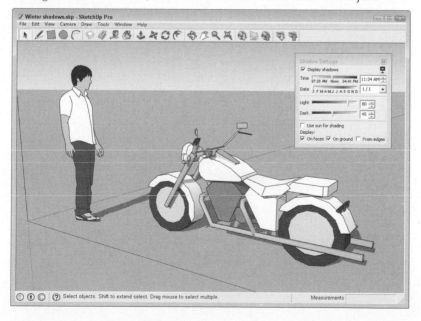

FIGURE 23.10

For the summer months, the shadow stays close to the object.

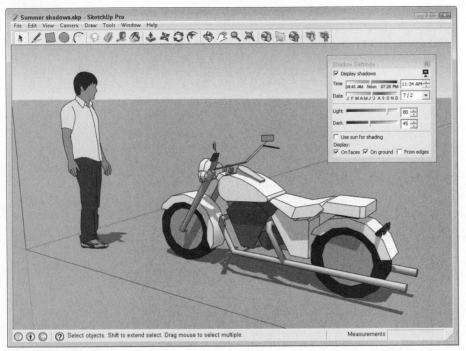

FIGURE 23.11

From the Shadow Settings panel, you can select a specific date from a pop-up calendar.

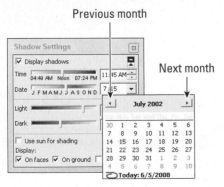

Brightening lights and shadows

The Light slider is used to brighten (or darken) the illuminated surfaces in the model. The Dark slider is used to change how dark the shadows appear. Each slider also has a value that you can change to its right.

Figure 23.12 shows a model with an increased light intensity, and Figure 23.13 shows the same model with a dark shadow setting.

FIGURE 23.12

The Light slider is used to adjust the light's intensity and to brighten illuminated surfaces.

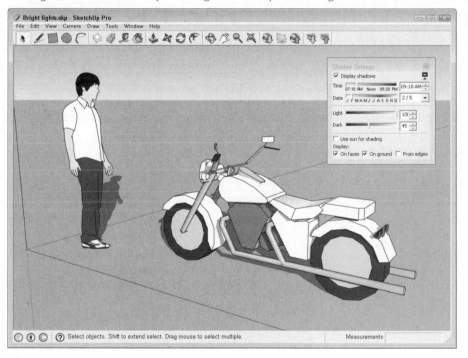

FIGURE 23.13

The Dark slider is used to adjust how dark the shadows are.

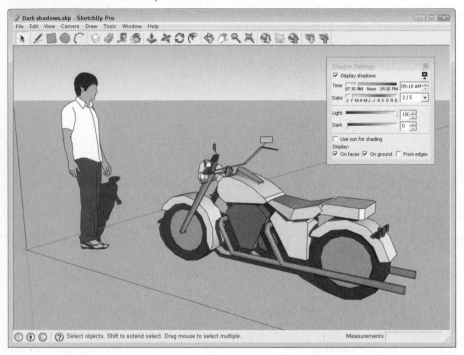

Controlling where shadows fall

At the bottom of the Shadow Settings panel are three Display options for controlling where the shadows are cast. Using these options, you can select to have the shadow only appear on the ground plane or only on the object faces and/or edges.

Figure 23.14 shows the model without any self-shadowing, which happens when one object casts a shadow on another part of the same object, and Figure 23.15 shows the opposite where self-shadowing is enabled and the ground shadows are removed.

FIGURE 23.14

When the On faces option is disabled, self-shadowing is turned off.

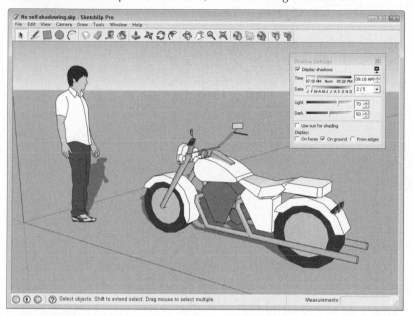

FIGURE 23.15

When the On ground option is disabled, the ground shadows are turned off.

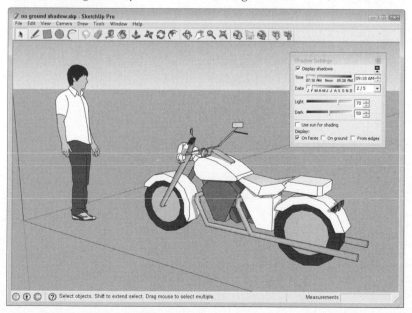

Allowing Which Models Cast and Receive Shadows

Using the Entity Info dialog box, you can set an object so it doesn't cast any shadows. This provides a way to remove the shadow from only a single object in the scene.

The Entity Info dialog box, shown in Figure 23.16, also includes a Receive Shadows option that you can disable. If disabled, shadows that are cast onto an object aren't displayed. This is another way to eliminate self-shadowing.

FIGURE 23.16

The Entity Info dialog box includes options to Cast and Receive Shadows.

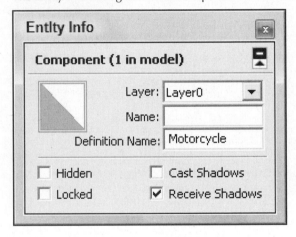

Figure 23.17 shows a shadow being cast from the man onto the motorcycle, but in Figure 23.18 the Receive Shadows option has been disabled, so the shadow is no longer cast onto the motorcycle.

FIGURE 23.17

All objects receive shadows by default.

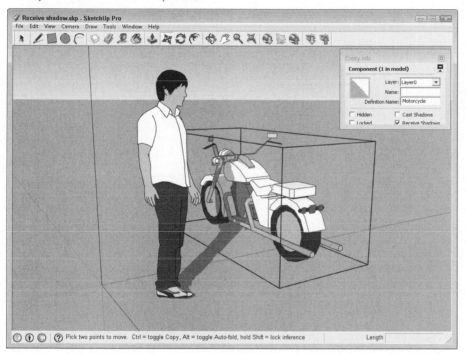

FIGURE 23.18

Objects can be set to not receive shadows.

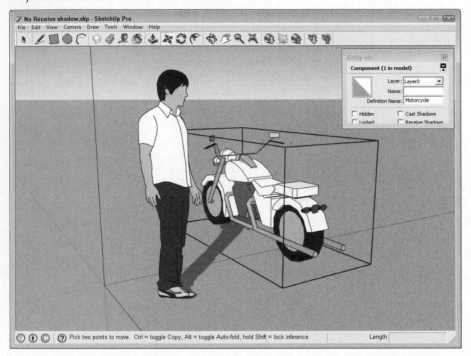

Summary

Shadows are a simple addition that can add a lot to a drawing. Using the Shadow Settings panel, you can turn shadows on and off, control the light and shadow brightness, and set the time and date for shadows.

This chapter covered the following topics:

- Accessing the Shadow Settings panel
- Enabling and disabling shadows
- Setting shadow time and date
- Changing light and shadow intensity
- Controlling which objects cast and receive shadows

In the next chapter, you look at the new Layout tool for presentations.

Part VI

Presenting SketchUp Scenes

Chapter 24

Using LayOut

S ketchUp is designed to enable users to quickly sketch and flesh out 3-D designs, but often drawings created in SketchUp are used in presentations. The SketchUp development team has purposely left many of the desktop publishing features out of SketchUp to keep the software focused on what it does best.

SketchUp drawings can be exported as 2-D images, and these images can easily be used in a desktop publishing presentation or image-editing package to create presentations. However, if you find after exporting that the perspective is a little off, then you need to make the changes in SketchUp and re-export the image file again. Users have found that a software package that lets you work with 3-D SketchUp files that also includes all the layout and presentation editing features would be ideal and thus LayOut was created.

LayOut is a presentation package that includes many of the same features as SketchUp. It also includes many editing features not found in SketchUp. This chapter covers the features that are unique to LayOut and refers to the other chapters for features that are common among SketchUp and LayOut.

The latest version of LayOut is LayOut 2.0, which is part of SketchUp Pro 7.

CROSS-REF This chapter is intended to be an introduction to the LayOut interface, and the features for working with layout content are presented in Chapter 25.

Learning the LayOut Interface

Many of the interface elements found in LayOut are identical to those found in SketchUp, including a Title Bar, menus, toolbars, and a status bar. The status bar also includes a Measurements Toolbar field and a drop-down list for selecting a zoom amount. Figure 24.1 shows the default interface.

CROSS-REF **You can learn more about using these various interface elements in Chapter 2.**

FIGURE 24.1

Many of the interface elements in LayOut are identical to SketchUp.

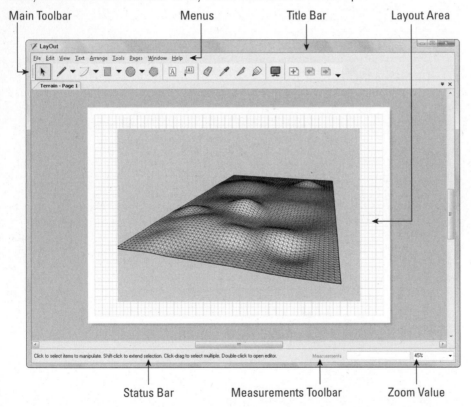

Main Toolbar Menus Title Bar Layout Area

Status Bar Measurements Toolbar Zoom Value

Learning the main toolbar

The main toolbar is positioned directly underneath the menus. LayOut by default only includes a single toolbar, but it includes customization features for creating new toolbars. If you click-and-drag the separator bar to the left of the main toolbar, you can pull the toolbar away from the interface and make it a floating toolbar, as shown in Figure 24.2. Double-clicking the toolbar's title returns it to its last docked location.

Moving the mouse over a toolbar button displays the button's name in a tooltip. Some of the buttons have stacked buttons. You can select the other tools by clicking the down arrow to the right of the button. These stacked buttons are listed in Figure 24.2.

FIGURE 24.2

The main toolbar includes the most common tools.

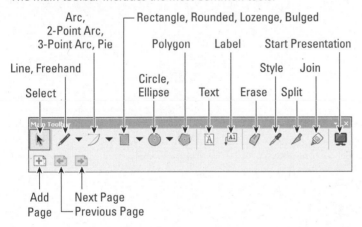

Using document tabs

The LayOut interface supports having multiple documents open at the same time. Each open document appears as a horizontal tab along the top edge of the layout window directly under the main toolbar, as shown in Figure 24.3. You can switch between the different documents using these tabs. You can also switch to a different document by selecting it from the Window menu.

The name of the saved document along with the document's current page is listed on the tab. If the document hasn't been saved, then the tab is listed as <Untitled>.

If you want to view two different pages of the same document, you can open a new window for the current document by choosing Window ⇨ New Window For. This creates a new tab with a second view of the current document. The new window can also show the same page with a different zoom value, as shown in Figure 24.4.

Each open document appears as a tab at the top of the interface.

Document tabs

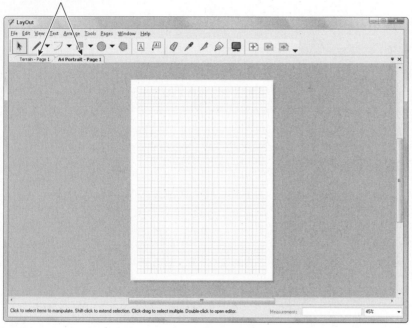

FIGURE 24.4

Each document can have multiple window views.

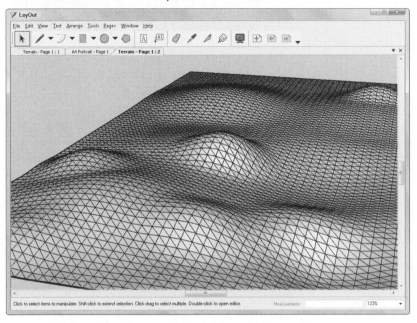

Using trays

One interface element that is unique to LayOut is the tray. The tray is a series of panels that are conveniently aligned along the right edge of the interface, as shown in Figure 24.5. You can make the tray appear by choosing Window ➪ Show Tray. Tray panels stack up nicely in rows and can be expanded by clicking the title. You can also close the entire tray by clicking its Close Tray button, the X to the right of its name. You can also close individual panels by clicking on Close button to the right of each panel name. Closed trays and panels can be reopened using the Window menu.

All trays can be hidden by choosing Window ➪ Hide Tray, or made visible again with the same command. Using the Window ➪ New Tray menu command, you can create a new tray that only has those panels that you want using the Add Tray dialog box, as shown in Figure 24.6. The new tray appears as a vertical tab on the right side of the interface, as shown in Figure 24.7.

Clicking the Auto-Hide button next to the Close Tray button causes the tray tabs to be automatically hidden whenever the mouse is moved away from the tray. If you move the mouse over the tray tabs, the tray slides open again. Disabling the Auto-Hide option causes the tray to remain open at all times.

FIGURE 24.5

Setting panels are stacked together in trays at the right of the interface.

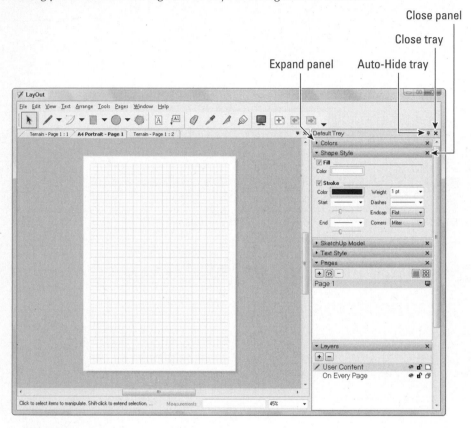

FIGURE 24.6

The Add Tray dialog box lets you choose which panels are displayed in the new tray.

FIGURE 24.7

All defined trays are displayed as vertical tabs to the right of the tray.

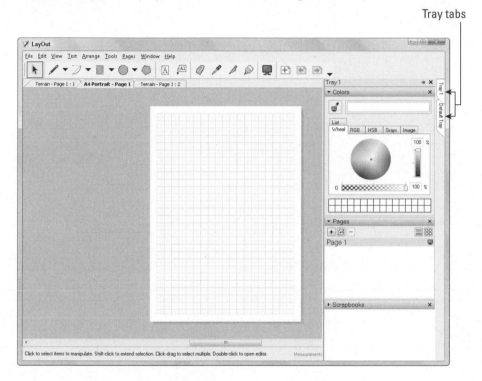

Working with LayOut Files

LayOut lets you combine multiple pieces of content together into a presentation. Whether you are working with SketchUp models, images, or text, LayOut is the platform for bringing it all together. Learning to work with files is one of the keys to using LayOut.

Creating a new LayOut file

The first step in creating a LayOut presentation is to create a new project file. Choose File ➪ New to open the Getting Started dialog box, as shown in Figure 24.8, where you can select from one of the default templates. These templates define the document size and orientation and also the grid divisions.

Within the Getting Started dialog box are several different styles of templates. Each style shows a thumbnail of what the template looks like.

FIGURE 24.8

The Getting Started dialog box lets you choose the template to use.

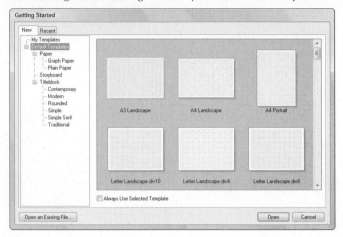

The Getting Started dialog box also includes a tab for accessing a list of Recent files. Each recent file is displayed as a thumbnail, as shown in Figure 24.9. Holding the mouse over the top of the file thumbnail displays a description of the file in a text balloon.

 **If LayOut crashes, any backed-up files are displayed in a tab labeled Recovered.**

Using the Startup panel in the LayOut Preferences dialog box, shown in Figure 24.10, you can specify what happens when the program is started and what appears when you choose File ⇨ New. Open the LayOut Preferences dialog box by choosing Edit ⇨ Preferences.

During startup, you can automatically have a new document appear, you can reopen the last document, or you can do neither. When you choose File ⇨ New, you can display the Getting Started dialog box, which is the default, you can have a blank new document appear, or you can have the default template show up. The Choose button opens the Getting Started dialog box and lets you specify which template is the default.

Opening existing files

The Getting Started dialog box also includes an Open an Existing File button. This button causes the Open LayOut File dialog box to appear, as shown in Figure 24.11. All layout files are saved with the .layout extension. Existing files can also be opened by choosing File ⇨ Open.

FIGURE 24.9

The Recent tab in the Getting Started dialog box displays all the recently opened files as thumbnails.

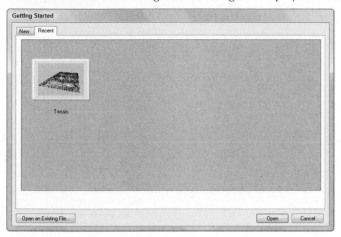

FIGURE 24.10

The Startup panel in the LayOut Preferences dialog box lets you turn off the Getting Started dialog box.

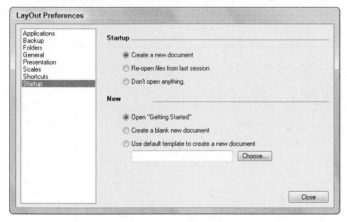

FIGURE 24.11

The Open LayOut File dialog box is a standard system file dialog box that lets you open LayOut files.

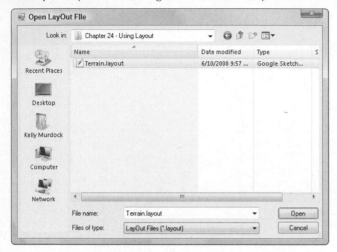

Inserting content

The File ➪ Insert menu command opens a file dialog box where you can select files to load into LayOut. The file types that are recognized include SketchUp models, Raster Images, Plain Text, and RTF Text.

You can also move SketchUp models to LayOut by choosing File ➪ Send to LayOut in SketchUp. This command opens LayOut, if it is not already open, and moves the current SketchUp model to the current layout document automatically.

CROSS-REF   More on inserting content into LayOut is covered in Chapter 25.

Saving LayOut files

You can choose File ➪ Save or the File ➪ Save As to save LayOut files. The File menu also includes an option to Save As Template that opens the Save As Template dialog box, as shown in Figure 24.12.

Choose File ➪ Save as Scrapbook to save the layout file to a scrapbook folder using the Save As Scrapbook dialog box, as shown in Figure 24.13.

CROSS-REF   More on using scrapbooks is covered in Chapter 23.

FIGURE 24.12

The Save As Template dialog box lets you save the current document as a template.

FIGURE 24.13

The Save As Scrapbook dialog box lets you save the current document to an established scrapbook.

To save your current document in case of power failures, you can enable the Backup and Auto-Save features. Both of these features are located on the Backup panel in the LayOut Preferences dialog box, as shown in Figure 24.14. Choose Edit ➪ Preferences to access this dialog box.

Selecting the Create backup file when saving option causes the current saved file to be backed up every time you save the file. If you make and save a change that you don't want, you can recall the latest backed-up file, which doesn't include the most recent saved changes.

The Auto-Save feature automatically saves the current document every designated number of minutes. Keep in mind that this ties up the hard drive as often as you specify.

FIGURE 24.14

The Backup panel of the LayOut Preferences dialog box includes options for enabling backup and auto-save.

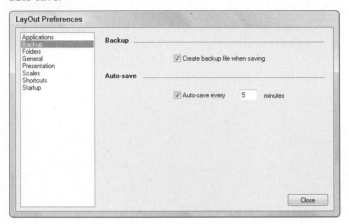

Export to Images

Choose File ➪ Export ➪ Images to export the current layout document as a series of PNG or JPEG images.

NEW FEATURE The ability to export a layout as images is new to LayOut 2.

Export to PDF

Choose File ➪ Export ➪ PDF to export the current layout document as a PDF file. This format is common on the Web and can be viewed using Adobe Reader. You can download Adobe Reader for free from the Adobe Web site at www.adobe.com.

Configuring the LayOut Document

Although the template choice determines the paper size and orientation, you can configure the document using the Document Setup dialog box, shown in Figure 24.15. Choose File ➪ Document Setup to open this dialog box.

The Document Setup dialog box is divided into five panels that are selected from the list at the left — General, Grid, Paper, References, and Units. The General panel includes fields for typing the layout's name and a description. The description information is displayed when you move the mouse over the file's thumbnail in the Recent panel in the Getting Started dialog box.

FIGURE 24.15

The Document Setup dialog box lets you configure the current document.

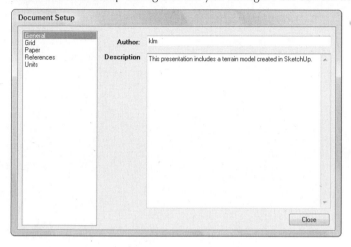

Establishing grids

The Grid panel, shown in Figure 24.16, includes Major Grid and Minor Grid options. For major grid lines, you can specify a Spacing dimension in measured units and a color. For minor grid lines, you can select the number of Subdivisions and a color. These subdivisions are spread equally between the major grid lines. There are also options to clip the grid to the page margins and to print the grid.

After a grid is established for a document, you can turn the grid on and off by choosing View ⇨ Hide/Show Grid.

Setting paper size, margins, and orientation

The Paper panel of the Document Setup dialog box, shown in Figure 24.17, includes settings for the size, orientation, and margins of the LayOut document. These settings are really intended for presentations that are printed. The drop-down list at the top of this panel includes a long list of standard paper size presets. There is also an option to change the orientation from Landscape to Portrait. The Landscape orientation is wider than it is tall, and the Portrait orientation is taller than it is wide.

If a standard paper size is selected from the drop-down list, the Width and Height values are automatically filled in. If you are printing to a nonstandard size, then you can type the custom dimensions in the Width and Height fields.

The Color swatch sets the background color for the document, and you can elect to have this color printed by selecting the Print Paper Color option. If this option is not selected, then the background color is not printed.

FIGURE 24.16

The Grid panel of the Document Setup dialog box lets you add grids and set the grid color.

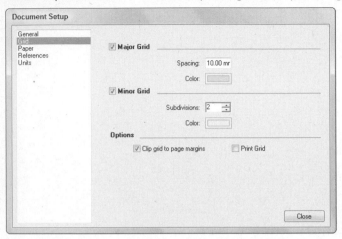

The paper margins can be turned on or off using the check box to the left of the Margins title. There are also dimension fields for setting the width of the margin at each paper edge. Margins can also have a color displayed, and you can set the margin lines to be printed.

The Rendering Resolution setting for SketchUp Models determines the dots per inch (dpi) of the included models. For laser printers, a dpi setting of 300 is common. Lower dpi settings will print quicker without as much memory, but at a reduced resolution. For presentations that aren't printed, a dpi setting of 72 is sufficient.

FIGURE 24.17

The Paper panel of the Document Setup dialog box lets you select from multiple standard paper sizes.

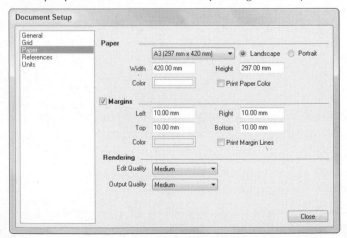

Referencing external content

The References panel, shown in Figure 24.18, shows lists of all external images that are loaded as part of the template. These references can be logos or images used as headers to the drawing. The list also records the status and the insertion date of the referenced images.

FIGURE 24.18

The References panel of the Document Setup dialog box lists all the external content included in the current layout.

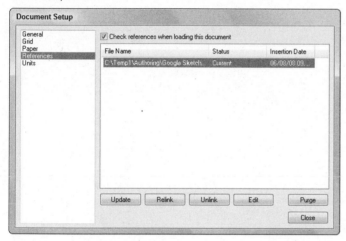

If you edit a referenced image outside of the LayOut interface, you can reload the image with its changes by clicking Update. Images that are inserted maintain a link to the image's location on the hard drive. If you click Unlink, you can break this link. Images with broken links cannot be updated if a change has been made to the image. Click Relink to reestablish a link, which lets you locate the image's file in a file dialog box.

Clicking Edit opens the selected image in its default image-editing package. The default image editor and the default text-editor applications can be set in the Applications panel of the LayOut Preferences dialog box, as shown in Figure 24.19. Simply click Choose and browse to the application that you want to open when you click Edit.

Clicking Purge removes any items from the list that are no longer included in the document.

FIGURE 24.19

The Applications panel of the LayOut Preferences dialog box lets you choose the default software to open when you click Edit.

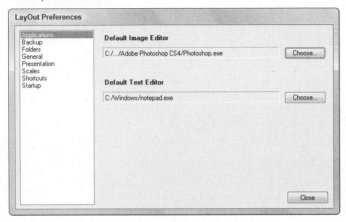

Setting layout units

The Units panel, shown in Figure 24.20, lets you set the units used by LayOut. The options include Decimal and Fractional units of Inches, Feet, Millimeters, Centimeters, Meters, and Points. You can also set the Precision of the selected units.

FIGURE 24.20

The Units panel of the Document Setup dialog box lets you set the units used by the current document.

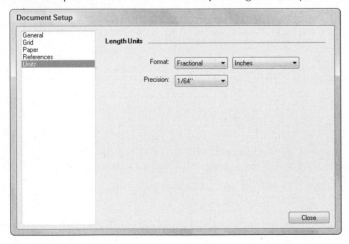

Printing a LayOut

One of the key features of the LayOut program is the ability to print the current document. Within the File menu are three commands for printing the current document: Page Setup, Print Preview, and Print.

The Page Setup dialog box, shown in Figure 24.21, lets you set the paper size, source, orientation, and margins. These values are taken by default from the Document Setup settings, but can be altered as needed.

The Print Preview dialog box, shown in Figure 24.22, shows a preview of what the printed document will look like. If the current document includes multiple pages, you can select a page to view from the Page drop-down list. You can also zoom in on the current page or display several pages side by side. There is also a Print button for printing the current page.

The Print dialog box, shown in Figure 24.23, lists the name of the default system printer. There is also a Properties button that lets you configure the selected printer. You can select the Print to file option to save the print job as a file. You can also select to print All the current pages, just a subset of the current document, or just the selected portion. If you want multiple copies, type a number in the Number of copies field, and you can select to collate the printed pages.

FIGURE 24.21

The Page Setup dialog box includes settings for preparing a document to be printed.

FIGURE 24.22

The Print Preview dialog box lets you see what the document looks like before being printed.

Print

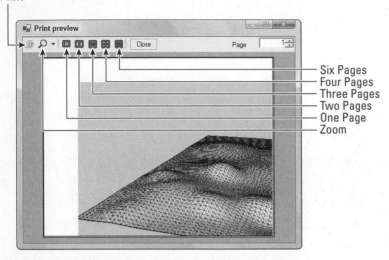

Six Pages
Four Pages
Three Pages
Two Pages
One Page
Zoom

FIGURE 24.23

The Print dialog box lets you select a printer.

Working with Pages

A single layout document can include multiple pages. Many of the default templates have only a single page, but you can easily add or remove pages from the current layout document using the Pages menu or the Pages panel.

Choosing Pages ➪ Add adds one new page to the current document. There is also an Add button on the default toolbar. The current page number is displayed on the document tab at the top of the interface. Choosing Pages ➪ Duplicate copies the current page as another page in the document including all its content. Choosing Pages ➪ Delete removes the current page from the LayOut document.

If several pages exist in the current document, choose Pages ➪ Previous or Pages ➪ Next to cycle through the pages. Previous and Next buttons are also on the default toolbar.

Another way to work with pages is with the Pages panel in the default tray, shown in Figure 24.24. This panel lists all the pages included in the current document.

FIGURE 24.24

The Pages panel lists all the pages in the current document.

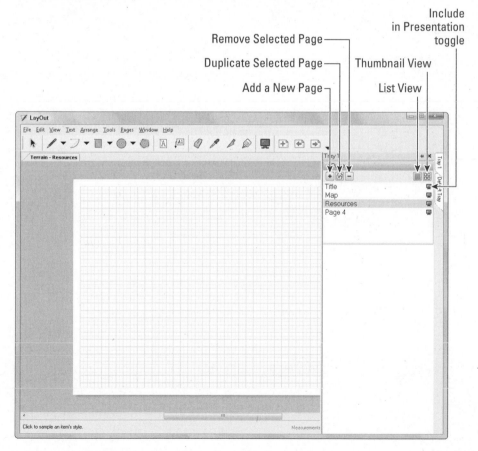

New pages can be added to the current document by clicking the Add a New Page button at the top of the panel. Selected pages can be duplicated or removed by clicking the other buttons, also at the top of the panel. Double-clicking the page name highlights the name and lets you type a new name. You can also display the pages as a list or as thumbnails, as shown in Figure 24.25.

FIGURE 24.25

The Pages panel can also display pages as thumbnails.

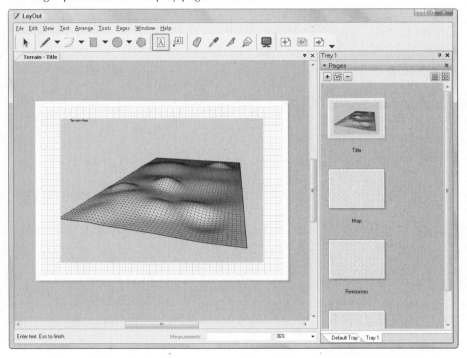

If the List option is enabled, each layer can be set to view or hide the master layer content using the row of icons to the right of the page name. There is also an Include in Presentation option that you can use to remove pages from a presentation without deleting them.

Navigating the LayOut View

As you begin to work with content, you'll want to zoom in to focus on details and move about the window as you work. The View menu includes several tools for navigating the LayOut view. The view navigation tools include the following:

■ **Pan**: This tool lets you move the window around by clicking and dragging. You can pan the current view by dragging with the mouse's scroll wheel held down, and you can pan the current window by dragging the scroll bars on the right and bottom of the layout window.

■ **Zoom**: This tool lets you zoom in and out of the current document by dragging the mouse. You can also zoom in and out at any time by scrubbing the scroll wheel.

■ **Zoom In**: This tool zooms in on the current document.

■ **Zoom Out**: This tool zooms out of the current document.

■ **Actual Size**: This tool zooms in to show the actual size of the current document.

■ **Zoom to Fit**: This tool automatically zooms the current document to show the entire document within the window.

■ **Full Screen**: This tool increases the layout window so that it fills the entire screen without any interface elements visible. Press the Escape key to return to the normal view.

Customizing the LayOut Interface

Although the LayOut interface is fairly simple, it still includes the options to customize various interface elements including shortcuts, toolbars, and menus. You can access the customization features by choosing View ⇨ Toolbars ⇨ Customize. This command opens the Customize dialog box, as shown in Figure 24.26. The Customize command can also be accessed by clicking the Toolbar Options button located at the right end of the main toolbar.

FIGURE 24.26

The Customize panel includes options for customizing toolbars and commands.

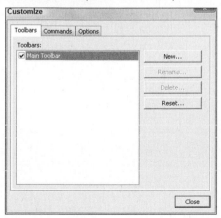

Altering toolbars

The quickest way to alter a toolbar is to add or remove buttons. Clicking the Toolbar Options button at the right end of the main toolbar offers a command to Add or Remove Buttons. For the main toolbar, all the buttons are presented in a list with check boxes to the left of the button names. Deselecting a check box removes that button from the main toolbar. There is also a Reset Toolbar option if you want to restore it to its default look.

The Customize dialog box includes buttons for creating, renaming, and removing new toolbars. There is also an option to Reset the current toolbar using the Reset button. When you click New, a New Toolbar dialog box, as shown in Figure 24.27, opens with options to name the new toolbar and to select the dock location, or you can choose to make the toolbar a floating toolbar.

FIGURE 24.27

The New Toolbar dialog box lets you name the new toolbar.

Once a new toolbar is created, it appears as an empty toolbar in the position that you specify. You can then open the Commands panel in the Customize dialog box, as shown in Figure 24.28, and click and drag any of the available commands to the empty toolbar. Commands with associated icons appear on the toolbar as icons, and those commands without icons appear as text, as shown in Figure 24.29. Buttons can be removed from the new toolbar by just dragging the button away from the toolbar.

Setting interface options

The Options panel of the Customize dialog box, shown in Figure 24.30, includes options for both menus and toolbars. All personalized menus and toolbars can be set to always show the full menu or to show the menu after a short delay. This is intended to keep the menus and toolbars smaller and only to display the full menu after you wait for a short delay.

There are also options for enabling large icons in the menus and toolbars. The Floating Toolbar Fade Display sets how long the floating toolbars stay around when not being used before they fade. The Show ScreenTips on toolbars option lets you turn off the tooltips if you find them getting in the way. You can also select to show any keyboard shortcuts in the tooltips. The Menu Animation options include None, Random, Unfold, Slide, and Fade. These options change the animation used to make the menus open.

FIGURE 24.28

The Commands panel of the Customize dialog box includes all the commands that you can add to a new toolbar.

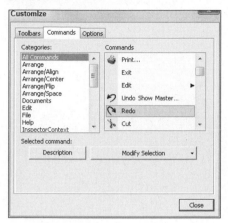

FIGURE 24.29

New toolbars can include text and buttons.

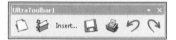

FIGURE 24.30

The Options panel of the Customize dialog box includes several interface options.

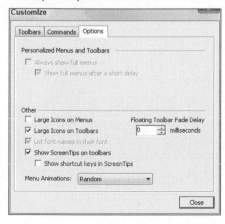

Adding keyboard shortcuts

All menu commands that include a keyboard shortcut have the shortcut listed to the right of the menu name. Only specific commands have shortcuts by default, but you can use the Shortcuts panel in the LayOut Preferences dialog box, as shown in Figure 24.31, to change any keyboard shortcuts. The LayOut Preferences dialog box is opened using the Edit ↦ Preferences menu.

FIGURE 24.31

The Shortcuts panel of the LayOut Preferences dialog box lets you change any keyboard shortcuts.

Shortcut field

Add shortcut — └ Remove shortcut

All commands are listed and any commands that have a keyboard shortcut assigned list the shortcut to the right. If you select a command that doesn't have a shortcut, you can type one in the field below the command list and click the Add Shortcut button. If the entered shortcut is already assigned to another command, a warning dialog box appears. The Remove Shortcut button can remove an assigned shortcut from the selected command. The Filter field lets you limit the number of commands that are displayed by typing in a text string. For example, entering View in the filter field limits the command list to only those commands that have the word View in them.

Changing tool color

In the General panel of the LayOut Preferences dialog box, shown in Figure 24.32, is an option to set the Tool Color. Using this color swatch, you can control the color used for the LayOut tools.

FIGURE 24.32

The color swatch lets you change the color of the LayOut tools.

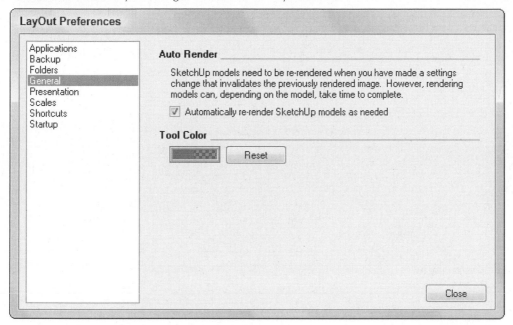

Getting Help

LayOut offers several ways to get help. They are accessible through the Help menu. Choose Help⇨ LayOut Help to open the help files in a Web browser. These same Web pages can also be viewed online, as shown in Figure 24.33, by choosing Help⇨ Online Help Center. The Help menu also includes options for checking for updates, accessing the SketchUp Community Web pages, sending a suggestion, and accessing the online video tutorials.

The Tip of the Day feature (choose Help⇨ Tip of the Day), shown in Figure 24.34, automatically appears when the software starts. You can disable it by deselecting the Show tips on startup option. There aren't a lot of tips, but they are worth reading once or twice.

The Quick Reference Card (choose Help⇨ Quick Reference Card) is a PDF file that shows the details of the toolbar buttons, as shown in Figure 24.35.

FIGURE 24.33

The Help ➪ LayOut Help menu command opens help pages in a Web browser.

FIGURE 24.34

The Tip of the Day dialog box presents a number of tips.

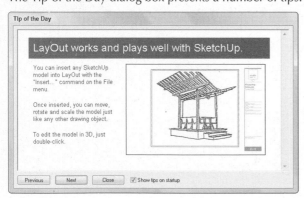

FIGURE 24.35

The Quick Reference Card is a printable guide for the LayOut main toolbar buttons.

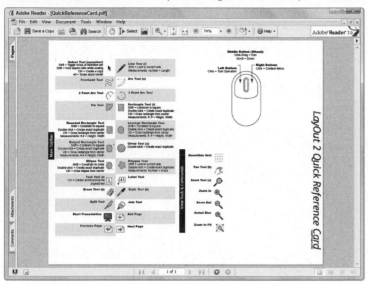

The Instructor panel, located in the tray, is another helpful guide. It lists details on how to use the currently selected tool along with an animated display of the tool in action, as shown in Figure 24.36.

FIGURE 24.36

The Instructor panel shows how to use the selected tool.

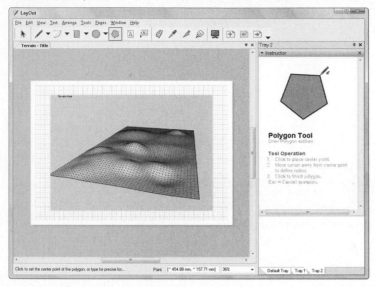

Summary

LayOut is a supplemental program that works in concert with SketchUp, enabling additional features for creating presentations. It includes many features not found in SketchUp and includes the ability to work with multiple documents and pages. It also has the ability to configure the document size, color, and grid, and to print the final presentation.

This chapter covered the following topics:

- Learning the LayOut interface, including trays
- Working with files, including opening, saving, and exporting
- Configuring the document with the Document Setup dialog box
- Printing the current document
- Adding pages and navigating the view
- Customizing the interface toolbars and shortcuts
- Getting help with the Help menu

This chapter introduced and explained the LayOut interface. The next chapter deals with how to handle content within the LayOut interface to create presentations.

Chapter 25

Editing LayOut Presentations

T he previous chapter presented the LayOut interface and showed how various aspects of the software worked, but it didn't get into actually using the program to create presentations.

Presentations are composed of content. That content can be SketchUp models, images, or text that is imported, or it could be lines, arcs, and shapes drawn in LayOut itself.

The power of LayOut is its ability to combine all these content pieces together into a coherent vision.

Assembling Content

Once you have a document template open and configured, you can begin to assemble the various pieces of content. This content is inserted into LayOut using the File ⇨ Insert menu command. The Open dialog box recognizes several different content formats including the following:

- **SketchUp files:** Models created in SketchUp can be opened and manipulated within LayOut. SketchUp also includes a File ⇨ Send to LayOut menu command that moves the current model directly to LayOut.

- **Image files:** Although the Insert File dialog box just lists images as Raster Images, LayOut recognizes and can insert JPEG, TGA, BMP, and TIFF image files.

- **Plain text files:** Plain text files have the .txt extension and they don't include any formatting.

- **RTF text files:** RTF stands for Rich-text format and its files are text files that include some basic style formatting.

Working with SketchUp files

The easiest way to get SketchUp files into LayOut is by choosing File ⇨ Send to LayOut in SketchUp. This menu command only works if the SketchUp file has been saved. If LayOut isn't open when this command is used, then LayOut is opened and the model is added to the center of the new document, as shown in Figure 25.1.

FIGURE 25.1

SketchUp models can be moved to LayOut using a command in SketchUp.

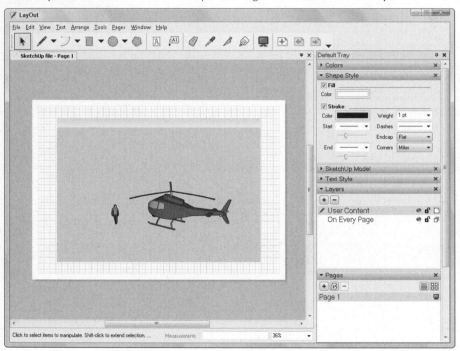

If you double-click on a SketchUp model in LayOut, the SketchUp view becomes active and you can orbit about the model using the left mouse button. Holding down the Shift key and dragging with the left mouse button lets you pan the view, and the scroll wheel lets you zoom in and out of the SketchUp view. Figure 25.2 shows the updated SketchUp file changed within LayOut.

If you double-click on a SketchUp model in LayOut, a pop-up menu of SketchUp commands appears. The pop-up menu commands include the various Camera tools including Orbit, Pan, Zoom, Zoom Window, Look Around, and Walk. There are also options to Zoom Extents, enable Perspective, Standard Views of Top, Bottom, Front, Back, Left, Right, and Isometric. You can also select from the available Styles and Scenes included with the document, and enable Shadows. Figure 25.3 shows the pop-up menu options for SketchUp files.

FIGURE 25.2

LayOut allows SketchUp models to be manipulated without having to return to SketchUp.

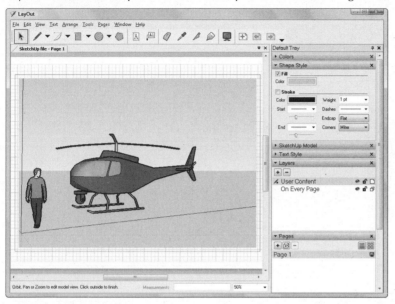

FIGURE 25.3

Right-clicking on an inserted SketchUp file lets you access a pop-up menu of SketchUp commands.

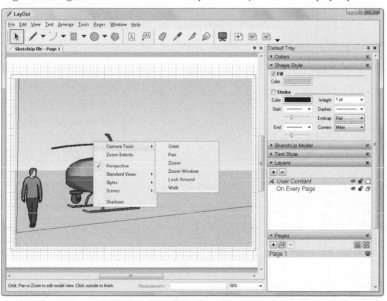

When you finish editing the SketchUp model, you can select the End Editing option from the pop-up menu or click on the LayOut document outside of the SketchUp model.

The settings for the opened SketchUp model are located in the SketchUp Model panel in the tray to the right of the interface. Within this panel is a drop-down list of the available scenes. There are also tabs for the View, Styles, Shadow, and Fog settings.

Working with image files

Inserted image files are displayed using their default resolution. Image files are added by choosing File ⇨ Insert, or they can be dragged and dropped from Windows Explorer or from Mac Finder. Figure 25.4 shows several images dropped onto a LayOut page.

Right-clicking on an inserted image file offers a pop-up menu with options to Cut, Copy, Delete, Move to Current Layer, Arrange, or Flip the image. There is also an option to Open the image in Photoshop (or whichever image-editing package that is designated in the Applications panel of the Preferences dialog box).

FIGURE 25.4

Images can be inserted or dropped onto LayOut pages.

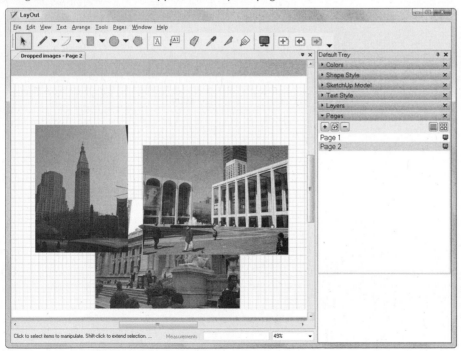

Inserting text files

TXT files and RTF files can be inserted into LayOut. The difference is that RTF files retain their formatting while TXT files lose all formatting when inserted. Text can also be cut and copied and pasted into LayOut by choosing Edit ⇨ Cut, Copy, and Paste features. Figure 25.5 shows some text that was copied and pasted into LayOut.

Right-clicking on a text entity displays a pop-up menu with options to Cut, Copy, Delete, Move to Current Layer, Arrange, or Flip the text as well as an option to Size to Fit the text.

Text style is changed in the Text Style panel. This panel is covered later in the chapter.

FIGURE 25.5

Text snippets can be copied and pasted into LayOut.

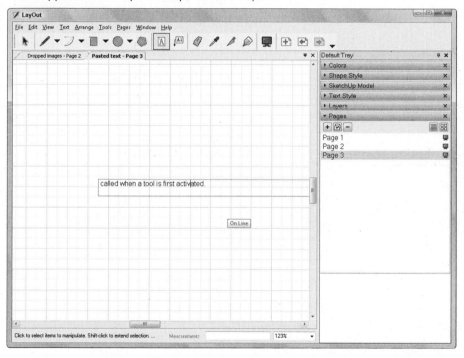

Transforming Content

Before a piece of content can be transformed, it needs to be selected. Selected objects — whether they're models, images, or text — can be transformed in a number of ways, including moved, rotated, and scaled.

Selecting objects

Each piece of content that is added to a LayOut page can be selected by clicking on the object. Several objects can be selected at once if you hold down the Shift key while clicking each item. Clicking a selected object with the Shift key held down deselects it.

You can also select multiple objects by dragging over them with the mouse. If you drag from left to right, then only those objects that are completely enclosed within the selection box are selected, but dragging from right to left only requires that a portion of the object be within the selection box. All objects that are selected are included in a highlighted area with corner icons. Figure 25.6 shows three images selected. At the center of the selected objects is the rotation center that is used to mark the center of rotation.

Choose Edit ⇨ Select All to quickly select all objects on the current page. Choosing Edit ⇨ Select None does the opposite.

FIGURE 25.6

Multiple objects can be selected at once.

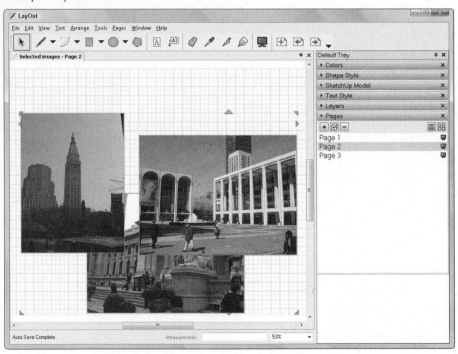

Deleting objects

Selected objects are deleted by choosing Edit ⇨ Delete or by simply pressing Delete.

Moving objects

To move a selected object, just click on the image and drag the object to its new location. The mouse cursor displays a four-way arrow icon when you can move an object. Figure 25.7 shows the page after moving the images.

FIGURE 25.7

Selected objects are moved by dragging them.

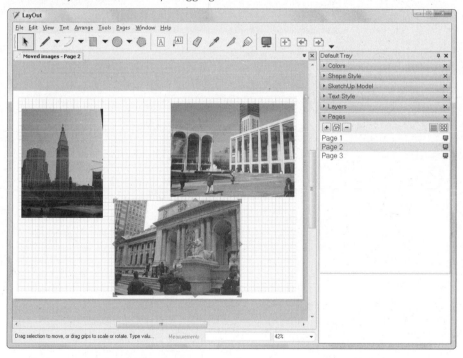

Rotating objects

To rotate a selected object, click on the center point and a small rotation handle appears to the right of the center point. Select and drag this handle to rotate the object. The cursor turns into a half circle when the object is ready to rotate. Figure 25.8 shows an image being rotated. The rotation control circle is highlighted with tick marks as it is rotated.

FIGURE 25.8

Selected objects are rotated by positioning the rotation center and dragging on the rotation handle.

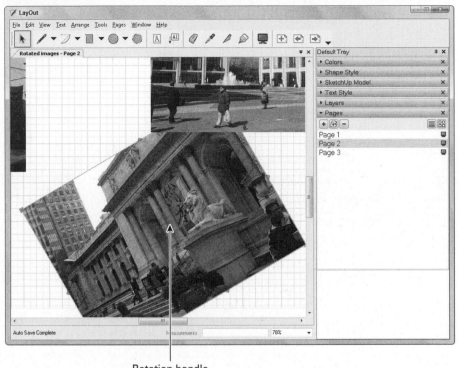

Rotation handle

Scaling objects

To scale the selected object, move the cursor over the object's edge or corner. The edge or corner is highlighted when it is ready to be scaled. Dragging on a corner causes a uniform scale and dragging on an edge causes nonuniform scaling. Figure 25.9 shows an image being scaled.

FIGURE 25.9

Selected objects are scaled by dragging on their corners or edges.

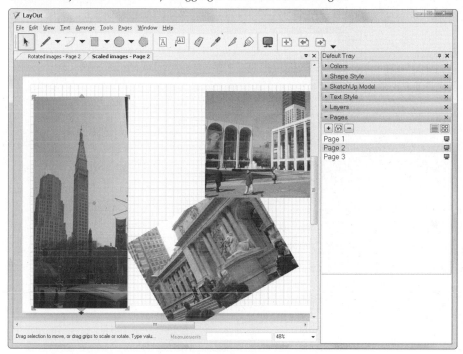

Duplicating objects

There are several ways to duplicate the selected object. One way is to use the Edit ⇨ Cut, Copy, and Paste commands. The Edit ⇨ Duplicate command also works and places the duplicated object offset from its original. You can also create a copy by holding down the Ctrl key while moving, rotating, or scaling an object. This causes the original to stay in its original position and the copied object to be transformed. Figure 25.10 shows an image being cloned as it is being moved by holding down the Ctrl key.

FIGURE 25.10

Holding down the Ctrl key creates a duplicate object.

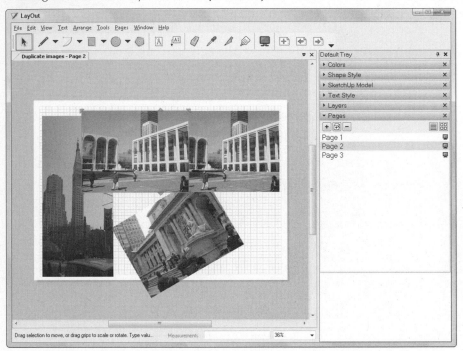

Snapping objects

Within the Arrange menu are two options that cause the objects to snap to either of the other objects or to the grid. Choose the Arrange ⇨ Object Snap toggle to make objects automatically snap to the edge of other objects. Choose the Arrange ⇨ Grid Snap toggle to cause the object being moved to snap to the grid intersections. These options are helpful when trying to align objects.

CROSS-REF The Grid settings are located in the Document Setup dialog box, which is covered in Chapter 22.

Aligning objects

When two or more objects are selected at once, you can choose Arrange ⇨ Align to line up the edges of the selected objects. The options in the Align menu include Left, Right, Top, Bottom, Vertically, and Horizontally. Figure 25.11 shows all objects aligned to the topmost edge. The Vertically and Horizontally options align the selected objects to the vertical or horizontal center of their selection.

Choose Arrange ⇨ Align to line objects up to a given edge.

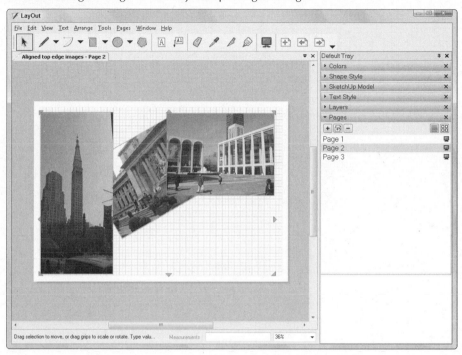

Spacing objects

Choose Arrange ⇨ Spacing when three or more objects are selected. It causes the center object to be centered between the other two objects. This is helpful if you have a row or column of small thumbnails that you need to position an equal distance from each other. The Spacing options include Horizontally and Vertically. Figure 25.12 shows three images that are equally spaced.

Centering objects

Choose Arrange ⇨ Center to center the selected object or objects in the very center of the page.

Flipping objects

Choose Arrange ⇨ Flip to flip the selected objects either Left to Right or Top to Bottom. Figure 25.13 shows the images flipped top to bottom.

FIGURE 25.12

Choosing Arrange ⇨ Spacing causes objects to be equally spaced from each other.

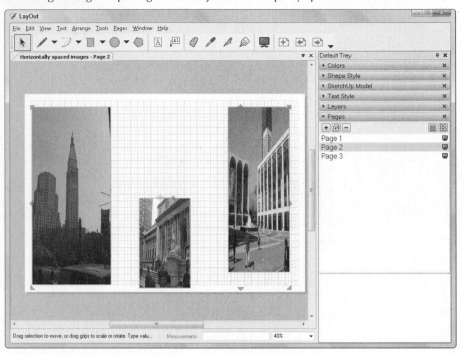

Changing the stacking order

When two or more objects overlap, one object covers the other. You can control which object is on top of the other in the stacking order using the Arrange menu options. The options include Bring to Front, Bring Forward, Send Backwards, and Send to Back. The Bring to Front and the Send to Back commands cause the selected object to move all the way to the top (or to the back) of the stacking order. The other commands move the objects forward (or backward) one level.

FIGURE 25.13

Choosing Arrange ⇨ Flip flips the selected objects.

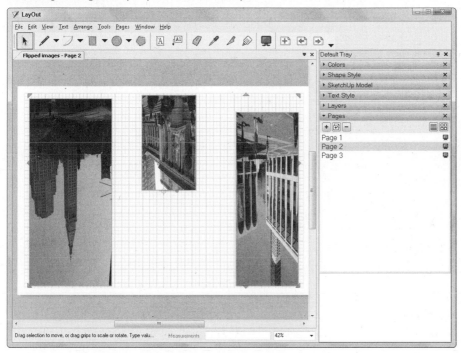

Using the LayOut Tools

In addition to the content pieces that you can insert, LayOut also includes several diverse tools that can draw lines, arcs, and shapes directly on the pages. These tools use the same inference points that SketchUp does. All of these tools can be found in the main toolbar and in the Tools menu.

CROSS-REF The various inference points are covered in Chapter 9.

Using the drawing tools

Included in the first set of tools in the toolbar (located under the Pencil icon) are the Line and Freehand tools. The Line tool draws straight and curved lines using the standard inference points. Lines that are parallel to the X-axis are red, and ones parallel to the Y-axis are green. As you draw with the Line tool, points and lines are highlighted so they can be edited by dragging them.

When using the Line tool, you can draw straight line segments by clicking at each corner's location or you can draw curves by clicking and dragging the Line tool. If you click and drag, then the line around the point becomes smoothed into a curve. The farther you drag away from the clicked point, the stronger the curvature at that point.

NEW FEATURE   The Line and Curve tools have been integrated together into the Line tool in LayOut 2.

After a line is created with the Line tool, you can edit the line points by simply clicking on the line with the Select tool.

The Freehand tool is another flyout button under the Line tool. It lets you draw freehand curves. Figure 25.14 shows examples of each of these tools. Closed curves form a shape that is filled with the default color.

FIGURE 25.14

There are three drawing tools for drawing lines: Line, Curve, and Freehand.

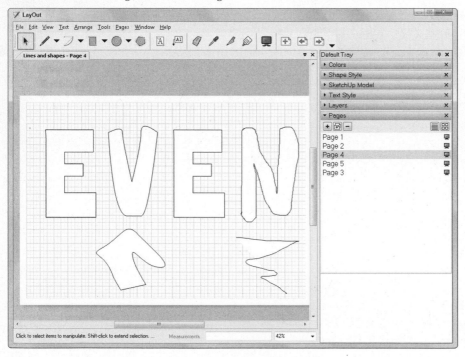

Drawing arcs

The LayOut tools include three ways to draw arcs. The Arc tool lets you click to place the center of the arc; click a second time to set the endpoint for the arc and then drag to form the arc. The 2-Point Arc tool lets you click at each endpoint for the arc and then drag to set the curvature of the arc. To use the 3-Point Arc tool, click once to set one of the arc's endpoints, click a second time to identify a point on the arc, and a third time to set the arc's other endpoint.

The Arc flyout also includes a Pie tool that creates an arc with the two endpoints connected to the center point, which looks like a pie wedge, as shown in Figure 25.15.

FIGURE 25.15

The LayOut tools include three ways to draw arcs and can even draw pie wedges.

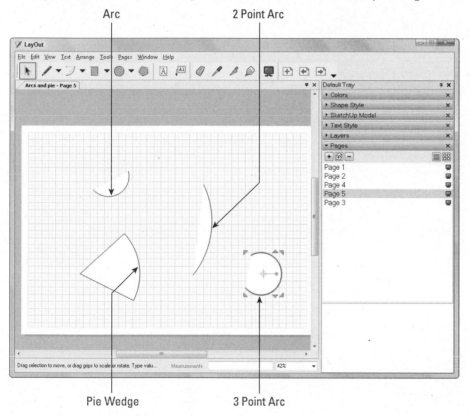

Drawing rectangles

The Rectangle tool comes in a variety of shapes. The standard rectangle has straight lines, the Rounded rectangle has rounded corners, the Lozenge rectangle has rounded edges at either end, and the Bulged rectangle has bowed length edges, as shown in Figure 25.16.

FIGURE 25.16

The LayOut tools include four rectangle shapes. From left, they are Standard, Rounded, Lozenge, and Bulged.

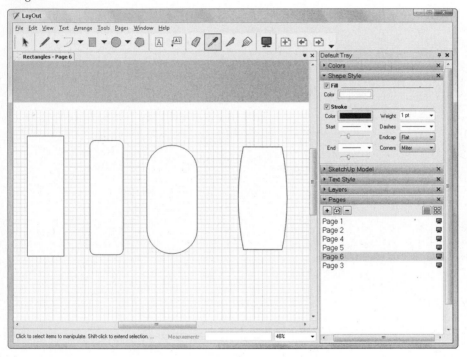

Drawing circles, ellipses and polygons

The Circle tool draws perfect circles, but there is also an Ellipse tool if you need a nonperfect circle. The Polygon tool draws polygon shapes with a given number of sides. You can change the number of sides as you create the polygon by pressing the up- and down-arrow keys.

Editing Shapes

The styles for any shapes created with the various tools are set using the Shape Style panel in the tray. This panel has settings for the Fill color, the Stroke color, and the Line Weight or thickness. You can also set the arrow type displayed at the Start and/or End of the line. There are also several options for Dashes, Endcaps, and Corners. The Endcap options include Flat, Round, and Square, and the Corner options include Miter, Round, and Bevel.

Copying style

If you define a style for one shape that you want to use on another shape, you can use the Style tool to select a style to copy. After a style is selected, the cursor changes to a Paint Bucket, allowing you to apply the copy style to another shape. Figure 25.17 shows the style applied to one shape applied to the adjacent shape using the Style tool. It also shows the Shape Style panel open.

FIGURE 25.17

The Style tool copies and pastes styles between shapes.

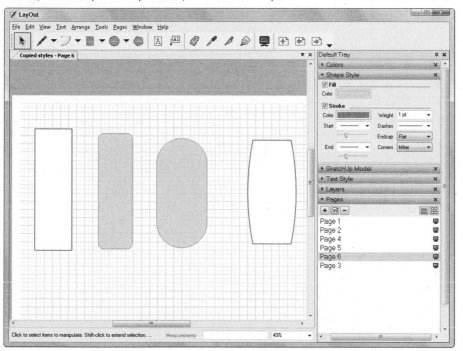

Erasing shapes

The Erase tool lets you remove shapes from the page by simply dragging the Erase tool over them.

Splitting and joining vertices

When shapes are created with the Rectangle tool, the shape consists of four edges and four corner points, but these are selected together and act as one unit. Using the Split tool, you can break the edges into separate objects. To use this tool, just click where you want the break to be located. Inferences points appear as you move the tool over the top of the object.

The Join tool does the opposite. It lets you combine two points that are lying on top of each other to be connected to make a single shape. To use this tool, simply click on the first point (or line) and then on the second point; the entities are then joined together.

Working with Text

Text can be inserted into the document by choosing File ➪ Insert, but text can also be added to the pages using the Text and Label tools. The Text tool creates a text field where you can type directly into the field. This is good for titles.

The Label tool works like the Text tool except it attaches the text field to an arrowed line that points to where you first click. After placing the arrow, you can drag to place the text field and then type to enter the text.

For both the Text and Label tools, the text style is defined in the Text Style panel, as shown in Figure 25.18. The Text Style panel includes settings for the text color, the font, the typeface, and the text size. The Text menu also includes options to make the selected text Bold, Italic, Underline, Strikethrough, Bigger, and Smaller. There also are several alignment options.

FIGURE 25.18

Style for the Text and Label tools are found in the Text Style panel.

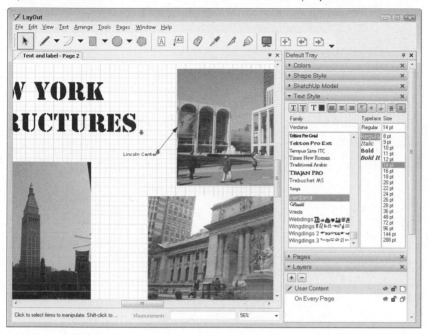

Summary

LayOut includes features for inserting and positioning a variety of objects including SketchUp models, images, and text. In addition to these object types, LayOut can also create a variety of its own objects including lines, curves, and shapes. It can also add text and labels natively. For its internal shape and text objects, you can configure the style and look using the various tray panels.

This chapter covered the following topics:

- Inserting models, images, and text
- Working with SketchUp models
- Selecting and transforming images and objects
- Duplicating objects
- Using the LayOut tools to draw lines, curves, and shapes
- Setting shape and text styles

In the next chapter, you look at how SketchUp can be used with Google Earth.

Chapter 26

Using SketchUp with Google Earth

hat do Google Earth and Google SketchUp have in common? They both are made and distributed by Google, but they share much more than that. Both programs are used to visualize 3-D environments and Google makes it possible to use the two together.

Location images in Google Earth can be imported into SketchUp, and models created in SketchUp can be uploaded and displayed in Google Earth. This synergy enables users around the globe to populate the virtual Earth with 3-D models, and the living online Google Earth is a testimony to this vision.

Installing Google Earth

Before you can retrieve and share models with Google Earth, you need to download and install Google Earth. You can find information about Google Earth at www.earth.google.com. Google Earth is available in three versions:

- **Google Earth:** This free version lets you view satellite images, maps, terrain, and uploaded 3-D objects.
- **Google Earth Plus:** This version is available for a nominal fee and adds GPS device support, faster performance, the ability to import spreadsheet data, and high-resolution printing.
- **Google Earth Pro:** The Pro version includes the ability to print at 4800-pixel resolution and offers many additional features that make it more accessible.

Once downloaded, run the installer and Google Earth is enabled on your system.

There are several interesting sites on the Google Earth Web site that you can view in Google Earth including geography awareness tours, turn-by-turn travel instructions, tours of famous locations such as the world of Shakespeare, and the Forbes.com list of the world's ten most expensive homes. These and other locations can be seen in the Google Earth Showcase gallery, as shown in Figure 26.1.

 **The latest version of Google Earth is version 4.3.**

FIGURE 26.1

The Google Earth Showcase gallery includes many interesting tours.

Using Google Earth

After you install Google Earth, you can run it on your system. The first view shows the entire globe from space, as seen in Figure 26.2.

Using the controls to the right, you can zoom in on the Earth and details begin to appear as you get close to them, as shown in Figure 26.3.

FIGURE 26.2

Google Earth begins with a view showing the whole Earth.

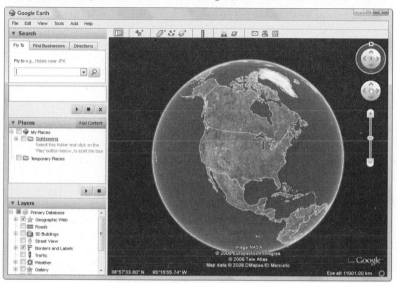

FIGURE 26.3

Zooming in reveals details such as city names.

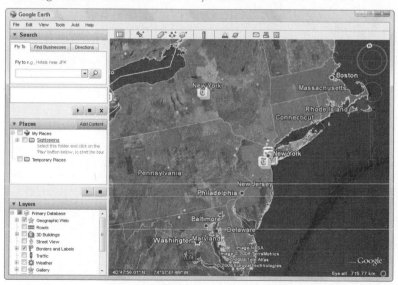

In addition to the interface controls, you can also zoom in using the scroll wheel. Clicking and dragging with the mouse, you can recenter the map. Dragging with the scroll wheel causes the map to spin about its center. Figure 26.4 shows a zoomed-in look at the south end of Central Park in New York.

FIGURE 26.4

Google Earth lets you zoom in to see individual buildings.

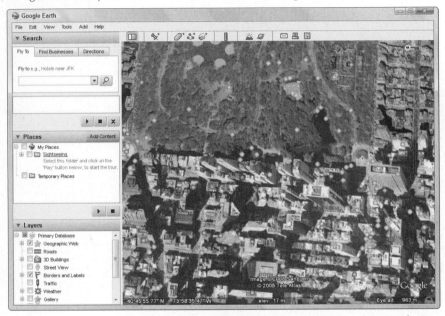

Retrieving the Current View

After you install Google Earth, you can take advantage of the links between Google Earth and SketchUp. The first way to use the two programs is to retrieve a view from Google Earth that you can use as a reference for your models.

When an image is retrieved from Google Earth, Georeferencing is automatically enabled and the location is set to the Longitude and Latitude values taken from Google Earth.

The first step in retrieving an image from Google Earth is to locate the image that you want to download in the Google Earth software. Zoom in on the building or the location until it is fairly detailed.

You can locate places in Google Earth by navigating the view, but you can also locate places by typing a specific address and having Google Earth locate the address.

Before downloading the Google Earth image, make sure that the Terrain option is selected in Google Earth or you will only get a flat, 2-D image. You can select this option at the bottom of the Layers panel, as shown in Figure 26.5.

After browsing in Google Earth, you can open up SketchUp and have the two programs connect with one another. When you have the image that you want, choose Tools ⇨ Google Earth ⇨ Get Current View within SketchUp, or you can click on the Get Current View button in the Google toolbar, as shown in Figure 26.6.

FIGURE 26.5

Make sure that the Terrain option is selected in Google Earth.

Terrain option

The Get Current View command queries Google Earth for its current view and imports the image into SketchUp. The image is locked to the current view so that it doesn't move as you navigate about the scene. Figure 26.7 shows an imported Google Earth image.

FIGURE 26.6

The Google toolbar in SketchUp includes buttons for interfacing with Google Earth.

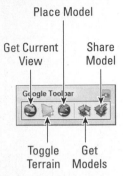

Place Model

Get Current
View

Share
Model

Google Toolbar

Toggle
Terrain

Get
Models

FIGURE 26.7

Google Earth images can be imported into SketchUp.

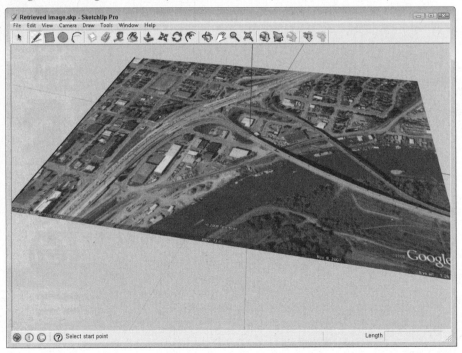

Imported images from Google Earth usually come in as 2-D images, like the one shown in Figure 26.8, but if the Terrain option is selected in Google Earth, you can choose Tools ⇨ Google Earth ⇨ Toggle Terrain menu in SketchUp, or click the Toggle Terrain button in the 3Google toolbar. This causes the terrain data to be viewed in SketchUp, as shown in Figure 26.9.

FIGURE 26.8

Google Earth images are imported as 2-D images.

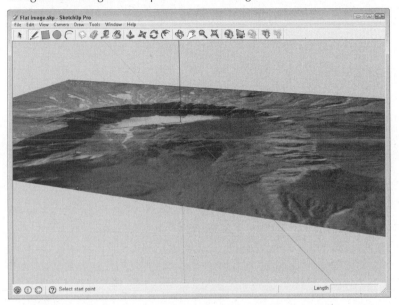

FIGURE 26.9

By toggling on the terrain, you can see the 3-D terrain data in SketchUp.

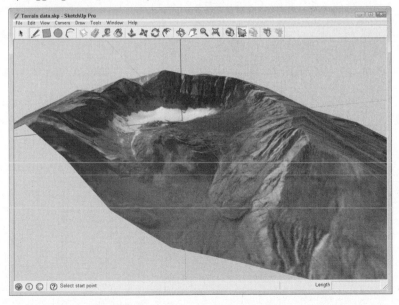

Placing Models

If you've spent time modeling a building, such as your own home or something more grand, like the Louvre museum in Paris, and you're anxious to show off your brilliant modeling, you can choose Tools ➪ Google Earth ➪ Place Model in SketchUp to add your model to the Google Earth database.

Figure 26.10 shows a simple platform that was added to the top of the mountain in SketchUp. Because the image was imported from Google Earth, the position relative to the Google Earth database is known and the Place Model command knows exactly where to place the model so it matches the work done in SketchUp.

> **NOTE** The objects placed with the Place Model command are displayed in your local installation of Google Earth only. To upload models to the actual online Google Earth database, you can use the Export feature.

After a model is completed in SketchUp, you can move it back to Google Earth. Figure 26.11 shows the same platform in Google Earth.

FIGURE 26.10

SketchUp models can be added to Google Earth.

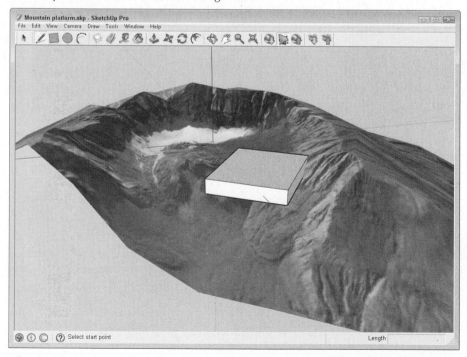

FIGURE 26.11

The same placed model appears in Google Earth at the same location.

Exporting Models

The Place Model command moves the current model to the local installation of Google Earth, but to integrate your model with the online Google Earth database, you need to export the model using the Keyhole Markup Language (KMZ) format.

The KMZ format is different in that it also contains latitude and longitude information that is used to globally line up the model on a global map.

You can export models to this format by choosing File ➪ Export ➪ 3D Model in SketchUp. In the Export Model dialog box, shown in Figure 26.12, select Google Earth (kmz) as the Export type, give the file a name, and click Export.

Exporting a model to the KMZ format doesn't make the model part of Google Earth. To actually add the model to the Google Earth database, you need to visit the Google Earth site and upload the exported file, or you can use the Share Models command in SketchUp.

FIGURE 26.12

The Export Model dialog box includes an option to export the model to the Google Earth (KMZ) format.

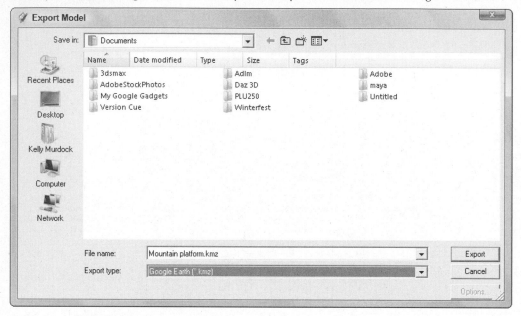

Sharing Models

Another way to distribute your work of art is to choose File ➪ 3D Warehouse ➪ Share Models within SketchUp or click the Share Model button on the Google toolbar. This command opens the 3D Warehouse Web site and asks you to log in to your account. If you don't have an account, you can easily create one.

CROSS-REF You can learn more about 3D Warehouse in Chapter 4.

After you log in, you are asked to complete a form to give the model a Title, a Description, and an Address, as shown in Figure 26.13. There is also a check box to mark if the model is real, current, and correctly located. Models built using an image imported from Google Earth are correctly located.

Other information that can be added to the 3D Warehouse login page includes a Web address to a site with more information, a logo of the model, and any tags that help categorize the model. You can also select an option to allow 3D Warehouse users to contact you about the model. After all the information is filled out, click Upload to add your model to 3D Warehouse.

FIGURE 26.13

You'll need to fill out a form describing your model before it can be uploaded to 3D Warehouse.

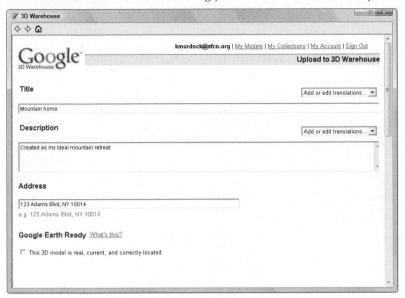

Getting Models

Choosing File ⇨ 3D Warehouse ⇨ Get Models in SketchUp or clicking the Get Models button on the Google toolbar opens the 3D Warehouse Web site, as shown in Figure 26.14. This site requires you to log in before you can access the various models.

After logging in, you can browse or search for models that you want. When you locate a file that you want to download, click on its thumbnail to view the details about the model, as shown in Figure 26.15. If the model is based on a Google Earth location, the description page will include an option to View in Google Earth, which you can use to download the model and view it in Google Earth.

FIGURE 26.14

The 3D Warehouse Web site is a great resource for getting new models.

FIGURE 26.15

You can view the details about a model by clicking on its thumbnail.

Summary

Learning to use Google Earth and SketchUp together gives you a powerful set of tools that ground the models in real locations. Terrain and images from Google Earth let you present an accurate view of your design's location. It also encourages users to share and upload their own models.

This chapter covered the following topics:

- Installing Google Earth
- Working with Google Earth
- Retrieving a location image from Google Earth and viewing its terrain data
- Placing SketchUp models in Google Earth
- Exporting SketchUp models to the KMZ format
- Sharing models with 3D Warehouse
- Getting models from 3D Warehouse

The next chapter shows how Ruby scripts can be used to extend the features of SketchUp.

Part VII

Extending SketchUp

Chapter 27

Scripting with Ruby

ketchUp was developed by a team of programmers using the latest programming techniques and tools. These tools keep the code secure and prevent hackers from altering the code. It preserves the code integrity and keeps it safe, but it also prevents the base code from being altered.

However, the programmers have also written the code in such a way that the internal structures of the program are open and can be accessed using a scripting language.

The scripting language that is supported by SketchUp is Ruby. Using Ruby scripts, you can add new functionality to the program.

Understanding Ruby Scripting

Scripting languages, such as Ruby, are founded on key programming concepts, but they are also generally easier to understand and write than a full-blown coding language like C++ or Java. Ruby scripts are interpreted, which means that they are written using normal text syntax. These text commands are read and interpreted by the code as the script is run.

Ruby scripts don't require any fancy development tool or compiler. The scripts are written using any standard text editor and are saved using the .rb extension.

Accessing the Ruby Help files

The textual syntax for interfacing with SketchUp comes from the established Application Programming Interface (API) developed by the SketchUp team. This API contains all the keywords that are needed to access the internal program feature. You can find the complete SketchUp API in the Ruby Help files, as shown in Figure 27.1, which are opened by choosing Help ⇨ Ruby Help.

FIGURE 27.1

The Ruby Help files include the SketchUp API.

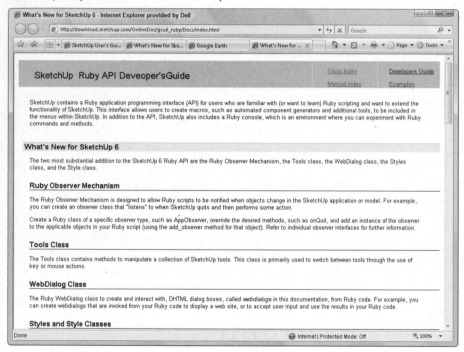

The Ruby Help file opens in a Web browser just like the SketchUp help files. An online version of the Ruby Help file is also available at the SketchUp Web site at `http://sketchup.google.com`.

The Ruby Help file also includes a Class Index, which lists all the available classes, as shown in Figure 27.2. Each class corresponds to a specific feature in SketchUp. Using the classes, you can extend and add to the functionality of the feature.

FIGURE 27.2

The Ruby Help files include a Class Index.

For example, the Toolbar class, shown in Figure 27.3, includes a description of the class and a list of its available methods. Each class method is a command for doing a specific task. For example, the Toolbar class includes a method to add_item. Using this method, you can add an item to the listed toolbar.

Methods are associated with each class, but there is also an index of available methods that you can use to work backward if you need to.

Getting Ruby help

In addition to the SketchUp API, you also need to understand the Ruby scripting syntax. The Ruby scripting language has specific keywords that it uses to do things like assign variables and loop through commands.

The Web has many sites that can provide this basic information. A good place to start is the Ruby user's guide at www.ruby-doc.org, as shown in Figure 27.4.

 **TIP** Another good Ruby learning site is www.rubycentral.com.

FIGURE 27.3

The Ruby Help files include detailed instructions on each class.

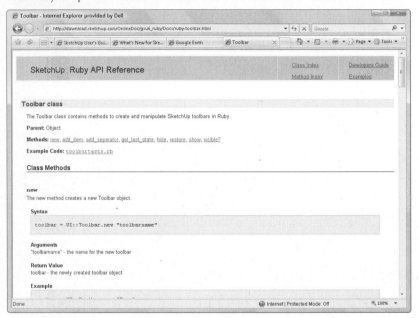

FIGURE 27.4

The Ruby user's guide is a good place to start learning Ruby scripting.

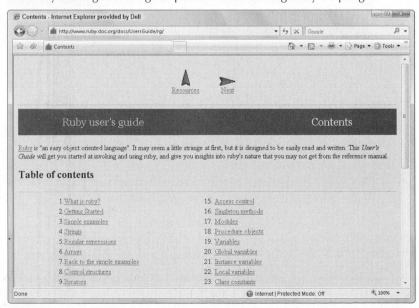

Reviewing the Ruby Samples

One of the best ways to start with Ruby scripting is to review an existing Ruby script to learn how certain things are accomplished. SketchUp includes several samples that you can review. All these samples have the `.rb` extension and can be viewed using a standard text editor such as Windows Notepad.

The Ruby scripting examples are located in the `Plugins\Examples` folder where SketchUp is installed. Additional Ruby scripts can be downloaded from the SketchUp Web site. Figure 27.5 shows a sample Ruby script in Notepad.

Some Ruby examples are made available as an extension. You can activate these samples using the Extensions panel in the System Preferences dialog box, as shown in Figure 27.6. You access the System Preference dialog box by choosing Window➪Preferences. Once enabled, these scripts are made available in the Plugins menu and in the Draw menu.

FIGURE 27.5

Ruby scripts can be opened and viewed within a text editor.

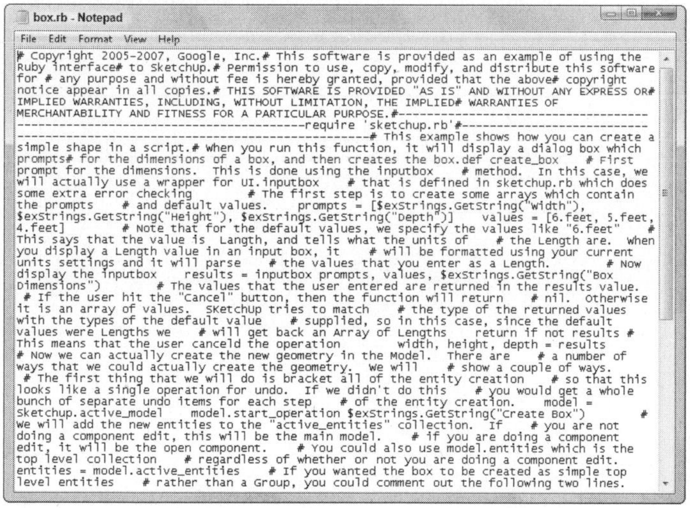


```
# Copyright 2005-2007, Google, Inc.# This software is provided as an example of using the
Ruby interface# to SketchUp.# Permission to use, copy, modify, and distribute this software
for # any purpose and without fee is hereby granted, provided that the above# copyright
notice appear in all copies.# THIS SOFTWARE IS PROVIDED "AS IS" AND WITHOUT ANY EXPRESS OR#
IMPLIED WARRANTIES, INCLUDING, WITHOUT LIMITATION, THE IMPLIED# WARRANTIES OF
MERCHANTABILITY AND FITNESS FOR A PARTICULAR PURPOSE.#------------------------------------
----------------------------------------require 'sketchup.rb'#---------------------------
-------------------------------------------------# This example shows how you can create a
simple shape in a script.# When you run this function, it will display a dialog box which
prompts# for the dimensions of a box, and then creates the box.def create_box    # First
prompt for the dimensions.  This is done using the inputbox    # method.  In this case, we
will actually use a wrapper for UI.inputbox    # that is defined in sketchup.rb which does
some extra error checking          # The first step is to create some arrays which contain
the prompts    # and default values.    prompts = [$exStrings.GetString("Width"),
$exStrings.GetString("Height"), $exStrings.GetString("Depth")]    values = [6.feet, 5.feet,
4.feet]        # Note that for the default values, we specify the values like "6.feet"    #
This says that the value is  Langth, and tells what the units of    # the Length are.  When
you display a Length value in an input box, it    # will be formatted using your current
units settings and it will parse    # the values that you enter as a Length.        # Now
display the inputbox    results = inputbox prompts, values, $exStrings.GetString("Box
Dimensions")        # The values that the user entered are returned in the results value.
 # If the user hit the "Cancel" button, then the function will return    # nil.  Otherwise
it is an array of values.  SketchUp tries to match    # the type of the returned values
with the types of the default value    # supplied, so in this case, since the default
values were Lengths we    # will get back an Array of Lengths    return if not results #
This means that the user canceld the operation        width, height, depth = results
# Now we can actually create the new geometry in the Model.  There are    # a number of
ways that we could actually create the geometry.  We will    # show a couple of ways.
 # The first thing that we will do is bracket all of the entity creation    # so that this
looks like a single operation for undo.  If we didn't do this    # you would get a whole
bunch of separate undo items for each step    # of the entity creation.    model =
Sketchup.active_model    model.start_operation $exStrings.GetString("Create Box")        #
We will add the new entities to the "active_entities" collection.  If    # you are not
doing a component edit, this will be the main model.    # if you are doing a component
edit, it will be the open component.    # You could also use model.entities which is the
top level collection    # regardless of whether or not you are doing a component edit.
entities = model.active_entities    # If you wanted the box to be created as simple top
level entities    # rather than a Group, you could comment out the following two lines.
```

FIGURE 27.6

The Extensions panel in the System Preferences dialog box makes some Ruby samples active.

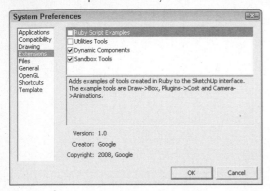

Accessing the Ruby Console

After you begin writing and working with Ruby scripts, you'll want to use the Ruby Console. This simple window is opened by choosing Window ⇨ Ruby Console. It provides an interface where you can type Ruby commands and see the results.

One such command is the `UI.messagebox()` command. This command opens a message box and prints inside the dialog box anything contained within quotes inside the parentheses. So, if you type **UI.messagebox("Ruby Rules")** in the text field at the bottom of the Ruby Console, as shown in Figure 27.7 and press Enter, the command executes and causes the message box shown in Figure 27.8 to appear.

FIGURE 27.7

The Ruby Console lets you type and execute Ruby commands.

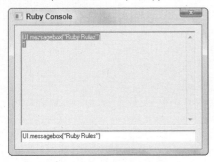

FIGURE 27.8

This message box appears as a direct result of the Ruby script command typed in Figure 27.7.

As you become more familiar with Ruby syntax and the SketchUp API, you can create more complex scripts.

Summary

Ruby scripting with the SketchUp API provides a way to extend the functionality of SketchUp. The Ruby Help files provide a detailed index of the available classes and methods, and several Web sites for learning Ruby are also available. Within SketchUp, the Ruby Console is available, along with multiple Ruby samples for testing and learning to write scripts.

This chapter covered the following topics:

- Accessing the Ruby Help files
- Reviewing the available Ruby sample examples
- Using the Ruby Console

Whether you write your own scripts or download one that someone else has written, you need to install it and work with plug-ins to get it to work in SketchUp. The next chapter covers working with plug-ins.

Expanding SketchUp with Third-Party Plug-Ins

I f you've mastered every menu and every command in SketchUp and still want the software to do more, you'll be happy to know that SketchUp is built around an open architecture that allows it to be extended using plug-in scripts.

These scripts help you gain additional functionality that may be just the tool that you need to save you tons of time. This chapter covers locating and installing plug-ins and takes a look at the available sample plug-ins from the SketchUp Web site.

Enabling Extensions

To show off the plug-in capabilities of SketchUp, the program includes three plug-in sets that you can enable in the System Preferences dialog box. These plug-in sets are known as extensions, and, although they are turned off by default, you can enable them in the Extensions panel of the System Preferences dialog box, as shown in Figure 28.1. The System Preferences dialog box is opened by choosing Window ⇨ Preferences.

Some extensions, such as the Sandbox tool, are available as soon as they are enabled, but others require you to restart SketchUp.

CROSS-REF The Sandbox tools are covered in more detail in Chapter 14.

FIGURE 28.1

Some plug-ins are enabled through the Extensions panel in the System Preferences dialog box.

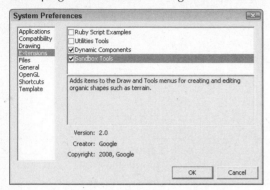

Locating Plug-Ins

Although SketchUp plug-ins can be found all over the Web, the SketchUp Web site is the best place to look for plug-ins. A list of available commercial and noncommercial SketchUp plug-ins can be found at `http://sketchup.google.com/download/plugins.html`, as shown in Figure 28.2.

FIGURE 28.2

The SketchUp Web site includes a list of available plug-ins.

CAUTION Although Google has created a number of valuable plug-ins, most plug-ins are developed by companies other than Google. If there's a problem that develops as a result of downloading a plug-in that is created by an outside vendor, the Google warranty does not cover this.

Exploring popular commercial plug-ins

The first plug-ins listed on the SketchUp Web site are popular commercial plug-ins that add significant features to the software. Some of this software must be purchased before it can be used, and others can be downloaded and installed for free. Table 28.1 lists many of the popular commercial plug-ins.

NOTE Some of these plug-ins are available for Windows, Mac, and Linux; others are only available for specific platforms. Check the plug-in's Web site for compatibility.

TABLE 28.1

Popular Commercial Plug-ins

Plug-in Name	Company	Description	Web Site
Podium	Cadalog Inc.	A photorealistic rendering engine that runs within SketchUp.	www.cadalog.com
TurboSketch	IMSI Design	A photorealistic rendering engine that runs within SketchUp. It also includes a lighting control feature.	www.imsidesign.com
iRender	Render Plus Systems	A photorealistic rendering engine that runs within SketchUp. It also includes a feature for creating reflections, lights, and mirrors.	www.renderplus.com
Artlantis	Abvent	Exports SketchUp models to a format that allows rendering within the Artlantis rendering engine.	www.artlantis.com
Maxwell Render	Next Limit Technologies	Allows SketchUp models to be rendered using the Maxwell Render system, which includes support for multilights, Maxwell Materials, Global Illumination, and Physical Sky.	www.maxwellrender.com
VRay	ASGVIS	This plug-in allows SketchUp models to be rendered in the VRay rendering engine, which features realistic ray-tracing renders.	www.asgvis.com
Hypercosm Teleporter	Hypercosm	This plug-in converts SketchUp models into an interactive Web page using the Hypercosm Player for viewing exported files.	www.hypercosm.com

continued

475

TABLE 28.1	*(continued)*		
Plug-in Name	**Company**	**Description**	**Web Site**
eDrawings Publisher	Geometric Software Solutions	This plug-in exports the SketchUp model to an eDrawings format that can be viewed and marked up using the eDrawings viewer. The eDrawings format is common among MCAD professionals.	`www.geometric software.com`
PRS 3D PDF Exporter	Render Plus Systems	Allows SketchUp models to be converted into popular 3-D PDF files that can be viewed in the Adobe Reader.	`www.renderplus.com`
Photoshop CS3 Extended Plug-In for Google 3D Warehouse	Google and Adobe	This plug-in installs into Photoshop CS3 Extended and allows Photoshop users to access 3D Warehouse models for importing into Photoshop.	`www.adobe.com`
SpecifiCAD	CADalytic Media	This plug-in is used to identify building components and match them to actual manufactured products available on the Sweets Network through 3D Warehouse. The plug-in can even replace the matched components with the selected product.	`www.cadalytic.com`
RPS RpReports	Render Plus Systems	This plug-in is designed to let you pre-define attributes and reports. It will automatically compute totals for the current project.	`www.renderplus.com`
RPS RpTools	Render Plus Systems	This plug-in is a suite of tools for working with downloaded 3-D components, allowing you to perform multiple transforms at once. It also includes a number of standard 3-D shapes and line tools.	`www.renderplus.com`
RPS Space Design	Render Plus Systems	This plug-in uses easy-to-follow wizards to create rooms of objects. It also includes a set of 3-D shapes.	`www.renderplus.com`
ArcGIS	Google	This plug-in helps to visualize GIS data using SketchUp models.	`www.sketchup.com`

Installing Plug-Ins

After you find a plug-in that you want to add to your SketchUp installation, you need to download it and unzip the file into your Plugins folder where SketchUp is installed on your system. Files that are added to the Plugins folder are automatically loaded the next time SketchUp starts.

After unzipping the downloaded plug-in file, look for a file that ends with the `.rb` extension. This is a Ruby file and is the plug-in file that needs to be placed within the Plugins folder.

You can look for information on how to use the downloaded plug-in in the downloaded Zip file. Most plug-in authors include a readme text file that explains how the plug-in works.

The SketchUp Web site has a section that features a number of sample Ruby scripts that add extra functionality to the program. These plug-ins can be downloaded from `http://sketchup.google.com/download/rubyscripts.html`, as shown in Figure 28.3.

FIGURE 28.3

Sample Ruby scripts can be downloaded from the SketchUp Web site.

Using Sample Ruby Scripts

Some of these Ruby scripts are libraries that include functions that the other plug-ins rely on. One of the best ways to become familiar with Ruby scripts is to download and install several. Several available scripts on the SketchUp Web site are helpful and add a lot to the functionality of the program. Once downloaded and placed in the Plugins folder, you need to restart SketchUp before these new features can be used. Several of these sample plug-ins with their new functionality are described in the following sections.

Bezier curves

Bezier curves are a special type of curve developed by Pierre Bezier, an engineer for Renault. He developed the curves while working to create a curve that mathematically could represent the curves of a car body. Bezier curves are computed from a set of straight hull lines that define the borders of the curve. A key advantage to Bezier curves is that they are always smooth, which makes them the basis for many computer-drawn vector curves such as fonts.

 **Bezier curves always intersect with the first and last endpoints of the hull lines.**

With the `Bezier.rb` plug-in installed, the Bezier Curves option appears in the Draw menu. With this tool selected, you can click to place the points used by a Bezier curve, and a smooth curve is drawn within the hull lines, as shown in Figure 28.4.

FIGURE 28.4

The Bezier Curve tool draws smooth curves based on a hull of straight lines.

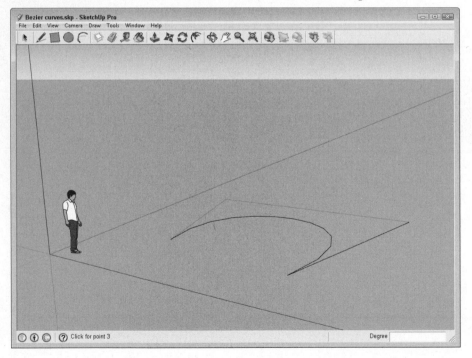

When drawing a curve with the Bezier Curve tool, the Measurements Toolbar displays the degree of the curve. This value determines how many points can exist in the hull. A degree setting of 1 only allows straight lines with 2 points. A degree setting of 3 allows 4 points, which creates a smooth curve. Higher degree curves allow more complexity, such as the 7-degree curve shown in Figure 28.5.

FIGURE 28.5

Bezier curves with a higher degree value can be more complex.

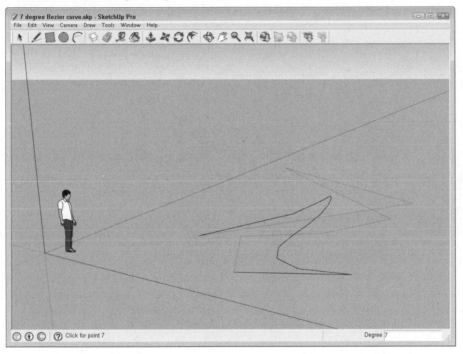

Rotated Rectangle

The Rotated Rectangle tool is added to the Draw menu after the `rectangle.rb` plug-in is installed. This tool lets you click and drag to set the rectangle's width; the rectangle's length is set by dragging about the drawing. Using inference points, the rectangle's length can be set to be rotated to any angle. This is convenient because you don't need to create a flat rectangle and rotate it into place.

Figure 28.6 shows a new rectangle that is being added to span the two parallel rectangles. Using the Rotated Rectangle tool, you can select the upper edge and click to create the rectangle in place.

FIGURE 28.6

The Rotated Rectangle tool lets you rotate and create a rectangle in place.

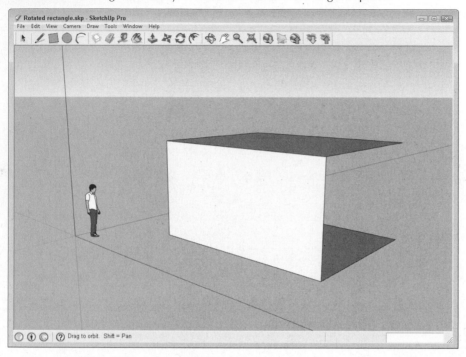

Adding new shapes

The Shapes.rb plug-in adds a Shapes menu to the Draw menu. The available shapes, which appear as submenus, include Box, Cylinder, Cone, Torus, Tube, Prism, Pyramid, and Dome. Each of these shapes is shown in Figure 28.7.

 The Shapes plug-in requires that the parametric.rb and the mesh_additions. rb scripts are also included.

For each of these shapes, a dialog box like the one in Figure 28.8 appears where you can type the exact dimensions of the shape. All new shapes appear at the origin.

Creating windows

The window.rb plug-in adds a Window option to the Tools menu. When selected, the Create Window dialog box, shown in Figure 28.9, appears. Using this dialog box, you can specify the dimensions of the window to create. You can also select the window type to be Slider or Double Hung. Figure 28.10 shows an example of each of these types.

FIGURE 28.7

The `Shapes.rb` plug-in makes several 3-D basic shapes available.

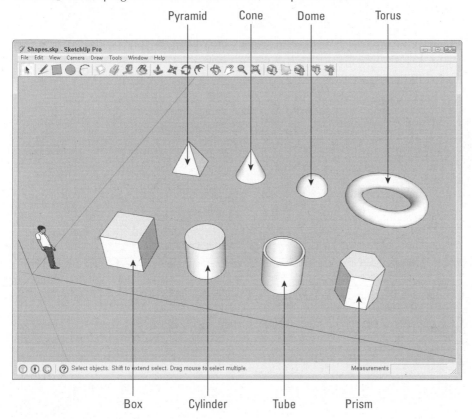

Pyramid · Cone · Dome · Torus

Box · Cylinder · Tube · Prism

FIGURE 28.8

A simple dialog box appears where you can type the dimensions of the shape you're creating.

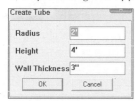

NOTE The Windows plug-in requires that the `parametric.rb` script is also included.

FIGURE 28.9

The Create Window dialog box enables you to set the window's dimensions and type.

FIGURE 28.10

Two kinds of windows can be created with the Window plug-in.

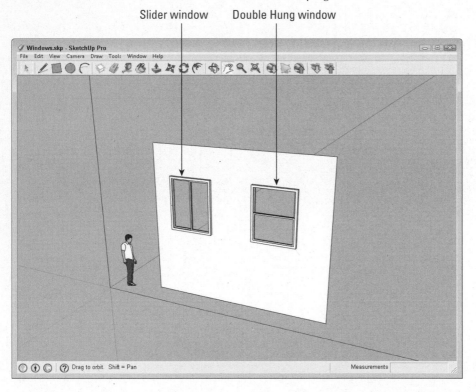

Creating grids

The Grid plug-in lets you create dashed-line grids by clicking and dragging in the scene. This option is available from the Tools menu after the plug-in is installed. To create a grid, click and drag to set the width and click and drag to set the length. The Spacing between grid cells is set in the Measurements Toolbar. Figure 28.11 shows a sample grid.

The Grid plug-in can create grids in the scene.

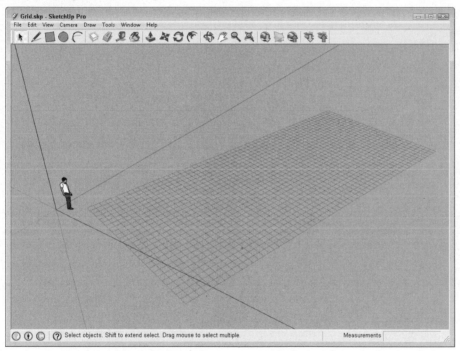

Making onion domes

An onion dome is the architectural roof type commonly found in Russia with the pointy top and the rounded sides. Once installed, the Onion Dome plug-in appears in the Draw menu. When selected, the Create Onion Dome dialog box appears, as shown in Figure 28.12. Using this dialog box, you can set the dimensions for the onion dome.

NOTE   The Onion Dome plug-in requires that the `parametric.rb`, `bezier.rb`, and the
`mesh_additions.rb` scripts are also included.

FIGURE 28.12

The Create Onion Dome dialog box includes all the dimension settings for the onion dome object.

Figure 28.13 shows the completed onion dome object.

FIGURE 28.13

Onion domes are sometimes used to cap the top of turrets on buildings in Russia.

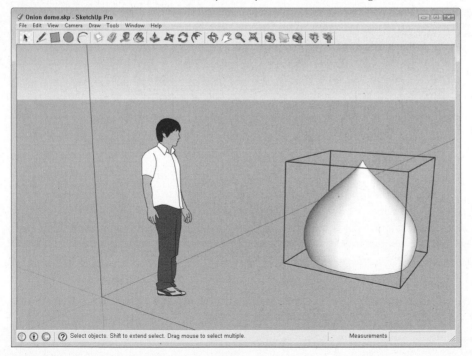

Simplifying contours

The Simplify Contours menu command appears in the Plugins menu after the plug-in is installed. It is used to simplify a large set of contour lines that are typical when received from a surveyor. After simplifying the contour lines, choose Draw ➪ Sandbox ➪ From Contours to create a terrain surface.

 **More on creating surfaces from contour lines is covered in Chapter 14.**

Summary

Using plug-ins, you can add new features to SketchUp. A search of the SketchUp Web site and other community sites will reveal a large assortment of available plug-ins. Some plug-ins are commercial and available to buy, and others are free to download and try. Installing plug-ins is simply a matter of dropping the script file into the Plugins folder where SketchUp is installed. This chapter also looked at the available sample plug-ins found on the SketchUp Web site.

This chapter covered the following topics:

- How to enable extensions
- Locating plug-ins on the SketchUp Web site
- A list of available commercial plug-ins
- How to install plug-ins
- The various sample plug-ins on the SketchUp Web site

This is the final chapter, but the appendixes include a lot of valuable information including the new features in SketchUp 6, how to install and configure the software, and a list of keyboard shortcuts.

Part VIII

Appendixes

Appendix A

What's New with Google SketchUp 7

W ith each new version of the software, there are a host of new features. There are also several minor improvements that make the software more efficient and which improve your productivity.

Many of the improvements in this version are a direct result of feedback from existing users. The SketchUp development team is committed to making software that works for you, and part of this effort involves listening to their users. If you have an idea for the development team, you can choose Help ⇨ Contact Us to access a Web page where you can provide feedback, report a bug, or present your idea.

IN THIS APPENDIX

New features in SketchUp 7

Minor improvements in SketchUp 7

New Features in SketchUp 7

This category of improvements is designated as major because it represents a new set of features that haven't been in the software previously. These new features let you do things that weren't possible in the previous editions.

Dynamic Components

Probably the biggest new addition to SketchUp 7 is the Dynamic Components. Within these components, you can control the behavior of objects using custom parameters such as the ability to open and close windows or to add and subtract stairs. All SketchUp 7 users can include and use dynamic components in their designs, and SketchUp 7 Pro users have the ability to create custom dynamic components.

CROSS-REF Dynamic Components are covered in Chapter 16.

Search in Components Browser

The Components Browser has been improved to allow you to search the 3D Warehouse directly from within the Components Browser. There is also a Save to Favorites option where you can save custom searches. All items found from a search of 3D Warehouse can be saved as a local collection providing you access to the model offline.

CROSS-REF The improved Components Browser is covered in Chapter 15.

Custom Templates

Design and rendering styles can be saved as a template providing a way to standardize all your documents. Custom templates let you specify the working units, style, ground, sky, and rendering attributes. Defined templates can then be selected when creating a new document.

CROSS-REF Saving a custom template is covered in Chapter 4, and defining the template's style is described in Chapter 20.

Georeferencing

Within the Model Info dialog box is a Location panel for setting the location, longitude, and latitude for the current model. You can also set the solar orientation. A status bar button is available for turning georeferencing on and off.

CROSS-REF The new Georeferencing features are covered in Chapter 15.

Style Builder

The new Style Builder application lets you create and save your own custom styles for SketchUp.

CROSS-REF The new Style Builder feature is covered in Chapter 21.

Improved LayOut interface

Included with the SketchUp Pro 7 version is the new LayOut 2.0 application. This program lets you combine SketchUp content with text, images, and photos to create interactive presentations.

CROSS-REF The new Layout program is introduced in Chapter 24 and continued in Chapter 25.

Better performance

Many of the underlying algorithms in SketchUp have been improved, making the software faster. In some configurations, the software runs as much as five times faster.

Minor Improvements in SketchUp 7

Minor improvements are changes made to an existing feature, but often these small changes may be an even more important improvement for the work you do.

Model Credits

All models that are built in SketchUp 7 are identified with credits. These credits stay with the model to record the creator as the model is uploaded to 3D Warehouse and downloaded and used by others. The credits even record individuals that make changes to an existing model.

Measurements Toolbar

The Value Control Bar (VCB) has been renamed the Measurements Toolbar. You can also change this toolbar's location.

Help Center

All the various Help resources have been integrated into a single help dialog box called Help Center.

Appendix B

Installing and Configuring Google SketchUp 7

I nstalling the software is usually the first task that is required before you can work with the software. However, for most experienced users, the process of installing software is quite simple, so rather than spend time covering installation and configuration issues in the early chapters of this book, they have been placed in this out-of-the-way appendix.

If you've had no trouble installing and configuring the software, then you won't need to read this appendix. But if you have any trouble, or if you are curious, then you can use this appendix to guide you through the process and get some tips along the way.

Choosing an Operating System

If you're purchasing a new computer to run SketchUp and have the luxury of customizing your system, you can do several things to make life easier. One of your first decisions is what operating system to use. Google SketchUp can run on both Windows and Macintosh. Both operating systems enable you to run multiple copies of SketchUp at the same time on a single machine.

Installing to Windows

If you choose to run SketchUp on a Windows system, you can use Windows 2000, Windows XP, and Windows Vista. Whichever Windows system you use, make sure that the latest Service Pack is installed (which you can download for free from Microsoft's Web page at www.microsoft.com). Also note that Windows NT, Windows 98, and Windows Me are not supported.

 Google SketchUp can also run on a 64-bit version of Windows, but it runs as a 32-bit application.

Installing to Mac

If you choose to run SketchUp on a Macintosh system, you can use Mac OS X 10.4.1+ or 10.5+. SketchUp is fully compatible with OS X Leopard, but there have been some problems reported when trying to authorize a Pro version. If you have such problems, try launching and typing your license key while disconnected from the Internet.

 Be aware that neither Boot Camp or Parallels is supported by Google SketchUp.

Understanding System Requirements

To get good performance from SketchUp, you need at least a 2 GHz Pentium 4 processor with 2GB of RAM for Windows or at least a 2.1 GHz G5/Intel processor with 2GB of RAM for Mac. If your computer isn't that new, you can get away with the minimum requirements, but these systems will cause the software to run sluggish.

 SketchUp can run on multiple-processor computers, but it runs as a single thread on only one processor.

Minimum requirements

The minimum hardware requirements for running Google SketchUp on Windows 2000 or Windows XP are:

- 600 MHz Pentium III processor
- 128MB of RAM
- 128MB of hard drive space

The minimum hardware requirements for running Google SketchUp on Windows Vista are:

- 800 MHz Pentium III processor for Vista Home Basic or a 1 GHz Pentium III processor for other Vista versions
- 512MB of RAM for Vista Home Basic or 1GB of RAM for other Vista versions
- 15GB of hard drive space

The minimum hardware requirements for running Google SketchUp on Mac are:

- 1 GHz PowerPC G4 processor
- 512MB of RAM
- 160MB of hard drive space

Graphics cards

One element of your system that will probably have the greatest impact on the performance of SketchUp is the graphics card. Any good graphics card has specialized hardware that takes much of the workload off your computer's CPU, freeing it up to do other tasks. SketchUp is very graphics-intensive, and a little extra money in the graphics card department goes a long way toward boosting your performance.

The good news is that hardware-accelerated graphics cards are becoming cheaper: You can get great cards for $200–$300. When searching for a graphics card, make sure that it can support a resolution of at least 1024×768 at 16-bit color with 3-D graphics acceleration including support for OpenGL. You also want a card with 512MB on the graphics card for the best performance, but look for cards with at least 256MB or more for 3-D graphics acceleration. You can use some of the graphics boards built to run computer games; however, be aware that some boards claim to support OpenGL but actually support only a subset of it. Before going out to make your purchase, visit the SketchUp Web site at www.sketchup.google.com to see if the graphics cards you are considering are supported.

 **A video card is only as good as the drivers that are available. SketchUp relies heavily on these drivers, and if the driver has trouble, then your display will flicker, have speed problems, or just plain won't work. Both nVidia and ATI video cards have excellent drivers with broad support.**

Other requirements

For the complete installation, you need 650MB of hard drive space. You can get by with less if you choose the Compact installation option. Another handy piece of hardware to have is a three-button scrollable mouse. A three-button scrollable mouse gives you a third button, which can be used to navigate the scene.

If you're running SketchUp on a Windows-based machine, then you also need to install the .NET 1.1 framework. The installer checks for this framework and automatically provides a link for downloading and installing the framework if it is missing.

To access and view the video tutorials, you need to have either Windows Media Player or QuickTime 5.0 installed on your system.

NOTE **If you plan on downloading the videos to your local system, then you'll need to also download the EnSharpen codec for viewing the videos.**

Installing Google SketchUp

Installing Google SketchUp is straightforward. It can be installed from a downloaded Web file or from a purchased CD. The setup process installs three separate applications: SketchUp 7, LayOut 2, and Style Builder. To install from the Web, follow these steps:

1. Locate and download the installation file from the Google SketchUp Web site at `http://sketchup.google.com/download.html`. If you choose to download the Pro version, you need to complete an online form.

2. Once downloaded, locate and run the installation file by double-clicking it. This starts the Installation Wizard, shown in Figure B.1. You can move through the Installation Wizard by clicking Next.

FIGURE B.1

The installation Wizard guides you through the setup process.

3. The second page of the Installation Wizard shows the License Agreement and requires that you accept the license terms before the Next button becomes active, allowing you to continue.

4. The next page of the Installation Wizard lets you specify the location on the hard drive where you want the software installed. After completing the wizard, the software is installed to your system.

5. The last page of the wizard shows that the installation was successful. Click Finish to exit the Installation Wizard.

If you've installed the standard version, the software should be ready to go. You can open the software using the desktop icon or by double-clicking the icon in the Google SketchUp 7 folder.

If you run the setup file after the software is installed, you'll see a maintenance wizard, as shown in Figure B.2, that lets you Modify, Repair, or Remove the installation.

Running the setup file after installing the program lets you access the maintenance wizard.

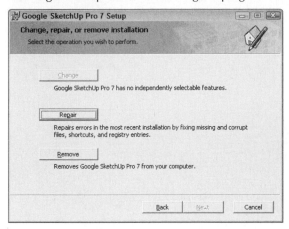

Authorizing Google SketchUp Pro

If you've installed the Pro version, you have one more step to complete. Authorizing the software lets you type the license code. If you don't have a license code, the Pro version runs in trial mode for eight hours after which the software is simply converted to the standard version.

NOTE   **The standard and Pro versions are exactly the same except that some of the export features are disabled in the standard version. If you upgrade the software by typing a valid license, then new features are simply unlocked and you have access to use the LayOut interface.**

A license code can be purchased directly from the Google SketchUp Web site. Once purchased, Google e-mails you a serial number and an authorization code. When you get this information, type it in the SketchUp Authorization dialog box, shown in Figure B.3. This dialog box is accessed by choosing Help ⇨ License ⇨ Authorize. Just copy and paste the serial number and the authorization code into this text field. You should copy all of the license information including the Contact into the SketchUp Authorization dialog box. If you have any trouble pasting in the license information, click Skip, which opens another dialog box where you can manually type the Registered User Name, Company Name, Serial Number, and Authorization Number.

After the software is authorized, you can view the License Information by choosing Help ⇨ License ⇨ License Info.

FIGURE B.3

The SketchUp Authorization dialog box lets you enter a license code.

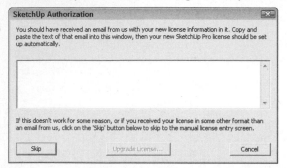

Authorizing a network version

The Help ⇨ License menu also includes a command to Set Network License File. This command lets you locate on the network a `SketchUp7.if` file that holds the license for authorizing a network version of the software.

 **The SketchUp licensing engine doesn't support mapped drives, so when locating the network license file, you need to access the shared network drive directly.**

The Help ⇨ License menu also includes a command to Set Network License File. This command lets you locate on the network a `SketchUp7.if` file that holds the license for authorizing a network version of the software.

If you have trouble locating the network license file, you can also authorize the other installations of the software by locating the `server.dat` file located where the original installation was authorized and copying it to the `Program Files\Google\Google SketchUp 7` folder for the other network installations.

To view the installations available over the network, open the LAN License Monitor application with the Help ⇨ License ⇨ Lan License Monitor menu command. This dialog box lists all the licenses on the network that are currently in use.

Updating SketchUp

Google SketchUp also includes a feature for checking for and automatically installing updates. From within SketchUp, choose Help ⇨ Check for Updates. This menu queries the SketchUp Web site and informs you if any new updates are available.

If you want to see which version you currently use, choose Help ⇨ About SketchUp to display the Google SketchUp information dialog box. This dialog box, shown in Figure B.4, shows the current version number.

The Google SketchUp information dialog box also includes links to the SketchUp Web site.

FIGURE B.4

The information dialog box displays the current version number.

Contacting Support

If you run into a problem that requires support, you can access customer support by choosing Help ⇨ Contact Us. This opens a Web page on the SketchUp Web site and takes you to a link where you can get Pro Technical Support. To access support, you need to fill out a form and type in your license number.

Moving SketchUp to Another Computer

A non-network license of SketchUp can exist on only one computer at a time. If you reinstall SketchUp on a different computer, you need to choose Help ⇨ License ⇨ Unauthorize to remove the license from the old computer. Once unauthorized, you can install and authorize the license on the new computer.

Appendix C

SketchUp Keyboard Shortcuts

The key to working efficiently with Google SketchUp is learning the keyboard shortcuts. If you know the keyboard shortcuts, you don't need to spend time moving the mouse cursor all around the interface; you can simply press the keyboard shortcut and get instant access to commands and tools.

IN THIS APPENDIX

Main interface shortcuts

Miscellaneous shortcuts

Main Interface Shortcuts

Most of the major menu commands and tools have their own keyboard shortcuts. This appendix breaks them up into logical groupings.

If you want to change any of the keyboard shortcuts, System Preferences includes a Shortcuts panel for making changes. Choose Window ⇨ Preferences to display this dialog box.

CROSS-REF Chapter 2 offers more details on creating custom keyboard shortcuts.

If you find that the keyboard shortcuts aren't working, then you can reset all shortcuts to their defaults using the Reset All button in the Shortcuts panel of the System Preferences dialog box.

CAUTION When installing an update, the default keyboard shortcuts are deleted and the new defaults are not enabled by default. Use the Reset All button to enable the new defaults.

Table C.1 presents the shortcut keys for the menu commands.

TABLE C.1

Menus

Command	Shortcut	Command	Shortcut
File ⇨ New	Ctrl+N	Camera ⇨ Zoom	Z
File ⇨ Open	Ctrl+O	Camera ⇨ Zoom Window	Ctrl+Shift+W
File ⇨ Save	Ctrl+S	Camera ⇨ Zoom Extents	Ctrl+Shift+E, Shift+Z
File ⇨ Print	Ctrl+P	Draw ⇨ Line	L
Edit ⇨ Undo	Ctrl+Z, Alt+Backspace	Draw ⇨ Arc	A
Edit ⇨ Redo	Ctrl+Y	Draw ⇨ Rectangle	R
Edit ⇨ Cut	Ctrl+X, Shift+Delete	Draw ⇨ Circle	C
Edit ⇨ Copy	Ctrl+C, Ctrl+Insert	Tools ⇨ Select	Spacebar
Edit ⇨ Paste	Ctrl+V, Shift+Insert	Tools ⇨ Eraser	E
Edit ⇨ Delete	Delete	Tools ⇨ Paint Bucket	B
Edit ⇨ Select All	Ctrl+A	Tools ⇨ Move	M
Edit ⇨ Select None	Ctrl+T	Tools ⇨ Rotate	Q
Edit ⇨ Make Component	G	Tools ⇨ Scale	S
View ⇨ Animation ⇨ Previous Scene	Page Up	Tools ⇨ Push/Pull	P
View ⇨ Animation ⇨ Next Scene	Page Down	Tools ⇨ Offset	F
Camera ⇨ Orbit	O	Tools ⇨ Tape Measure	T
Camera ⇨ Pan	H	SketchUp Help	Shift+F1

Tables C.2 through C.6 present the shortcut keys for the toolbar tools and buttons.

TABLE C.2

Camera Toolbar

Command	Shortcut	Command	Shortcut
Orbit tool	O	Zoom tool	Z
Pan tool	H	Zoom Extents tool	Shift+Z

TABLE C.3

Drawing and Construction Toolbars

Command	Shortcut	Command	Shortcut
Line tool	L	Arc tool	A
Rectangle tool	R	Tape Measure tool	T
Circle tool	C		

TABLE C.4

Edit and Principal Toolbars

Command	Shortcut	Command	Shortcut
Move/Copy tool	M	Offset tool	F
Rotate tool	Q	Select tool	Spacebar
Scale tool	S	Paint Bucket tool	B
Push/Pull tool	P	Eraser tool	E

TABLE C.5

Standard Toolbar

Command	Shortcut	Command	Shortcut
New	Ctrl+N	Paste	Ctrl+V
Open	Ctrl+O	Erase	Delete
Save	Ctrl+S	Undo	Ctrl+Z or Alt+Backspace
Cut	Ctrl+X	Redo	Ctrl+Y
Copy	Ctrl+C	Print	Ctrl+P

TABLE C.6

Views Toolbar

Command	Shortcut	Command	Shortcut
Iso view	Shift+1	Back view	Shift+5
Top view	Shift+2	Right view	Shift+6
Bottom view	Shift+3	Left view	Shift+7
Front view	Shift+4		

Miscellaneous Shortcuts

In addition to specific shortcuts for the main interface and the dialog boxes, SketchUp provides several general shortcuts that can be used in many different places, as listed in Table C.7.

TABLE C.7

General Shortcuts

Command	Shortcut	Command	Shortcut
Apply settings	Enter	Highlight any text field	Double-click current value
Highlight next text field	Tab	Display First Tab	Alt+1
Highlight previous text field	Shift+Tab	Help	F1

Appendix D

What's on the CD

Throughout this book, you'll find many tutorials that help you to understand the principles being discussed. All the example files used to create these tutorials are included on the CD that comes with this book.

This appendix provides you with information on the contents of the CD. For the latest and greatest information, please refer to the ReadMe file located at the root of the attached CD.

IN THIS APPENDIX

System requirements

Using the CD with Windows

Using the CD with Mac

What's on the CD

Troubleshooting

Customer Care

System Requirements

Make sure that your computer meets the minimum system requirements listed in this section. If your computer doesn't match up to most of these requirements, you may have a problem using the contents of the CD.

For Windows Vista, Windows XP Professional SP2 (recommended), Windows XP Home Edition SP2, or Windows 2000 SP4:

- Intel® Pentium® III or AMD® processor, 500 MHz or higher (dual Intel)
- Xeon® or dual AMD Athlon® or Opteron® (32-bit system recommended)
- 512MB RAM (1GB recommended)
- 500MB swap space (2GB recommended)
- Graphics card supporting 1024×768×16-bit color with 64MB RAM (OpenGL® and Direct3D® hardware acceleration supported; 3-D graphics accelerator 1280×1024×32-bit color with 256MB RAM recommended)

- Microsoft® Windows®–compliant pointing device (optimized for Microsoft IntelliMouse®)
- Microsoft Internet Explorer 6
- A CD drive

For Macintosh OS X:

- Mac OS X® 10.4.1+ and 10.5+
- 1 GHz PowerPC™ G4
- 512MB RAM
- 160MB of available hard disk space
- Safari
- QuickTime 5.0 and web browser
- 3-D class Video Card with 128 MB of memory or higher. The video card driver must be 100 percent OpenGL-compliant and up to date.
- Three-button, scroll-wheel mouse
- A CD drive

Using the CD with Windows

To install the items from the CD to your hard drive, follow these steps:

1. Insert the CD into your computer's CD drive. The license agreement appears.

NOTE The interface won't launch if you have autorun disabled. In that case, click Start ➪ Run. In the dialog box that appears, type D:\start.exe. (Replace D with the proper letter if your CD drive uses a different letter. If you don't know the letter, see how your CD drive is listed under My Computer.) Click OK.

2. Read through the license agreement, and then click the Accept button if you want to use the CD. After you click Accept, the License Agreement window won't appear again.

   The CD interface appears. The interface allows you to install the programs and run the demos with just a click of a button (or two).

Using the CD with the Mac

To install the items from the CD to your hard drive, follow these steps:

1. Insert the CD into your Mac's CD drive.

2. Click the CD's icon on your desktop. The interface launches and the license agreement appears.

3. Read through the license agreement, and then click the Accept button if you want to use the CD. After you click Accept, the License Agreement window won't appear again.

4. The CD interface appears. The interface allows you to install the programs and run the demos with just a click of a button (or two).

What's on the CD

The following sections provide a summary of the software and other materials you'll find on the CD.

Author-created materials

The example files used in the tutorials throughout the book are included in the "Chapter Example Files" directory. Within this directory are separate subdirectories for each chapter. Supplemental files, such as models and images, are also included in these directories. For each tutorial, the resulting example after all steps are completed has the word "final" in the filename. Using these final examples, you can compare the results to your own work.

Applications

The following applications are on the CD:

- Google SketchUp 7
- Google SketchUp Pro 7 Trial

Trial, demo, or *evaluation versions* are usually limited either by time or functionality (such as being unable to save projects). Some trial versions are very sensitive to system date changes. If you alter your computer's date, the programs will "time out" and will no longer be functional.

Troubleshooting

If you have difficulty installing or using any of the materials on the companion CD, try the following solutions:

- **Turn off any anti-virus software that you may have running.** Installers sometimes mimic virus activity and can make your computer incorrectly believe that it is being infected by a virus. (Be sure to turn the anti-virus software back on later.)

- **Close all running programs.** The more programs you're running, the less memory is available to other programs. Installers also typically update files and programs; if you keep other programs running, installation may not work properly.

- **See the ReadMe file.** Please refer to the ReadMe file located at the root of the CD for the latest product information at the time of publication.

Customer Care

If you still have trouble with the CD, please call the Wiley Product Technical Support telephone number: (800) 762-2974. Outside the United States, call 1 (317) 572-3994. You can also contact Wiley Product Technical Support at `http://support.wiley.com`. John Wiley & Sons will provide technical support only for installation and other general quality control items. For technical support on the applications themselves, consult the program's vendor or author.

To place additional orders or to request information about other Wiley products, please call (800) 225-5945.

Index

Symbols and Numerics

Wiley Publishing, Inc.
End-User License Agreement

READ THIS. You should carefully read these terms and conditions before opening the software packet(s) included with this book (*"Google SketchUp and SketchUp Pro 7 Bible"*). This is a license agreement ("Agreement") between you and Wiley Publishing, Inc. ("WPI"). By opening the accompanying software packet(s), you acknowledge that you have read and accept the following terms and conditions. If you do not agree and do not want to be bound by such terms and conditions, promptly return the Book and the unopened software packet(s) to the place you obtained them for a full refund.

1. **License Grant.** WPI grants to you (either an individual or entity) a nonexclusive license to use one copy of the enclosed software program(s) (collectively, the "Software") solely for your own personal or business purposes on a single computer (whether a standard computer or a workstation component of a multi-user network). The Software is in use on a computer when it is loaded into temporary memory (RAM) or installed into permanent memory (hard disk, CD-ROM, or other storage device). WPI reserves all rights not expressly granted herein.

2. **Ownership.** WPI is the owner of all right, title, and interest, including copyright, in and to the compilation of the Software recorded on the disk(s) or CD-ROM "Software Media." Copyright to the individual programs recorded on the Software Media is owned by the author or other authorized copyright owner of each program. Ownership of the Software and all proprietary rights relating thereto remain with WPI and its licensers.

3. **Restrictions on Use and Transfer.**

   (a) You may only (i) make one copy of the Software for backup or archival purposes, or (ii) transfer the Software to a single hard disk, provided that you keep the original for backup or archival purposes. You may not (i) rent or lease the Software, (ii) copy or reproduce the Software through a LAN or other network system or through any computer subscriber system or bulletin-board system, or (iii) modify, adapt, or create derivative works based on the Software.

   (b) You may not reverse engineer, decompile, or disassemble the Software. You may transfer the Software and user documentation on a permanent basis, provided that the transferee agrees to accept the terms and conditions of this Agreement and you retain no copies. If the Software is an update or has been updated, any transfer must include the most recent update and all prior versions.

4. **Restrictions on Use of Individual Programs.** You must follow the individual requirements and restrictions detailed for each individual program in the "What's on the CD-ROM" appendix of this Book. These limitations are also contained in the individual license agreements recorded on the Software Media. These limitations may include a requirement that after using the program for a specified period of time, the user must pay a registration fee or discontinue use. By opening the Software packet(s), you will be agreeing to abide by the licenses and restrictions for these individual programs that are detailed in the "What's on the CD-ROM" appendix and on the Software Media. None of the material on this Software Media or listed in this Book may ever be redistributed, in original or modified form, for commercial purposes.

5. **Limited Warranty.**

   (a) WPI warrants that the Software and Software Media are free from defects in materials and workmanship under normal use for a period of sixty (60) days from the date of purchase of this Book. If WPI receives notification within the warranty period of defects in materials or workmanship, WPI will replace the defective Software Media.

(b) WPI AND THE AUTHOR(S) OF THE BOOK DISCLAIM ALL OTHER WARRANTIES, EXPRESS OR IMPLIED, INCLUDING WITHOUT LIMITATION IMPLIED WARRANTIES OF MERCHANTABILITY AND FITNESS FOR A PARTICULAR PURPOSE, WITH RESPECT TO THE SOFTWARE, THE PROGRAMS, THE SOURCE CODE CONTAINED THEREIN, AND/OR THE TECHNIQUES DESCRIBED IN THIS BOOK. WPI DOES NOT WARRANT THAT THE FUNCTIONS CONTAINED IN THE SOFTWARE WILL MEET YOUR REQUIREMENTS OR THAT THE OPERATION OF THE SOFTWARE WILL BE ERROR FREE.

(c) This limited warranty gives you specific legal rights, and you may have other rights that vary from jurisdiction to jurisdiction.

6. **Remedies.**

    (a) WPI's entire liability and your exclusive remedy for defects in materials and workmanship shall be limited to replacement of the Software Media, which may be returned to WPI with a copy of your receipt at the following address: Software Media Fulfillment Department, Attn.: *Google SketchUp and SketchUp Pro 7 Bible,* Wiley Publishing, Inc., 10475 Crosspoint Blvd., Indianapolis, IN 46256, or call 1-800-762-2974. Please allow four to six weeks for delivery. This Limited Warranty is void if failure of the Software Media has resulted from accident, abuse, or misapplication. Any replacement Software Media will be warranted for the remainder of the original warranty period or thirty (30) days, whichever is longer.

    (b) In no event shall WPI or the author be liable for any damages whatsoever (including without limitation damages for loss of business profits, business interruption, loss of business information, or any other pecuniary loss) arising from the use of or inability to use the Book or the Software, even if WPI has been advised of the possibility of such damages.

    (c) Because some jurisdictions do not allow the exclusion or limitation of liability for consequential or incidental damages, the above limitation or exclusion may not apply to you.

7. **U.S. Government Restricted Rights.** Use, duplication, or disclosure of the Software for or on behalf of the United States of America, its agencies and/or instrumentalities "U.S. Government" is subject to restrictions as stated in paragraph (c)(1)(ii) of the Rights in Technical Data and Computer Software clause of DFARS 252.227-7013, or subparagraphs (c) (1) and (2) of the Commercial Computer Software - Restricted Rights clause at FAR 52.227-19, and in similar clauses in the NASA FAR supplement, as applicable.

8. **General.** This Agreement constitutes the entire understanding of the parties and revokes and supersedes all prior agreements, oral or written, between them and may not be modified or amended except in a writing signed by both parties hereto that specifically refers to this Agreement. This Agreement shall take precedence over any other documents that may be in conflict herewith. If any one or more provisions contained in this Agreement are held by any court or tribunal to be invalid, illegal, or otherwise unenforceable, each and every other provision shall remain in full force and effect.